The Sardinian Neolithic:
An Archaeology of the 6th and 5th Millennia BCE

Gary Webster

with a contribution from Maud Webster

BAR INTERNATIONAL SERIES 2941 | 2019

Published in 2019 by
BAR Publishing, Oxford

BAR International Series 2941

The Sardinian Neolithic: An Archaeology of the 6th and 5th Millennia BCE

ISBN 978 1 4073 5511 5 paperback
ISBN 978 1 4073 5521 4 e-format

© Gary Webster 2019

COVER IMAGE *Bonu Ighinu 'volumetric' statuette from Cuccuru
S'Arriu, tomb 386 (after Lilliu 1999, figs. 196-198).*

BAR
PUBLISHING

BAR titles are available from:

BAR Publishing
122 Banbury Rd, Oxford, OX2 7BP, UK
EMAIL   info@barpublishing.com
PHONE   +44 (0)1865 310431
FAX   +44 (0)1865 316916
www.barpublishing.com

Acknowledgements

My sincere thanks to Didier Binder, Charleston Chiang, Laura Fanti, Timothy Insoll, Gianmarco Loddi, Carlo Lugliè, Stefano Masala, Irene Assunta Molinari, Alberto Moravetti, Kewin Peche-Quilichini, Robin Skeates and Isabelle Vella Gregory for generously responding to queries and sharing information and publications pertinent to this project.

Books by the same author

Studies in Nuragic Archaeology
Village Excavations at Nuraghe Urpes and Nuraghe Toscono in West-Central Sardinia
Edited by Joseph W. Michels and Gary S. Webster

Oxford, BAR Publishing, 1987   BAR International Series **373**

Duos Nuraghes - A Bronze Age Settlement in Sardinia
Gary S. Webster

Oxford, BAR Publishing, 2001   BAR International Series **949**

Punctuated Insularity
The Archaeology of 4th and 3rd Millennium Sardinia
Gary Webster and Maud Webster

Oxford, BAR Publishing, 2017   BAR International Series **2871**

Related titles

Studies in Sardinian archaeology III
Nuragic Sardinia and the Mycenaean World
Miriam S. Balmuth

Oxford, BAR Publishing, 1987   BAR International Series **387**

Analisi tecnologica e funzionale dell'industria in pietra non scheggiata del Neolitico medio dell'Italia settentrionale
Tre casi studio dell'area veneta
Anna Lunardi

Oxford, BAR Publishing, 2017   BAR International Series **2864**

Vida y muerte en el asentamiento del Neolítico Antiguo de El Prado (Pancorbo, Burgos)
Construyendo el Neolítico en la Península Ibérica
Carmen Alonso-Fernández

Oxford, BAR Publishing, 2017   BAR International Series **2876**

For more information, or to purchase these titles, please visit **www.barpublishing.com**

Contents

List of Figures

Abstract

Despite Sardinia's rich Neolithic record, very little of it has entered into European scholarly discourse. This volume responds to that omission by providing a detailed, interpretive synthesis of Sardinian Neolithic remains of the 6th and 5th millennia. It is laid out and written as a prequel and companion to *Punctuated Insularity. The archaeology of 4th and 3rd millennium Sardinia* (Webster and Webster 2017) which deals similarly with the Sardinian Copper Age. The chapters treat in turn ceramics, settlement remains, mortuary and non-mortuary cult deposits, crafts, imagery, art and extra-insular links especially with neighbouring Corsica. Following a report on the evidence for a human presence during the Palaeo- and Mesolithic periods, by Maud Webster, individual chapters are devoted in turn to the pioneering so-called Impressa phase, Cardial- and Epicardial phases (Early Neolithic), the Middle Neolithic Bonu Ighinu phase and the Late Neolithic San Ciriaco phase. The Final Neolithic Ozieri phase, which bears the earliest evidence of metal use in Sardinia, is given only brief consideration as an Epilogue, having been recently examined in detail in the earlier volume (*Punctuated Insularity*).

Mesolithic deposits including habitations and burials are well confirmed but enigmatic regarding their implications for hunter-gatherer and Neolithic encounters. The material record suggests a hiatus between Mesolithic and Neolithic occupations, while genetic studies suggest enough entanglement to have instilled pre-Neolithic genetic markers traceable today. The first Neolithic groups – pastoralists bearing signature Impressa ware – can be dated on Sardinian and Corsica to the early centuries of the 6th millennium, roughly equivalent to datings from the northern Tyrrhenian mainland and only slightly later than those in the southern Italian peninsula, and would seem to document the rapidity with which Neolithic groups arrived into the northern regions from the south. Full colonisation by agro-pastoral communities commenced before the mid-6th millennium, probably involving new migrant groups, bearing Tyrrhenian Cardial-impressed pottery with close parallels in Tuscany – their most likely homeland. During the second half of the 6th millennium, the introduction of so-called Epicardial ceramics, which clearly diverge from the Cardial tradition, suggests a fresh influx of settlers. During the subsequent Middle Neolithic Bonu Ighinu phase of the early 5th millennium, traditional cultural features combined with unprecedented and unique socio-economic developments. Better-crafted wares in a wider range of forms appeared, some decorated with zoomorphic/anthropomorphic mouldings finding stylistic parallels among repertories of the southern Italian peninsula. Burials in unprecedented hypogeal tombs with accompanying carved stone statuettes suggest an incipient elite with privileged access to the island's obsidian resources. During the San Ciriaco phase of the later 5th millennium, ceramic expression featured an array of high-quality austere and generally unembellished forms, paralleling those in Corsica. Earlier so-called volumetric idols were replaced by slimmer steatopygeous forms, while customs and architecture of a European-wide megalithic burial cult took hold in northeast Sardinia and Corsica featuring slab-cist graves with cairns and aniconic monolithic uprights (stelai, menhirs or baetyls).

One overarching impression of the Sardinian Neolithic corpus is one of diversity. The island was probably not culturally 'unified', nor the adaptive undertakings specific to Sardinia. A notable finding is that plant cultivation was probably never the predominant subsistence mode. Both Sardinia and probably Corsica supported instead a patchwork of sub-insular and local regimes involving herding, hunting, collecting – and, at times, cultivation.

Introduction

About this account

The cover of the splendid *Oxford Handbook of Neolithic Europe* (Fowler, Harding and Hofmann 2015) features what is arguably one of the finest examples of Neolithic stone sculpture anywhere. At a first glance, it might conjure up comparisons with the famous mother goddess figurines of Anatolia. But this carving is Sardinian, dating to the Middle Neolithic – an expression of the rich material culture known as Bonu Ighinu. The intrigued reader, turning to the text for more about this, will find precious little, however: it is still the case, as it has long been, that despite Sardinia's important record, very little of it has made its way into the general discourse on the European Neolithic. The Sardinian Copper Age has fared somewhat better, and the Sardinian Bronze Age is well known for its megalithic tower-houses and tombs. But for the Neolithic phases of the sixth and fifth millennia BCE, detailed syntheses accessible to the scrutiny of European scholarship and written in English, are simply lacking. This omission has motivated the writing of this volume; it has moreover allowed its purpose to be straightforward and, to the degree that post-positivist epistemologies will permit, to justify its being primarily descriptive and interpretive.

The earliest evidence of a Neolithic presence in Sardinia comes from several upland caves in the form of so-called Impressa ceramics (see below) with associated C14 dates around 5700 cal BCE. These dates are comparable to assays from neighbouring Corsica, and only slightly later than those from Early Neolithic deposits on the mainland. The archaeology of sixth- and fifth-millennium Sardinia is thus an archaeology of the so-called neolithisation of the broader Tyrrhenian region which includes Sardinia and Corsica, and primarily a study of the frequentation and settling of Sardinia as a locale, a large, insular, west-Mediterranean landmass, by people with non-indigenous heritages. That this phenomenon was *ex oriente* is not in doubt: the earliest ceramics have clearly traceable eastern precedents, associated chronometric data trace the spread of Neolithic settlements across the Mediterranean from east to west, and a high percentage of eastern genetic markers (with minor pre-Neolithic contributions) persists among contemporary populations, especially Sardinian (Chiang et al. 2018; Omrak et al. 2016; Olivieri et al. 2017; Chikhi et al. 2002).

In short, the aim of this volume is to provide a detailed, interpretive synthesis of the Sardinian Neolithic archaeological record. The study is laid out and written as a prequel and companion to *Punctuated Insularity. The archaeology of 4th and 3rd millennium Sardinia* (Webster

Fig. 1. Sardinia in the west-central Mediterranean.

and Webster 2017) and, in the same way, addresses a wider scholarly readership interested in the Neolithic of the west-central Mediterranean, but not necessarily familiar with the less known Sardinia data. The chapters also conform more or less to the layout of the earlier volume, treating in turn ceramics, settlement remains, mortuary and non-mortuary cult deposits, crafts, imagery and art, and for each theme noting possibly significant extra-insular links and, where feasible, offering interpretive suggestions (Fig. 1).

The earliest Neolithic history of Sardinia is bound up with that of neighbouring Corsica, separated only by the short stretch of sea at the Straits of Bonifacio. Throughout much of the period under study here, Corsica supported ceramic repertories diverging from those in Sardinia mainly in name, made use of nearly exclusively Sardinian obsidian, and for similar industries, and deployed similar subsistence strategies combining the herding of domestic stock, the cultivation of cereals and pulses, and the exploitation of wild plants and animals. It is likely too that the Neolithic populations that first explored and eventually colonised Sardinia had traversed Corsica and/or its shores *en route* from the Italian mainland. Although the project at hand focuses on exploring the Sardinian evidence of neolithisation, it will also track events in Corsica to some extent.

This account begins with a report on the evidence for a human presence here during the remote Palaeo- and

Mesolithic periods, kindly contributed by Maud Webster. Following this, the account will step off the island in order to discuss what is known about the cultural landscape from which the first Neolithic groups to arrive here are likely to have come and, as far as possible, what repertory of resources, technologies, skills, experiences, customs and traditions will have accompanied them. This practical and intellectual baggage is commonly referred to as 'the Neolithic package', and its main distinctive feature is usually indicated as agriculture. With this backdrop in mind, Sardinia will then be considered on the eve of the Neolithic, as it were: as a location, a landscape with a set of conditions of potential interest or necessity to incoming pioneers bearing 'the Neolithic package', following which the material evidence for all of the Neolithic cultural adaptations in the island will be described and discussed in turn: the pioneering so-called Impressa phase first, followed by Cardial- and Epicardial phases (Early Neolithic), the Middle Neolithic Bonu Ighinu phase and the Late Neolithic San Ciriaco phase. For all, a range of developments will be traced, including productive industries, demography, technologies and land-use, as far as the evidence allows. A final chapter will then tease out and discuss the findings made in the course of the study regarding the nature and circumstance of the Sardinian Neolithic.

Sardinian cultures/phases

As for later periods of Sardinian prehistory, chronological divisions of the Neolithic are often referred to as facies, phases or cultures with reference to the diagnostic ceramics by which they are recognised archaeologically (see Fig. 2). This approach will be taken here as well, in order to provide consistency with previously published *corpora*. It would be a mistake, however, to regard such labels as

necessarily suggesting the presence of island-wide cultural unities, or modalities specific to Sardinia. It is clear, based on available evidence, that the cultural profiles of the period in question were diverse and sometimes local. Any insular-level 'unity' probably did not go beyond a common ceramic *koiné* which is, however, indicated, and the named phases (Impressa, Cardial, Epicardial, Bonu Ighinu and San Ciriaco) generally transcend insular boundaries and change names more on the basis of national geographies and academic traditions than on prehistoric cultural or demographic discontinuities. In light of this, one might view the island during the period under examination as supporting not one but multiple Neolithics. It is not until the early fourth millennium BCE, in the Final Neolithic-Initial Chalcolithic, that Sardinia can be recognised archaeologically as bearing something like a unified material culture and possibly a common identity specific to the island as such. It is also to that phase, known as Ozieri or San Michele, that the earliest evidence of metal use can be dated in the island.

The Ozieri repertories and their implications were examined and discussed in the volume *Punctuated Insularity* (Webster and Webster 2017). For the present volume I have attached an epilogue that reviews the defining and sometimes extraordinary features of this important *facies*.

Considerable new work on lithic remains – in particular flaked tools – by Carlo Lugliè and others have brought us closer to identifying phase-specific industries for the Early Neolithic. It is still unclear, however, how best to consistently differentiate Impressa, Cardial and Epicardial assemblages in the absence of associated ceramics or radiometric data, and the data are generally considered under the umbrella-rubric of 'Early Neolithic', including a

	SARDINIA	CORSICA	S. FRANCE	N. ITALY	C. ITALY	S. ITALY	SICILY
10000- Younger Dryas climatic event			Azilian				
Mesolithic 6.2K climatic event	Epipaleolithic	Epipaleolithic ?	Epipaleolithic Castelnovian	Epipaleolithic Castelnovian	Epipaleolithic Castelnovian	Epipaleolithic Castelnovian	Epipaleolithic Castelnovian
6000-						Archaic	*Impressa*
Early Neolithic	*Impressa* Cardial *Su Carroppu* Epicardial *Grotta Verde-Filiestru-M.Maiore*	*Impressa* *Filiestru-Basi-Pienza* Strette-a Petra	*Impressa* Cardial Epicardial Final Cardial	*Impressa* Cardial Pollera	*Impressa* Cardial Sarteano Sasso-Fiorano	Evolved *Impressa* Stentinello	
5000-	Tyrrhenian Linear Carved Ware			Tyrrhenian Linear Carved Ware			
Middle Neolithic	Bonu Ighinu	Curasien	Chasséen	VBQ/Chiozza	Ripoli	Serra d'Alto	Passo di Corvo
Late Neolithic	San Ciriaco	Présien					
4000-				Lagozza	Diana	Diana	Diana
Final Neolithic	Ozieri	Basien	Verazien/ Ferriéres				
3500-		Terrinien	Couronnien				
Cal. BC							

Fig. 2. Cultural-chronological sequence for the west-central Mediterranean (after Manen 2007, fig. 89; Manen and Sabatier 2003, fig. 17; Lugliè 2018; Tanda 1998; Lo Vetro and Martini 2016, table 2; M.G. Melis 2011; Tramoni and D'Anna 2016).

number of non-ceramic deposits. For the present synthesis, however, I will take into consideration only such aceramic sites that have radiometric dates or associated diagnostic material like sculptures or adornments.

Sea-level changes and the archaeological record

There have long been suspicions based on finds of submerged archaeological deposits that significant parts of the Neolithic landscape have escaped detection due to post-Pleistocene sea-level rise (e.g. Antonioli et al. 1994). Recent data indicate that the Neolithic sea-level around Sardinia was as much as 20 m lower than today, and in consequence, the shoreline lay up to 10 km further out in some places (Lambeck et al. 2004, fig. 12; Antonioli et al. 2007). The most affected landscapes are the coastal areas with gentler topography, namely the larger gulfs and river mouths. The current shoreline at the Gulf of Oristano, for example, may have been some five km further out than today (Pittau et al. 2012, fig. 1), while smaller bays have been modified to a lesser degree. Recent work in the now submerged caves at Porto Conte near Alghero, for example, have shown that although they are now under 8-10 metres of sea water, they were c. 15 m above sea-level and about a kilometre from the shore in the sixth millennium BCE (Palombo et al. 2017).

From an archaeological perspective, these facts imply a likelihood of significant *lacunae* in the Neolithic landscape record. As will be discussed further, the gulfs and the mouths of the island's waterways were probably the very settings targeted by Neolithic settlers seeking pasturage and fertile soils. Coastlines with steeper topography have been less altered by sea-level changes, but would also have been less attractive to early agro-pastoralists. The generally rugged and precipitous east coast, for example, probably appears today much as it did during the Neolithic. Similarly, the topography along the likely routes in and out of the island have changed very little: Corsica to the north lay across a 12 km stretch of sea, the Tuscan archipelago eastward from there some 60 kms away, and the mainland another 35 km (see Figs. 1, 3).

A note on interpretation

The evidence discussed here supports some interpretive statements regarding the possible social significance of certain patterns perceived in the data. It should go without saying that any and all such statements are necessarily tentative and ideally hypothetical. As elsewhere, the Sardinian record and its archaeology are attended by uncertainties regarding the representative nature of the evidence, dependent as it is on the variable and generally unaccountable vagaries of preservation and sampling inadequacies. Much of the Neolithic evidence on Sardinia has moreover been revealed through rescue operations, a circumstance which probably aggravates the situation. But such realities are part and parcel of archaeological inquiry, which perforce must proceed from and return to the available material evidence as both source and interrogator

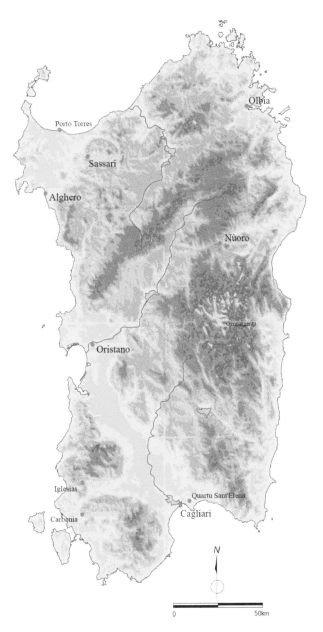

Fig. 3. Topographic map of Sardinia. (J.M. Borràs for WikiMedia Commons).

of its statements. Each chapter therefore closes with an attempt at interpreting or making sense of the evidence such as it stands today, with the understanding that future findings – and future approaches – will be brought bear on them.

Beginnings: The Palaeo- and Mesolithic Record

By Maud Webster

It is a well-confirmed understanding that the colonisation of Sardinia, i.e. its full and sustained peopling, is largely a Neolithic phenomenon. The following chapters of this book will explore that sequence of events from its pioneering phases onward, in terms of material cultures and their implications as far as current evidence allows. But the Neolithic influxes did not represent the first human inroads here. The island has long been thought to have hosted Palaeolithic presences, albeit poorly attested, and reports of epi-palaeolithic assemblages have increased in recent years, warranting the conceptualisation of a Sardinian Mesolithic. In a general sense, these findings add to the Mediterranean-wide picture regarding post-glacial sea travel and landfalls on the part of hunter-gatherer groups, because Sardinia (or, rather, the Sardinia-Corsica bloc) was always insular, even if not always as distant from other shores as it is today: coming here always involved seafaring. Beyond such elementary reflections, however, the currently patchy nature of the material record for these remote periods does not allow for much in the way of detailed or far-reaching conclusions. Results from genetic research offer complimentary leads, however, and in sum, the Palaeo- and Mesolithic evidence currently available for Sardinia provides some food for thought, and will be surveyed and briefly discussed here, by way of a background to following chapters (see Fig. 4).

A debated Lower and Middle Palaeolithic

In the 1980s and early -90s, there was considerable interest on the part of some archaeologists and local administrations to explore the possibility of a hominin presence in Sardinia, in the Middle Pleistocene (780000-125,000 years ago), and thus to trace a Lower or Middle Palaeolithic culture here (see Martini 2017 for an overview). Surface sampling of chert fields in the flint-rich northern part of the island, and excavations of two sites deemed to have stratigraphic integrity (see below), led some of these scholars to define some of the finds as Clactonian (from the English type-site where a flint tool industry is dated to c. 400,000 years ago). Meanwhile, excavations in Corbeddu cave in eastern Sardinia yielded Mesolithic human remains whose unusual features, in conjunction with faunal and environmental considerations, led the excavators to propose that they had belonged to an individual with endemic traits, developed over a long time in isolation, and implying a Middle Pleistocene, pre-sapiens presence here (Spoor

and Sondaar 1986; Klein Hofmeijer 1987; Sondaar 1998). This notion was later reviewed and retracted (Spoor 1999), and has found no supporting evidence since.

Indeed, the propositions of a Middle Pleistocene occupation of Sardinia was not well received by the wider scientific community generally, and led to divisive debates (Martini 2009; 2017). It is with some awe that one notes the seemingly unbridgeable gap between the advocates of a Middle Pleistocene occupation on the one hand, repeatedly presenting their interpretation of chipped stone assemblages as established fact (Sondaar 1998; Martini 2009 and 2017), and its detractors on the other, considering the very notion of an early hominin presence here 'wildly anomalous' (Cherry 1992, 34, cf. Vigne 1989; Simmons 2016, 109-13), also in view of its inapplicability for other Mediterranean islands – including neighbouring Corsica, where there are no reliable indications of human presence before the Mesolithic (e.g. Costa 2004, but see Bonifay et al. 1998 for a controversial report of a putative late Pleistocene Corsican site). The absence of new evidence, and perhaps also the infected nature of the very issue, has led, more recently, to its simple dismissal or outright omission in some general texts (e.g. Broodbank 2015, 95, cf. Luglié 2018). But given the humbling fact that when it comes to hypotheses such as these, even a single new discovery – if well-dated and incontrovertible – could turn the tables, a review of the published data is in order.

To begin, several hundred of the thousands of flint pieces surveyed and excavated at the open site of Sa Coa de Sa Multa-Perfugas in northern Sardinia appear to result from knapping activities which, according to the excavators, can be dated on pedological stratigraphy to well over 300,000 years ago (Martini 2009 and 2017 with references). The flint items present no bifacials and were defined as denticulates and scrapers obtained by simple so-called SSDA knapping (système par surface de débitage alterné), comparable to the English Clactonian assemblage from High Lodge (Martini 2009, cf. Forestier 1993). A recent, more detailed study of the chipped stone from Sa Coa has, however, opened up for the possibility that it may date to almost any period of time (Romagnoli and Martini 2012, 366). Also at Ottana, in central Sardinia, assemblages of chipped volcanic rock described as 'Lower Palaeolithic looking' have been reported, consisting of denticulates, scrapers and flakes purportedly obtained by both SSDA and discoid/

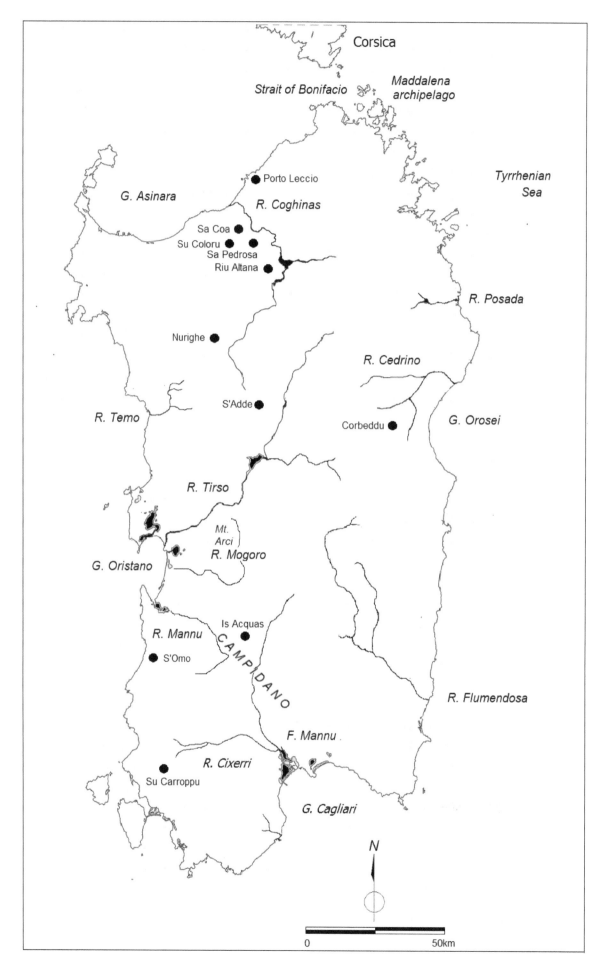

Fig. 4. Map of Sardinian pre-neolithic sites mentioned in this chapter.

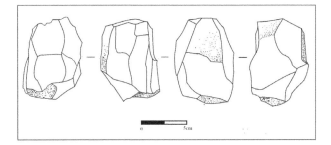

Fig. 5. Nucleus from Sa Coa de sa Multa-Perfugas (after Romagnoli and Martini 2012, fig. 4).

Levallois techniques. But given their generic nature and surface location, the samplers urged for caution regarding specific interpretations and limited themselves to suggest a date 'prior to the arrival of the first Neolithic communities in the island' (Fenu et al. 2012, 374). Neither of these sites provided any evidence other than the lithics (see Fig. 5).

At Sa Pedrosa-Pantallinu, the same team that ascribed nearby Sa Coa de Sa Multa to the early Middle Pleistocene excavated what was described as an open-air mine-cum-workshop, again with thousands of pieces of flint in what was deemed to be a stratified context (but lacking any evidence other than the lithics). The worked elements here were referred to the late Middle Pleistocene (c. 200,000-125,000 years ago) and said to include denticulates, scrapers, flakes and blades described as belonging to an advanced phase of Clactonian expression (Martini 2009 and 2017). But a separate study of the knapping technology employed here indicated that it is more characteristic of the late Pleistocene or, culturally speaking, the Upper Palaeolithic, and should be dated after 35000 years ago (Aureli 2012; a study which led to outright conflict with the excavating team, cf. Martini 2009, 21). Several surface collections of chipped stone at nearby locations were also said to reflect Clactonian industries. At Riu Altana-Perfugas specifically, flint items were ascribed to both of the Pleistocene horizons proposed for Sa Coa and for Sa Pedrosa, and some were compared to mainland proto-Levallois tools (Martini and Palma di Cesnola 1993). Again, the claims were found 'not convincing' by the wider scholarly community (se f.ex. Simmons 2016, 109, cf. Cherry 1992). Lastly, a fossil found by a speleology group in Nurighe cave at Cheremule in northwest Sardinia in the late 1990s was said to represent a hominin phalanx dating to well before 100000 years ago (Ginesu et al. 2003), thus raising the debate once more. When the bone was re-examined, however, it was found to probably have belonged to a large bird (Mallegni 2011). In sum, a Lower-Middle Palaeolithic human occupation of Sardinia remains very largely a field of contested claims, awaiting diagnostic data for its clarification.

The Upper Palaeolithic

The evidence from the period of time following the Late Glacial Maximum presents a curiously contradictory

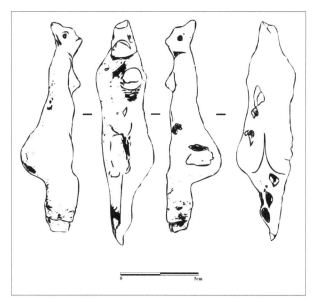

Fig. 6. Late Upper Palaeolithic figurine from Macomer (after Mussu 2012, fig. 2).

picture regarding human activities in the island. The environmental conditions of this phase should have been propitious to a colonisation of Sardinia – and Corsica, with which it essentially formed one landmass when sea levels were at their lowest around 18000 years ago (a circumstance leading to the coining of the term 'Corsardinia'; Broodbank 2015, 121; 126-28). There was a large deer here at this time, *megaloceros cazioti*, but no carnivores larger than a small canid, *cynotherium sardous*, so hunting would have presented a fruitful – even safe – prospect. But the archaeological evidence of a human presence is scarce in the extreme, with nothing yet confirmed from Corsica and the data from Sardinia amounting to one stone figurine of late Upper Palaeolithic type (c. 12,000-10,000 years ago; Mussi and Melis 2002, 89) and one human phalanx fragment approximately dated to 20,000 years ago (Sondaar et al. 1995) (see Fig. 6).

The former, the figurine, comes from Macomer in west-central Sardinia where it was found in 1949, stashed away in the depths of a rock-shelter at S'Adde. During the excavations that followed, the site yielded thousands of artefacts from the Neolithic through the Bronze Age, mainly lithics, and a scattering of Roman artefacts as well (Pesce 1949). The figurine was doubtless the most remarkable of the finds: standing c. 13.5 cm tall, made from basalt (or possibly andesite), it depicts a one-breasted, armless and footless human female with pronounced buttocks and a lagomorph head. An iconographic and stylistic study has recently dispelled early, misguided speculations relating it to the Neolithic and convincingly framed it within a late Upper Palaeolithic sphere (Mussi 2012). But how and when it came to be lodged in the Macomer shelter is not clear, and all other artefacts here are thousands of years younger. Given the wealth of Neolithic debris in particular, reflecting intense use of the shelter as an obsidian workshop at that time, one might wonder whether the figurine might not have been brought in then, discovered by Neolithic knappers somewhere, by chance, and picked up and stashed for the striking-looking piece that it is. Although entirely conjectural in this case, an instance of such curation is documented at the Neolithic village of La Marmotta at Bracciano lake in Italy, where an Upper Palaeolithic figurine was found in the lowest levels of the settlement, dated to the mid-sixth millennium BCE (Robb 2007, 55).

The other Upper Palaeolithic item known from Sardinia, a human phalanx, was discovered deep in the sediments of Corbeddu cave near Oliena in the east during regular excavations in 1993. Found in relative isolation, it was not directly dated but under- and overlying strata determined its deposition to have occurred c. 20000 years ago (Sondaar et al. 1995). Time-correspondent strata elsewhere in this large cave were rich in terms of late Pleistocene faunal remains including bones of the majestic deer and the small canid mentioned above, as well as *prolagus sardus*, a pika which is now extinct but whose skeletal remains constitute a near-ubiquitous feature of many prehistoric sites in Sardinia and Corsica (see further below). Indeed, perhaps it was such a pika – or a canid – that unwittingly caused the phalanx to be brought to its lonely resting place at Corbeddu (incidentally, the *prolagus* is likely the animal which lent its features to the distinctive Macomer figurine; Mussi 2012). In any event, the excavators at Corbeddu saw the late Pleistocene faunal remains as indicative of human exploitation and, citing the presence of the phalanx, argued for a 'permanent colonisation' by Upper Palaeolithic hunters c. 16000-10000 years ago (Sondaar 1998, 49, cf. Sondaar et al. 1995, 149).

All told, then, two material data currently constitute the sum total of securely attributable finds from the Sardinian Upper Palaeolithic (excepting the debated lithics from Sa Pedrosa noted above). But genetic studies have added several suggestive strands of evidence for this period of time. These relate to the so-called haplogroups identified among present-day Sards, i.e. assemblages of genes sharing a common ancestor and capable of indicating origin in terms of both time and space (female inheritance is traced through mitochondrial DNA; male through Y-chromosome haplogroups). Already in 2003, beta-globin analyses suggested the presence of palaeolithic ancestral genetics in Sardinia and southern Corsica (Latini et al. 2003), and support for this has increased since, at least regarding Sardinia (cf. Calò et al. 2008). In their recent study of mitogenome diversity, Olivieri et al. (2017, 1234) came to the tentative conclusion that haplogroups K1a2d and U5b1i1, specific to Sardinia and present in c. three per cent of its population today, appeared here 18,700-11,000 years ago and 13,000-9,700 years ago respectively, the former of Near Eastern origin; the latter Western European (Modi et al. 2017 would narrow the latter range to post-11,000 years ago or kya, as it is commonly abbreviated). To Olivieri et al., these data imply a reproductive base of 500-1500 people living in Sardinia 15-12 kya (2017, 1235) – translating to an Upper Palaeolithic population

which, as we have seen, left almost no material traces (but was nevertheless indeed envisioned by the Corbeddu excavators).

Similar conclusions have been reached by studying Y-chromosome evidence. Y-haplogroup I2a1a-M26 is well known among geneticists working with Sardinian data, as it is very rare elsewhere (and indeed absent in Corsica), but reaches a remarkable incidence of c. 40 per cent in Sardinian males (e.g. Pardo et al. 2012; Chiang et al. 2018; this haplogroup is also relatively well represented in northern Iberia, see f.ex. Contu et al. 2008). To Chiang et al. (2018), its trajectory in Sardinia suggests reproductive groups with relatively few males responsible for its early propagation, a sex-bias compatible f.ex. with polygynous practices. Contu et al. (2008) have estimated its origin to 18-10 kya, and suggest a population expansion around 14 kya from a founder group of some 1000 people; Calò et al. (2008) also envision a small but viable palaeolithic population in Sardinia, based on wider-ranging genetic indications. Regarding haplogroup I2a1a-M26 specifically, however, some researchers estimate its appearance to c. 9-7 kya (Pala et al. 2009), thus potentially shifting the data – in cultural terms – to a late Mesolithic sphere. This phase will be surveyed below, before discussing some implications of the pre-neolithic evidence as a whole.

The Mesolithic

The concept of a Sardinian Mesolithic is quite recent: until a decade or so ago, the remnants in question were referred to as either pre-neolithic or epi-palaeolithic. But recent discoveries have added up to a more consistent panorama for the ninth through seventh millennium BCE, for which the more specific concept of a Mesolithic phase has become justified. These millennia were bounded by two significant climatic events: the Younger Dryas (12.9-11.7 kya; see Carlson 2013; Alley and Agustsdottir 2005), and the briefer so-called 8k-event (8.4-8.0 kya; see Alley and Agustsdottir 2005; Berger and Guilaine 2009), both involving rapid onsets of cold, dry weather. The former coincides with the Pleistocene-Holocene transition, which in Sardinia probably saw the disappearance of the large deer *megaloceros cazioti* and thereby the reduction of the island fauna to one lacking big game animals *tout court* (cf. e.g. Martini 2017). It should be noted that a single find of a fossilised deer apparently belonging to this species has been dated to 7.5 kya (Benzi et al. 2007), and thus might represent the latter end of an extinction process much slower than assumed, but it remains an exceptional case – and there are to date no instances of *megaloceros* remains associated to evidence of Mesolithic human activities. The later, so-called 8k-event instead coincides with a period of at least 300 years for which no C14-dates have been related to archaeological sites or materials at all, so far (6210-5895 BCE; Fenu et al. 2002, Tab. 1; Lugliè 2018, Tab. 1). This apparent hiatus has led some scholars to posit that the island was deserted at that time (Lugliè 2009a; 2018), and that the Neolithic influxes would have taken place in a landscape devoid of people. This picture is challenged, however, by genetic evidence to which we will turn further below.

The archaeological panorama of Mesolithic Sardinia is sparse and homogeneous, currently comprising seven sites dated either directly or circumstantially to the ninth-seventh millennia BCE. Five of them are rock-shelters with mainly lithic residues and, in three cases, human remains as well; two sites are instead open-air camps with lithic remains only. Of these sites, one is located more than 25 km from the coast (Santa Maria de is Acquas), one is instead right on the shore (Porto Leccio, in the north); the others are 12-15 km from the sea. Sardinia and Corsica will have become separated by or around this time, as the post-glacial sea levels had by now risen considerably, but they still remained much lower than they are today (-35 m at 8000 BCE; see Vigne 1998, 57), and these sites were all further inland when in use. It is not known what – if anything – of a Mesolithic age might be hidden under water beyond the present-day shoreline, but as it appears today, the geographical distribution of the known Mesolithic sites in Sardinia suggests an off-coast preference while also keeping well away from the inland/uplands.

The oldest Mesolithic site so far known is also the southernmost, the rock-shelter of Su Carroppu-Sirri in the southwest, where a robust Neolithic component overlay – and partially intermingled with – three fragmentary burials C14-dated to 9124-7851, 8227-7596 and 7938-7525 cal BCE (Modi et al. 2017), later recalibrated to 9131-7941, 8228-7596 and 7938-7599 (Lugliè 2018, Table 1). The bones were also examined for DNA, resulting in complete mitochondrial sequences for two of the individuals, revealing their divergent heritage as likely Near Eastern and Western European respectively, and also indicating their non-relation to later, Neolithic lineages (Modi et al. 2017). In uncertain association, quartzite flakes, pierced shells and an animal bone implement imbued with ochre may have accompanied the burials (Lugliè 2018, cf. Atzeni 1978). Moreover, four calibrated C14-dates on charcoal from here range between 7576 and 6831 BC (Lugliè 2018, Table 1).

The recently calibrated but very wide range of the C14-dates from the Mesolithic component at Corbeddu cave in Sardinia spans much of the ninth-seventh millennium BCE (Lugliè 2018, Table 1), and relates to a slim assemblage comprising animal bone, a very few lithic tools and a human maxilla and temporal bone (it was this maxilla, with its unusual morphology, that first led the excavators to propose that it had belonged to an individual with endemic traits implying a pre-sapiens presence in the island; see above). Another cave, Su Coloru at Laerru in northern Sardinia, has more recently returned calibrated C14-dates ranging between c. 7700-6210 BC from stratified contexts evincing intermittent use (Fenu et al. 2002 and Lugliè 2018, Table 1), and Neolithic data from the early sixth millennium BCE and later. The Mesolithic component which was investigated included small hearths and more

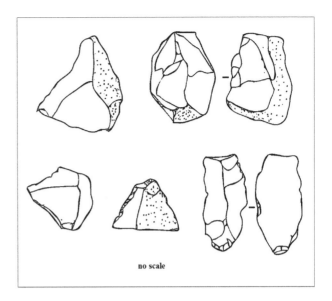
no scale

Fig. 7. Undifferentiated epi-palaeolithic assemblage from Porto Leccio-Trinità d'Agultu (after Tozzi and Dini 2012, fig. 1).

than 800 pieces of local flint of less than excellent quality, documenting a *chaîne opératoire* of the production of mainly short scrapers (Martini et al. 2012). The typology is known as 'undifferentiated epipalaeolithic' or 'undifferentiated Mesolithic', a less invested, more expedient version of contemporary mainland industries (e.g. Martini and Tozzi 2012) (see Fig. 7).

The repertory bears similarities f.ex. with the c. 530 lithics recovered in a rock-shelter near the shore at Porto Leccio, likewise in the north and similarly covering a full *chaîne opératoire* (this site also presents Middle Neolithic data). Here, the investigators stressed close similarities with Corsican Mesolithic assemblages of the seventh millennium BCE, but C14-dates were not reported (Dini and Tozzi 2012). The preponderant material was quartz (c. 92 per cent, including some rock crystal), along with flint and some rhyolite, suggestive of an opportunistic-experimental approach in both the inclusion of variable rock types and the range of artefacts. The open site of Sa Coa de sa Multa also returned a Mesolithic flint assemblage dominated by short scrapers but including some blades as well (this site has been studied mainly for its putative Middle Pleistocene strata and the Mesolithic horizon has as yet received little attention; see Martini and Saliola 1999).

In the southwest, at Santa Maria de is Acquas-Sardara, another open-air setting with ample lithic scatters has been revealed – in the excavators' words, not so much a site as a part of a vast, sandy 'palaeolandscape' (Mussi and Melis 2002, 84). A selection of some 70 flint artefacts at first resulted in an ascription to the Upper Palaeolithic on typological grounds, and the pedological stratigraphy was interpreted as defining the finds within the late Pleistocene (Mussi and Melis 2002, 75 and 88). This affirmation led to the site's inclusion in general texts on the Mediterranean Palaeolithic (e.g. Broodbank 2015, 128, cf. Martini 2017), but it now carries an IRSL date of 9000 +/- 500 years ago (c. 7000 BCE; Melis et al. 2012, calling the same site Sardara), framing it within the Holocene/Mesolithic even if its material record does not conform to the undifferentiated epi-palaeolithic horizon. This curious circumstance prompts some consideration: might the findings represent a Mesolithic workshop producing artefacts resembling much older tools and, if so, what might that signify? Or are there instead problems with the date and/or its referent? As the excavators stressed, the assemblage reveals a clear ambition toward making blades, which is otherwise unusual in the Sardinian Mesolithic record where short scrapers account for a majority of the finds. The implications of the data from Santa Maria de is Acquas are thus unclear, and the query is compounded by the fact that similar chipped stones have been found at nearby Puisteris where they have been ascribed to the Neolithic (Locci 2000; Lugliè 2000). As the investigators at Sardara suggested, these too might refer to a preceding occupation (2002, 88), but preceding by how much is uncertain indeed.

Not far away, at S'Omu e S'Orku near Arbus in the west, a chance unearthing of human skeletal remains in the 1980s has more recently led to extensive archaeological investigations (Melis et al. 2012; Floris et al. 2012; Melis and Mussi 2016). The context is a collapsed rock-shelter containing three burials, one of which carries a calibrated C14-date of 8596-8373 years ago, i.e. c. 6600-6400 BCE (Melis and Mussi 2016). The upper and lower shelter boundaries carry dates of 8148-7800 and 8953-8545 years ago respectively, indicating that the burial episodes

preceded the climatic 8k-event around 6200 BCE. This shelter had also preserved evidence of the funeral rites, and constitutes the only Sardinian Mesolithic site discovered so far that allows for insights of this intimate kind. The burial labelled SOMK2 (carrying the C14-date) represents the remains of a young adult woman in a flexed position with arms cross-folded and hands on the shoulders, accompanied by sea shells including four pierced *Columbella* specimens and considerable amounts of ochre (Melis et al. 2012; Floris et al. 2012). The SOMK1 burial (accidentally revealed, prior to excavation) represents instead the remains of an adult man in a flexed position on his left side, with plenty of ochre and a large *Charonia* shell, commonly known as a 'triton', carved seemingly to serve as a trumpet of sorts. On the bottom of the rock-shelter was the burial called SOMK3, likewise of an adult (man?) with a large *Charonia*-trumpet as accompaniment. In addition, along the left side was a row of superimposed *Cypraea* shells and a dozen *Columbella* specimens, all ochred (Melis and Mussi 2016). Found less discriminately within the shelter were ochre lumps, two flint pieces and four obsidian flakes, as well as bones from the endemic pika, *prolagus sardus* (found also at f.ex. Su Carroppu, Corbeddu and Porto Leccio). For now, the burial *ensemble* at S'Omu e S'Orku may represent the oldest find of obsidian in association with humans, likely attesting to a late Mesolithic use of this local volcanic glass whose exploitation is otherwise commonly assumed to have begun with the Neolithic (see Fig. 8).

The contemporary Corsican Mesolithic appears in most respects very similar to that of Sardinia, hence the concept of a *mésolithique insulaire* (de Lanfranchi 1998). Characterised by a near-identical repertory of lithics of the utmost simplicity, Corsica currently counts nine sites of this phase (Martini 2017, 30), and more seem likely to be revealed in coming years. Two burials are located in inland valleys in the southwest, while the other Corsican sites cluster – interestingly – in the far northern and far southern infra-coastal stretches respectively (de Lanfranchi and Alessandri 2012). Two of these are open sites, one is a cave and the remainder are rock-shelters, most of them evincing periodic visitations and abandonments (e.g. Martini and Tozzi 2012, 402), and several bearing also later, Neolithic strata.

Interestingly, the important site of Punta di Caniscione in southern Corsica yielded, in its Mesolithic strata, two pieces of flint from Perfugas in Sardinia, indicating movement and interaction (Pasquet and Demouche 2013). A possible difference between the Corsican and the Sardinian Mesolithic might relate to the sustenance of the people occupying these landscapes: the evidence for this is slight, but suggests a heavily meat-based diet with some input from seafood at Corsican sites (Vigne 1998; Costa 2004; Martini and Tozzi 2012), while the very rare data from Sardinia indicate a plant-based diet supplemented by some meat (Floris et al. 2012). Regarding genetic studies of Corsica, these have so far yielded largely contradictory data regarding its peopling and early context (see f.ex. Di Cristofaro et al. 2018, also for references), perhaps in

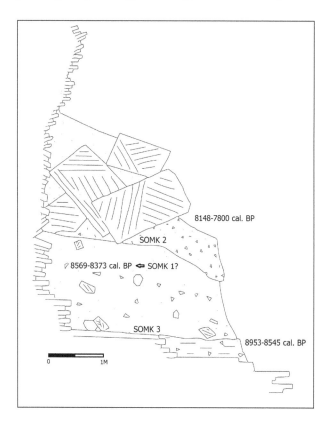

8148-7800 cal. BP

SOMK 2

8569-8373 cal. BP ⇐ SOMK 1?

SOMK 3

8953-8545 cal. BP

0   1M

Fig. 8. Section of the burial shelter of S'Omu 'e S'Orku-Arbus (after Melis and Mussi 2016, fig. 3).

part because this island, always sparsely inhabited, was also resettled by Italian and French groups after severe population contractions for example in the Middle Ages (Francalacci et al. 2003, 271 and 274; Contu et al. 2009).

To return to Sardinia, the deposits at S'Omu e S'Orku and at Su Coloru-Laerru represent the latter end of Mesolithic activities here to date, followed – as noted – by an apparent archaeological hiatus between c. 6200 and 5900 BCE preceding the Neolithic influxes. Adding to this paucity the deleterious climate event of 6200, it has seemed plausible to argue for a depopulation (e.g. Lugliè 2018, 290). As also noted, however, genetic evidence challenges this picture. Generally, genetic studies involving the origin of the Sardinian population do indicate that it was largely Neolithic, with later admixture (e.g. Chiang et al. 2018; Modi et al. 2017; Olivieri et al. 2017), but the evidence of pre-neolithic heritage seems solid, if slight, and cannot be dismissed. Regarding the Mesolithic specifically, Rootsi et al., in their phylogeographic work (2004), concluded that Y-haplogroup I1b2 is likely to reflect a founding population in Sardinia around 9 kya, and Contu et al. (2008) proposed that Y-haplogroup R-M18, apparently unique to the island, originated around the same time (10.5-7.8 kya), i.e. within a Mesolithic panorama. Regarding maternal heritage, Olivieri et al., in the study cited above (2017, 1236), proposed that mitochondrial haplogroup H3 expanded in Sardinia 10.5-9 kya, and Francalacci et al. (2003, 276) suggested that mitochondrial haplogroup V, present in interior Sardinia, is likewise a Mesolithic marker – both of these probably of Iberian origin. Meanwhile, mitochondrial haplogroup U5b3 (probably of Italian mainland origin) has been estimated to 9-7 kya here (Pala et al. 2009, 818; Pardo et al. 2012), adding to the Mesolithic – and/or earliest Neolithic – data.

Discussion

The genetic evidence touched upon here is lacunous and likely to grow significantly in coming years. Nevertheless, its suggestion of a heterogeneous makeup among the early visitors to Sardinia, including Western European (Iberian) as well as Near Eastern input well before the Neolithic, would appear solid. In a general sense, this attests to the periodic mobility of hunter-gatherers in the post-glacial Mediterranean world, overseas as well as overland, but that aside, what might be concluded from the present survey? First, the genetic and the archaeological evidence diverge in a seemingly contradictory fashion, and it is clear that any interpretation must be provisional as future research may fill in current gaps and modify proposed hypotheses. At present, however, the apparent contradiction primarily brings up old questions regarding human presence without archaeological traces. For this is what the genetic data – if at all reliable – must imply: an unbroken propagation of at least some Upper Palaeolithic and Mesolithic genetic matter into the Neolithic period, despite the paucity of material finds attesting to the former, and across the apparent void suggested by the lack of dated traces for

some centuries preceding the latter – and into the present day. If so, the apparent hiatus is rather an archaeological lacuna and, as such, it may well prove temporary.

But while a tenuous thread does seem to stretch across these vast time-spans, it is not indicative of colonisation, in the sense of sustained human permeation and conditioning of a territory. Little can be made of the meagre material record of the Sardinian Upper Palaeolithic, but genetic research nevertheless points to a small, if archaeologically elusive, population here following the Late Glacial Maximum. In this regard, it has been suggested that 'Corsardinia' may have served as a refuge due to a milder climate than that of the mainland at this juncture (Broodbank 2015, 128). For the better attested Mesolithic, however, when Modi et al. reported the burial data from Su Carroppu, they felt that they were documenting 'the first colonisers of the island' (2017). This *ensemble* indeed represents the oldest well-dated human remains-in-context so far found in Sardinia, but there is nothing to suggest that the Mesolithic groups that the buried individuals belonged to did any actual colonising. That would have resulted in detectable traces at least in the regional flora and fauna – the normal consequences of steady human presence documented in many contexts world-wide (Leppard 2014; Cherry and Leppard 2017) but not attested for the Sardinian Mesolithic. This negative evidence may indeed clarify the nature of the archaeological remains: the small size and suggestive location of most of the few known sites (i.e. not penetrating the inland), the local and spare nature of their assemblages (for short-term, low-demand applications), and the stratigraphies indicating brief occupations and periodic abandonments have all led some scholars to propose that the people buried at Su Carroppu, and their later Mesolithic sequels at Corbeddu, Su Coloru, Porto Leccio, Sa Coa, Sardara and Arbus, were visitors, seasonal or longer-term (Lugliè 2018, 289; Martini 2017, 34).

In all honesty, however, it is difficult to see the reasons for their presence here at all, if our contextual understanding is correct. Unlike in the Palaeolithic, there was no big game to hunt (with the *megaloceros* all but extinct), marine foodstuffs were apparently not utilised to any extent in Sardinia, and no effort seems to have been made to exploit the better lithic resources available in the island (tools being instead summarily fashioned from the variable rock present at the camp-sites). One could say, of course, that the presumed absence of game animals (and of any practices involving cultivation) would have obviated most needs for specialised lithics. It is also clear that the lifestyles that can be inferred from the Mesolithic data in Sardinia appear exceedingly simple: shelter was sought in caves and under overhangs, and sustenance was drawn from foraged plants and presumably the meat of the small *prolagus*. No art of any kind has been associated to this period in Sardinia, and the few burial rites attested so far, while carefully effected, were minimal. Future findings are likely to add to this sketchy picture, but it seems clear that the full colonisation of Sardinia was effected only later, with the more robust and essentially different Neolithic influxes to which the slight Palaeo- and Mesolithic substrata contributed very little – but still a little, which is genetically detectable. The contexts and circumstances by which that admixture came about is another intriguing matter awaiting more evidence for its elucidation.

3

The Northern Tyrrhenian at the Dawn of the 6th Millennium BCE: The Archaeology

The advent of *ceramica impressa*

Until recently, finds of the regionally distinct Tyrrhenian or Geometric Cardial-impressed ware, which begins to appear in the record between 5700-5600 cal BCE, were believed to document the initial appearance of agro-pastoral communities in Sardinia and Corsica and the Tyrrhenian region generally. It has become increasing clear, however, that this phase of Neolithisation was preceded by an earlier 'pioneer' or 'scouting' phase dating roughly from the first centuries of the sixth millennium (e.g. Luglië 2018). Its diagnostic ceramics, widely if confusedly referred to as *ceramica impressa* or Impressa ware, bear clear stylistic affinities to ceramics of the earliest Neolithic assemblages in the southern Italian mainland, from which it is believed to have derived (Manen 2003; Guilaine and Manen 2007; Manen and Covertini 2012) (see Figs. 9-10).

Importantly, a mapping of these Impressa-phase sites has revealed rather clearly a discontinuous distribution from south to northwest, with wide geographical gaps consistent with a demic pattern of marine-based leap-frog expansion involving implantations at select Tyrrhenian coastal settings (Richards 2003, 165; Bergin 2016). Radiometric data document a rapid diffusion of Impressa sites from southern Italy and Sicily from ca. 6000 cal BCE (Archaic Impressa) northward, within a couple of centuries into the Tyrrhenian region of the north Italian peninsula, Liguria, and Provence and Languedoc in France (Peiro Signado, Pont de Roque-Haute; e.g. Luglië 2018, Binder and Sénépart 2010; Manen 2007; Guilaine 2017). Confirmed examples of these pre-Cardial 'pioneer' implants are not numerous – fewer than a dozen mainland sites present dates ranging over the first two centuries of the sixth millennium cal BCE (Battentier et al. 2017, Table 1).

The prime diagnostic of the eponymous phase is, then, the ceramics. Recent inventories have identified Impressa ware at some 11 northern mainland sites. These include deposits in caves/rock-shelters as well as open settlements distributed along the Tyrrhenian coast from Marmotta in Abruzzo to La Grotta in Languedoc. Of these, eight have provided reliable radiometric dates falling roughly within the first half of the sixth millennium cal BCE (Battentier et al. 2017, fig. 1; Marchand and Manen 2010; Manen 2007).

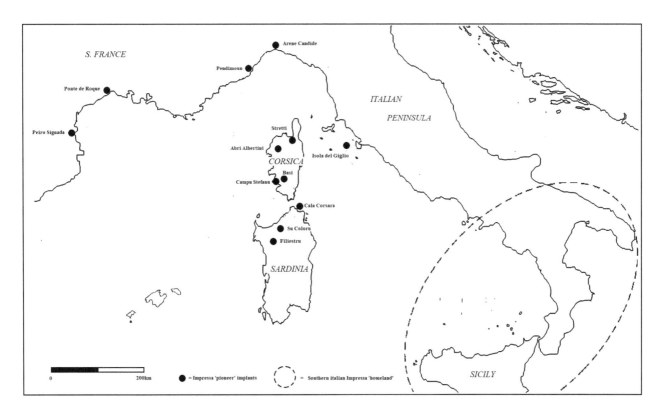

Fig. 9. West-central Mediterranean diffusion of Impressa-phase sites (elaborated after Marchand and Manen 2010; Binder et. al 2017).

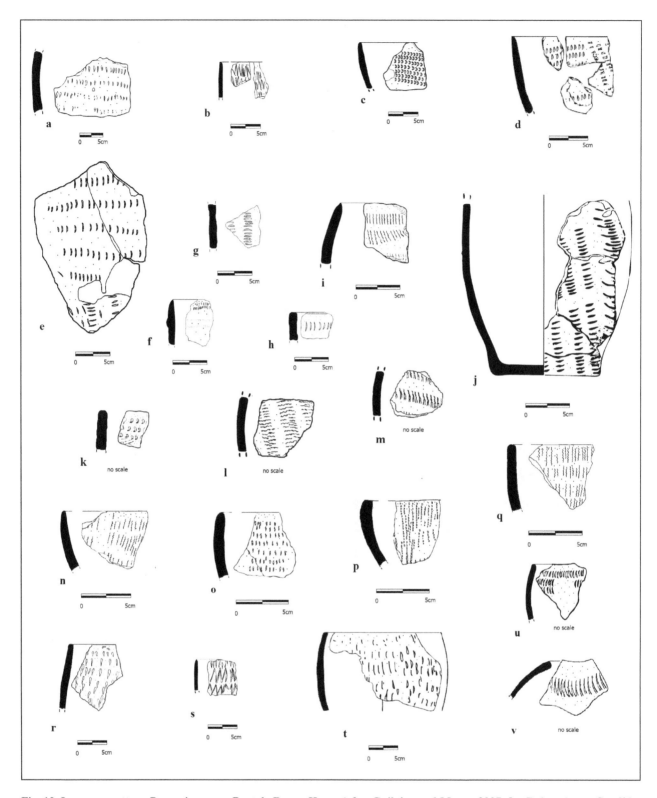

Fig. 10. Impressa pottery. Proveniences, a: Pont de Roque-Haute (after Guilaine and Manen 2007, fig. 5), b-c: Arene Candide (after Biagi and Starnini 2016, fig. 6:3, 7.5), d: Pendimoun (after Binder and Sénépart 2010, fig. 4.4), e: Campu Stefanu (after Cesari et al. 2012a, fig. 5.1), f: Strette (after Costa et al. 2002, fig. 3.9), g-h: Basi (after Paolini-Saez 2010, fig. 2-2-3), i-j: Isola del Giglio (after Manen 2007, fig. 87.2-7), k: Cala Corsara (after Ferrarese Ceruti and Pitzalis 1987, fig. 3.2), l: Su Coloru (after Fenu et al. 2002, fig. 5), m-q: Filiestru (after Trump 1983, figs. 6 and 8), r-s: Guadone-San Severo (after Manen 2007, fig. 85.10-11), t: Ripa Tetta-Lucera (after Manen 2007, fig. 85.12), u-v: Mersin (Anatolia; after Garstang 1953, fig. 3-4).

The pottery is recognised by its distinctive decorations that comprise various spaced impressions, incisions, grooves and relief mouldings. While impressions were often executed with shells (*cardium, patella* and others), unlike the geometric motifs of later Tyrrhenian Cardial-impressed ware, Impressa designs are characteristically simple, composed of vertical or horizontal lines or parallel bands (e.g. Guilaine and Manen 2002; 2007; Fugazzola Delpino 2002). Forms include various narrow-necked bottles, trunco-conical open vessels, often with flat bases and lateral tongue handles, sometimes vertically perforated. Based on formal attributes, Impressa is felt to have originated in southeast Italy (e.g. Guilaine and Manen, 2002, 42; Binder et al. 1993; Guilaine and Grifoni Cremonesi 2003), although certain decorative schemes, such as the so-called nail-impressed wares (usually made with a small shell edge, however), can be traced further east through the Aegean (Benvenuti and Metallinou 2002) and the Near East (Balossi and Frangipane 2002; Garstang 1953).

Impressa-phase lithics

Flaked stone industries are similarly diagnostic of this earliest Neolithic phase, although as much by the choice of raw material as by the knapping techniques. The exploitation of volcanic glass (obsidian) for flaked tools is widely considered indicative of a Neolithic presence, despite some exceptional finds in Mesolithic contexts such as S'Omu e S'Orku-Arbus in Sardinia (see the previous chapter and Lugliè 2012, 174; 2018, 296; Ceruleo 2003). Why obsidian was little used prior to the Neolithic is less than obvious, since the locations of known Mesolithic sites in the central Mediterranean suggests an awareness of the major obsidian sources on Sardinia, Lipari, Palmarola and Pantelleria among hunter-gatherer groups (Tykot 1995, 205). This apparent indifference to volcanic glass by pre-Neolithic groups here is made even more curious by the relative wealth of evidence for its extensive use and marine-based circulation in the Aegean and Near East prior to agriculture (Ceruleo 2003, 41; Horejs et al. 2015, 294). In any event, the incorporation of obsidian into the Impressa-phase stone industry was neither immediate nor thorough,

and flints of various kinds dominated in most Impressa contexts such as at Peiro Signado and Pont de Roque-Haute in France (Guilaine and Manen 2007, 33, 35), and Arene Candide (Starnini 1999, 231) and Le Secche-Giglio in Italy (Brandaglia 2002, 415). Importantly, the rare occurrences of obsidian, as at Arene Candide and Peiro Signado, represent imports from Sardinia and Palmarola (Briois et al. 2009; Ammerman and Polglase 1993; 1997; Lugliè 2018).

Apart from the selection of raw materials, knapping technologies also document discontinuities, generally represented by the replacement of the typical Mesolithic flake- or debitage-based so-called undifferentiated industry toward the systematised blade-based microburin industry. The transition was not necessarily abrupt, but it involved both the intensification of previously little employed but known Mesolithic procedures of blade production and microburin techniques for trapezoidal or triangular microlithics, as well as the elaboration of especially the microlithic industry into a variety of new forms, now more often realised with pressure-flaking methods, including trapezoids, triangles, rhomboids, re-touched bladelets – some of which were hafted as sickle-blades and/or arrow-heads (Guilaine and Manen 2007; Binder et al. 2003; Briois et al. 2009). At the important single-component deposits of neighbouring Peiro Signado and Pont de Roque-Haute, Mesolithic (Castelnovian) lithic traditions are in evidence in the Impressa industries: chert was worked into blades and double-truncated trapezoids by the percussion microburin technique, and the rarer obsidian was worked into blades following comparable methods (see Fig. 11 and Briois et al. 2009).

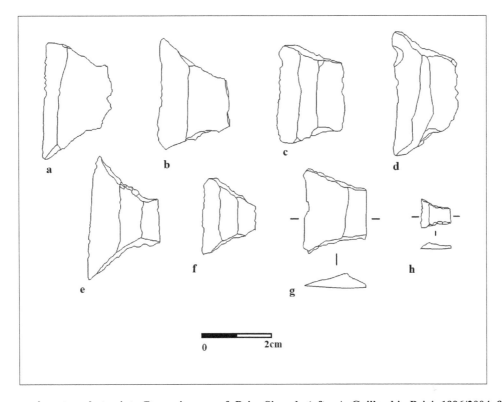

Fig. 11. Impressa-phase tranchet points. Proveniences, a-f: Peiro Signado (after A. Gaillaud in Briois 1996/2004, fig. 8), g-h: Su Coloru (after Sarti et al, 2012, fig. 1).

Impressa-phase subsistence

Needless to say, economic indexes of animal and plant domestication constitute crucial diagnostics of the Mesolithic-Neolithic transition. Several Impressa sites on the mainland – both open-air and caves – report cultivated emmer, einkorn and barley, with some gathered plant remains at Pendimoun near Castellar, France (Guilaine and Manen 2007). Unfortunately, faunal remains that can be reliably associated with Impressa contexts are rare (e.g. Vigne 2007). But butchered bones from the deepest Early Neolithic stratum (XXVIII) at Arene Candide in Italy were dominated numerically by those of domestic sheep/goats, with lesser numbers from swine (*Sus scrofa*), red deer (*Cervus elaphus*), roe deer (*Capreolus capreolus*), and hare (*Lepus capensis*), with cattle (*Bos taurus*) notably absent (Rowley-Conway 1997, fig. 3). Pont de Roque-Haute revealed a similar range of herded and hunted animals but also included cattle (n=11), and showed caprines (n=411) to have greatly outnumbered all other species (3 swine, 13 red or fallow deer, 10 roe deer, 1 hare; Vigne 2007, Annexe 3). Anne Tresset and Jean-Denis Vigne (2007) have regarded the Pont de Roque-Haute remains as evidence for a pastoral specialisation.

Given the proximity of these sites to the sea, finds of marine molluscs at Arene Candide and Pendimoun, including shells of *Cardium edule* used in pottery decoration, is not surprising (Binder and Sénépart 2010; Binder et al. 1993). However, it appears from recent stable isotope analyses of bone remains at these shelters that marine shell-fish were not much consumed (Le Bras-Goude et al. 2006, 45).

Grinding implements are not frequent in mainland Impressa deposits, but a few are reported at Peiro Signado and Pont de Roque-Haute (Guilaine and Manen 2007, 35-37). As key components of the so-called Neolithic package, such tools have typically been considered reliable indicators of domestic cereal processing. But recent reports from Iberian hunter-gatherer sites bearing rich ground-stone assemblages (Gilabert et al. 2016) warn against too much confidence in interpreting these implements as necessarily agricultural unless accompanied by macrobotanical remains of domesticates. The site of Le Secche on the island of Giglio (Italy) is a case in point. Apart from sherds of Impressa ware, finds of ground-stone axes, pestles, hammerstones and shredding tools as well as traces of wear and gloss on certain obsidian elements would seem to suggest some plant use. But the only food remains recorded were fractured shells of marine molluscs and animal (Brandaglia 2002; Ducci and Perazzi 2000).

Impressa-phase settlement

As regards settlement patterns, two modes are evident among the Tyrrhenian mainland Impressa sites: natural caves or rock-shelters and open settlements, in rare cases preserving architectural remains (as at Peiro Signado and Pont du Roque-Haute). The evidence from caves/rock-shelters suggest multi-purpose use: near-permanent habitation with corralling of domestic stock is suggested by finds of teeth, coprolites and fodder remains at Arene Candide (Traverso 2002, 299-300; Maggi 2002, 93), while seasonal encampments appear more likely for Pendimoun and Caucade (Guilaine and Manen 2002, 43).

Of the open sites, only Peiro Signado in Languedoc has provided settlement details (Guilaine and Manen 2007; Briois and Manen 2009). Here, the stripping of topsoil exposed a clearly delineated habitation area of some 90 sqm with interior features, but no indication of any circuit ditch or wall. A single dwelling demarked by nine post-holes (20-30 cm dia., reflecting 8 wall-posts and 1 central post) with an oval plan measuring ca. 5.5 by 8 m occupied the northeast sector. Finds of clay lumps/cob (also found at neighbouring Pont de Roque-Haute) suggest a wood-and-daub construction. Lithics and ceramics were recovered inside with little functionally significant spatial patterning. A number of pits containing mixed fill flanking the hut mainly on the west are of special interest and have tentatively been identified as extraction pits for mining underlying clays for building cob. Other finds, from plow-disturbed and fill deposits, included quartz gravel, fragments of basalt stones, and a single large millstone (*in situ*) near a small pit with carbonised cereal grains. That the structure is a domestic dwelling seems likely. Its size (an interior space of ca. 40-50 sqm), suggests a small family group (assuming 10 sqm per person on ethnographic grounds, see Narroll 1962).

A consideration of the locations of the Impressa sites – both the placement of open sites in the landscape and/or the choice of natural shelters – suggests a common appeal of coastal/littoral settings at low elevation (Battentier et al. 2017, 4), a mode also favoured, it seems, for Impressa settlements in southern Italy (Palmiotti 2004). Access to easily worked arable has otherwise been considered important (Guilaine and Manen 2007, 309), as well as proximity to coastal resources as exemplified in the shell middens at Le Secche-Giglio. The pattern is in clear contrast to known Mesolithic placements – assumed to represent seasonal camps – which tended to favour uplands (above 800 m) and lowlands (below 200 m) with few at medium elevation. These differences have been viewed as significant, and explained alternatively in terms of diversified niches between farmer-herders and hunter-gatherers, or perhaps resulting from mutual social avoidance (Binder and Guilaine 1999; Binder 2000; Binder and Maggi 2001; Battentier et al. 2017, 4).

Interestingly, there is currently no evidence of ritual observances at Impressa sites. Even burials appear to be absent from the mainland record generally (Starnini et al. 2018, 306). Claire Manen (2007) has suggested that this might reflect an adherence to customs that de-emphasised or excluded the dead from the landscapes of the living – an approach which, if applicable here, would be in stark contrast to eastern Neolithic practices.

The picture gained from the patchy evidence of the initial or pioneer phase of Neolithisation in the Tyrrhenian mainland is thus one of small groups – perhaps individual families – applying an inherited 'Neolithic package' adjusted to local, mainly coastal, conditions, resulting in a diverse array of agro-pastoral adaptations supplemented by hunting and gathering. Settlement near the coast was favoured, perhaps in a context of strategic avoidance of late hunter-gatherer sites. Across this diversity however, a common cultural heritage or *koiné* is evinced in the Impressa ceramic tradition traceable to the south Italian peninsula and further east.

4

Pioneers of the *Ceramica Impressa*

Sardinia under a Neolithic gaze

It is uncertain to what extent the evidence at our disposal allows for a reconstruction of the island and its environments on the eve of the Neolithic. The general conditions that greeted the first agro-pastoralists coming here at the beginning of the sixth millennium BCE are, however, known. To begin, due to sea-levels 15-20 m lower than today, the landmass was slightly larger than its current 24,000 sq. km and its coastal plains extended as much as 10 km farther out at the gulfs (Antonioli et al. 2007, fig 8; Palombo et al. 2017; Pittau et al. 2012). The climate would have already have been typically Mediterranean, with hot, dry summers and cool, wet winters, supporting a range of low, bushy perennials and annuals (*macchia*) in the plains below 200 m elevation, somewhat lusher cover in the uplands including thin stands of oak (up to 600 m) and thicker cover still in the mountainous interior with oak, chestnut and lesser scrub clinging to the slopes ranging over 1200 m (see Webster 1996 for a detailed review of insular environments and traditional nineteenth-century CE land-use practices).

With an eye to land suited for planting the hulled grains and legumes favoured on the Italian peninsula at this time, or for grazing stock of sheep, goats, swine and cattle, moisture-retaining alluvium could be found as terrace formations along the larger rivers Mannu in the south and Tirso in the west, and near the mouths of a number of other flows (the Posada, Cedrino, Flumendosa, Coghinas, Temo, Palmas). The winter rainfall regime would have demanded the sowing of cereals and pulses in the fall towards an early summer harvest, likely coupled with the grazing of stock on harvested and fallowing fields. With the onset of the summer heat and aridity, animals could be fed in the humid gulley bottoms, or driven to higher pasture to graze on scrub and forage on acorns. The uplands too would have offered opportunities for cultivation, but here, alluvial bottoms were less common (e.g. restricted to the middle to upper Tirso and Coghinas valleys, and highland valleys such as Bonu Ighinu) and poorer, rockier soils were the norm, better suited to summer pasturing.

If ceramic affinities have been correctly read, the likely migration route for Neolithic pioneers venturing into Sardinia will have been from Tuscany by way of the intervening islands of Elba, Pianosa and/or Giglio to the southernmost tip of Corsica. From there, a 12 km sea crossing at the straits of Bonifacio accessed the islets of the Maddalena archipelago off northeast Sardinia toward landfall in Gallura and near present-day Olbia. From here, near-shore travel by boat would have been manageable around much of the island's shore save perhaps the rocky precipitous eastern coastline facing Italy, known in later

Fig. 13. Landscape of Gallura in northern Sardinia (Photo: B. Prieur for WikiMedia Commons).

Fig. 12. Approaching the northwest islet of Spargi (Photo: G. Careddu for WikiMedia Commons, cropped).

Fig. 14. The Coghinas river setting in northern Sardinia (Photo: M. Braun for WikiMedia Commons, cropped).

Fig. 15. Monte Arci 'obsidian landscape' today (Photo: M. Cau for WikiMedia Commons).

periods also for its forbidding currents, while overland travel would have been easy along the river valleys. Whether by boat or land, the extensive flint deposits of Perfugas in the upper Coghinas valley near the north coast would soon have been discovered, and eventually also the vast flows of obsidian glass covering the western slopes of the extinct volcano of Monte Arci just inland from the western Gulf of Oristano.

An unexpected challenge to Neolithic newcomers would perhaps have been the island's paucity of wild game. In stark contrast to the mainland's rich and diverse fauna that included several species of deer at this time (e.g. Battentier et al. 2017, 2), Sardinia was apparently bereft of wildlife at the start of the sixth millennium BCE, save small birds, reptiles, fish, marine and terrestrial molluscs, small rodents and one medium-sized lagomorph – the pika, *Prolagus sardus* (Vigne 2004; Sondaar and van der Geer 2000). Given the complete absence of natural predators, the small mammals will periodically have reached infestation levels. That the *prolagus* would have provided early settlers with a valuable source of meat, if not skins, we can be certain. It is fairly clear from the Mesolithic record that this animal had sustained hunter-gatherer exploitation without depletion (e.g. Sondaar and van der Geer 2000, 69). We must wonder though, whether it would not have posed a serious threat to crops later on (Fig. 16).

One could draw a similar picture of Corsica at this time, although this would feature fewer agricultural options and a lack of good lithic resources, while otherwise sharing in the paucity of game – and uncertainties regarding the presence of late Mesolithic groups. For we must wonder whether the first Neolithic pioneers found these islands uninhabited or occupied to some extent by late hunter-gatherers. At the moment, the answer eludes us. As discussed in the previous chapter, regarding Sardinia, the archaeological record suggests a hiatus of some centuries between the final Mesolithic and the earliest Neolithic remains. One the other hand, genetic evidence seems to leave little doubt that some pre-Neolithic biological heritage survived into modern day Sardinian populations, presumably by way of Neolithic ancestors.

Fig. 16. *Prolagus sardus* (Prolagussardus for WikiMedia Commons).

Corsican Impressa

Impressa ware has been tentatively at several locales on Corsica: in rock-shelter deposits at Campu Stefanu and Albertini, and in the open-air sites of Basi and Strette (Paolini-Saez 2010, Cesari et al. 2012a; Binder et al 2017). With the exception of Campu Stefanu, the finds amount to a few fragments of Impressa ware among predominantly Cardial assemblages. Only at Campu Stefanu has it been possible to differentiate the Impressa phase stratigraphically from that of overlying Cardial deposits.

Campu Stefanu-Sollacaro

Campu Stefanu is a multi-phase complex of deposits covering more than a hectare on a rocky granitic hill at 94 m asl near the Taravu river at Sollacaro in southern Corsica. In addition to a cyclopean masonry structure of the Bronze Age, it features a rock-shelter preserving stratified deposits from the Mesolithic through the Bronze Age (Cesari et al. 2012b). This remarkable feature consists in a large granite boulder, naturally hollowed by erosion (a not infrequent occurrence in Corsica and Sardinia), and offering interior living space of ca. 13 sqm. Of interest here is especially its stratum 108a (Fig. 17).

Approximately two metres of sediments preserved seven cultural strata. Stratum US108a was clearly differentiated from an overlying mixed Cardial-Epicardial deposit (US 105b) and an underlying Mesolithic layer containing burial remains (US 108b) dated to 6596-6469 cal BCE (Lugliè 2018). It contained a small assemblage of Impressa ware comparable to mainland examples (Apulia, Tuscany, Liguria, Herault) as well as the few specimens found at Strette and Basi. These were associated with a small collection of blades and bladelets in imported Sardinian (Perfugas) flint and obsidian (probably also Sardinia) (Cesari et al. 2012a; 2014; Lugliè 2018). The dozen Impressa

Fig. 17. Rock-shelter n. 1 at Campu Stefanu in Corsica, a: plan, b: section (after Cesari et al. 2012a, fig. 2).

finds were thick sherds probably from two or three large (storage?) containers, simply decorated with unmargined vertical lines of impressions made with a small scalloped shell, probably *Cardium edula* (Cesari et al. 2012a, 84). A small collection of bones was associated, representing birds and small mammals including *Lagomys*, burned and highly fragmented, as one would expect of food remains.

Impressa in Sardinia

Confirmed evidence for a pre-Cardial Impressa phase in Sardinia is limited and enigmatic. There are several possible explanations for this. One, of course, is that, pioneering Impressa settlements were never numerous, and amounted rather to temporary scouting ventures, as Luglè (2008) has implied. But there are also sampling issues that remain unresolved. Pure Impressa components like those at Peiro Signado, Pont de Roque-Haute, Pendimoun I, and Campu Stefanu on Corsica have not as yet been identified in Sardinia. Instead, Impressa finds comprise a few sherds within deposits dominated by classic Cardial-impressed ware. Problems of detection are evident as well, and made more challenging by typological issues: the recognition of Impressa as distinct from and probably ancestral to Cardial-impressed ware (alternatively Tyrrhenian Cardial or Geometric Cardial) is quite recent. Older reports tend to classify all shell-marked pottery as Impressed or even Cardial-impressed, making re-evaluations problematic, and it is likely that pre-Cardial Impressa specimens went unrecognised in older excavations. Nevertheless, the data which has been gleaned regarding an early, pre-Cardial presence on Sardinia is still informative, and moreover suggests several points of contrast with Corsican and mainland Impressa occupations. It centers on the caves

Fig. 18. Filiestru Cave mouth (Photo: G. Careddu for WikiMedia Commons).

of Filiestru and Su Coloru and the rock-shelter at Cala Corsara-Spargi.

Filiestru-Mara

Filiestru is a large cave in the interior Bonu Ighinu valley in northwest Sardinia (Fig.18-19). Excavations in the late 1970s and early -80s revealed deeply stratified occupational deposits representing facies known as Su Carroppu (Cardial), Filiestru (Epicardial), Bonu Ighinu, Ozieri, Bonnanaro (Early Bronze Age) and Sa Turricula (Middle Bronze Age). With associated carbon dates and faunal remains, the series has long served as a key chrono-cultural reference for the island.

The deepest three strata (11-13 of trench B, 7-9 of trench D) were dominated by ceramics of the Geometric (or

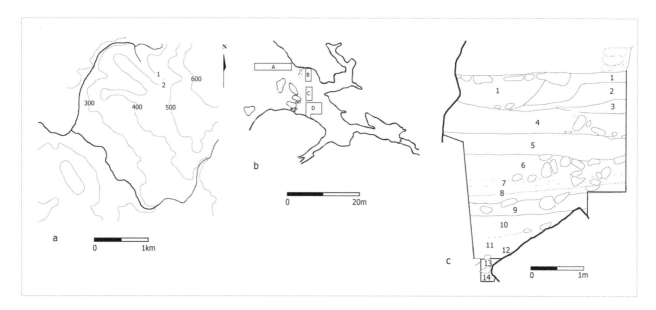

Fig. 19. a: The Bonu Ighinu basin with the caves of 1/ Filiestru and 2/ Sa Ucca de su Tintirriolu (after Trump 1983, fig. 1), b: plan of Filiestru cave (after Trump 1983, fig. 2), c: section of trench D at Filiestru cave (after Trump 1983, fig. 5).

Tyrrhenian) Cardial-impressed ware phase, and four radiocarbon dates range between 5702 and 5316 cal BCE (Lugliè 2018, Table 1). An inspection of the published figures shows that eight or nine of these sherds (ca. six per cent of the total) diverge in terms of decorative motif from the dominant geometric designs of Cardial wares. These bear short, vertical segments of shell-impressed lines, mostly arranged in irregular rows, comparable to examples of Impressa ware from Pont de Roque-Haute and Peiro Signado in southern France (Guilaine and Manen 2007, figs. 4:10; 5: 2-5), and to the Corsican Impressa finds noted below (see Cesari et al. 2012a, fig. 5:1-7; Paolini-Saez 2010, fig. 2:2-3; Costa et al. 2002, fig. 3:9-10). One specimen in particular revealed rows of rocker-shell impressions (see Natali 2003, fig. 2), similar to some found at Arene Candide in Liguria (Biagi and Starnini 2016, fig. 6:3), Guadone in southeast Italy (Manen 2017, fig. 85:10-11) and in Asia Minor (Garstang 1953, fig. 10). Open shapes (bowls, cups) with simple rims comparable to Impressa ware elsewhere in the region are indicated (Tanda 1995: fig. 3), although the thickened rim on one specimen is more reminiscent of impressed vases in Asia Minor (Garstang 1953, fig. 10; see also Balossi and Frangipane 2002).

No botanical remains appear to have come from these earliest strata at Filiestru, but a small collection of bone remains were identified as coming from stratum D9 and included domestic caprines and swine, as well as *prolagus* and a single element from a fox – this last presumably imported (Levine 1983). As these deposits are greatly dominated by Cardial-ware ceramics, these faunal data will be considered in some detail in chapter five below.

Su Coloru-Laerru

Su Coloru is situated in the upland plateau of Tanca Manna at about 350 m asl at Laerru, currently some 10

km from the north coast. It is an underground complex of tunnels running to over 600 m with entrances at both ends. Excavations during the 1990s in the mouth of the larger SE entrance revealed deep, stratified deposits resulting from periods of human occupation and intermittent episodes of flooding from an active interior spring. Although not as yet sounded to bedrock, 14 main strata and numerous micro-layers have revealed cultural remains dating from Late Mesolithic through Middle Neolithic (Fig. 20 and Fenu et al. 1999-2000; 2002; Pitzalis et al. 2002).

The earliest ceramic-bearing stratum (I) was deposited above Mesolithic stratum L, dating to 6380-6210 cal BCE (Beta-167932; Lugliè 2018, 290; Lugliè 2017, 38; Fenu et al. 2002, Tab. I). Like the underlying deposits, stratum I preserved a series of micro-sedimentary layers deposited during periods of intermittent occupations and alluviation. The small collection of sherds came from layer I1 carrying a date on charcoal of 5895-5571 cal BCE (Lugliè 2018, Tab. I). Unfortunately, although some specimens bore decoration, none have as yet been considered classifiable (Sarti et al. 2012, 456, 461). The associated lithic assemblage was also small and largely non-diagnostic, dominated (as in the Mesolithic layers) by flake tools in local flints of varying quality. But there were also blades in finer-quality flint imported from the Perfugas quarries nearby. Notable were two trapezes from snapped blades (microburin technique), one of which showed traces of wear from contact with soft material, consistent with use as a hunting projectile (Sarti et al. 2012, 458). Macrobotanical remains have not been reported from Su Coloru (cf. Ucchesu et al. 2017). But faunal remains from both domestic stock (swine, sheep/goats, cattle), as well as wild game (*prolagus*, fox, boar) and even the domestic dog were recovered from the Early Neolithic deposits, albeit not reported by individual strata (Masala 2008: fig. 8). These, like the Filiestru faunal data, will be discussed in chapter five.

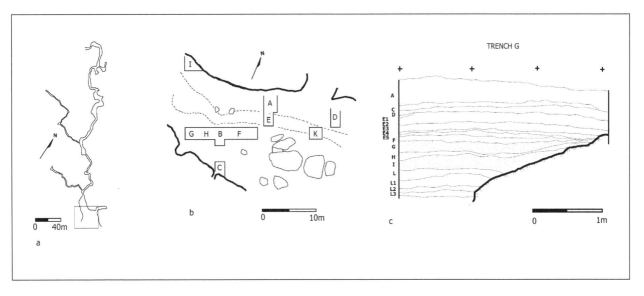

Fig. 20. Su Coloru Cave, a: plan (after Masala 2011, fig. 2), b: excavations (after Masala 2008, fig. 3), c: section of trench G(after Fenu, Martini and Pitzalis 1999-2000, fig. 1).

This earliest pottery-bearing horizon (I1) was separated by alluvial (Ia) and occupational horizons (I) from the next pottery-bearing stratum, H. The majority of shell-decorated sherds here were clearly identifiable as Tyrrhenian Geometric or Cardial-impressed ware with diagnostic, margin-band motifs. But a few others bore simpler shell-markings that appear to represent examples of the more archaic Impressa phase (see Lugliè 2017, 40-41; 2018, 290; Cesari et al. 2012a, 85; 2012b, 448). A superficial examination of decorative comparanda finds the closest parallels to be the Impressa ware from Le Secche on Giglio in the Tuscan archipelago (Manen 2007, fig. 87.12). An associated date on carbon, of 5901-5322 cal BCE (Lugliè 2018, Tab I), is in close agreement to that from underlying stratum I1. In light of the Filiestru ceramic series, it would not be surprising if underlying stratum I contained additional examples of Impressa ware.

Cala Corsara-Spargi

The so-called *tafone* of Cala Corsara is a small cave, (4 x 3.70 x 2-3 m) formed by the weathering of a granitic rock face (Fig. 21). It is situated at the water's edge of Cala Corsara Bay on the south coast of the small Isola di Spargi in the Maddalena archipelago off Sardinia's north coast (Ferrarese Ceruti and Pitzalis 1987). An intact basal deposit contained a few sherds of Impressed Ware, a small flaked stone assemblage and mollusc shells. The sherds are from simple bowls. One bears impressions typical of Geometric or Tyrrhenian Cardial ware (horizontal row below obliques within triangular fields, see Ferrarese Ceruti and Pitzalis 1987, fig. 3.1); the other, smaller sherds resemble Impressa wares. A second larger sherd bears rows of impressions made with the beak or umbo of a shell, possibly *Cypraea* (decorative category A1a3 in Bernabou Auban et al. 2010, Table 14.1), along with three

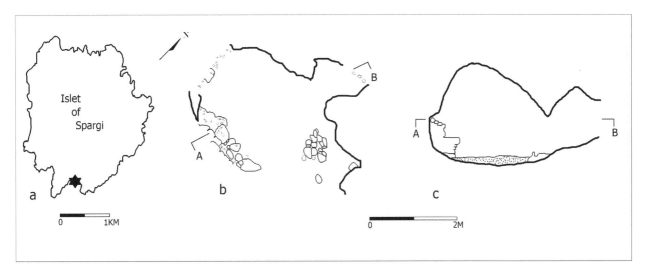

Fig. 21. Cala Corsara rock-shelter, a: location on the islet of Spargi (cf. Fig. 12), b-c: plan and section (after Ferrarese Ceruti and Pitzalis 1987, fig. 1).

oblique, linear Cardial shell impressions (Ferrarese Ceruti and Pitzalis 1987, fig. 3.2). The umbo-impressed specimen is notable as this decorative technique is quite rare, with specimens among Tyrrhenian sites on Giglio, at Peiro Signado and Arene Candide, and in Spain at Mas d'Is and Cariguela 16 (Biagi and Starnini 2016, fig. 7.5; Bernabou Auban et al. 2010, Table 14.3). A third, larger sherd carries a row of short, vertical fingernail impressions below the rim (Ferrarese Ceruti and Pitzalis 1987, fig. 3.4), similar to some sherds from Basi in Corsica and fairly common along with shell-impressed specimens in mainland sites from southern France (Binder and Sénépart 2010) to southeast Italy (Natale 2010, figs. 10-11).

Sardinian, Corsican and Tyrrhenian Impressa: contrasts and commonality

So far, only a handful of sites on Sardinia and Corsica have recorded finds of Impressa ceramics. Moreover, with the single exception of Campu Stefanu on Corsica, these have come from deposits dominated by Tyrrhenian Geometric ware. Still, the remains bear witness to a Neolithic presence in these islands at the beginning of the sixth millennium BCE. Whether these newcomers found the insular landscapes sparsely settled by hunter-gatherers or vacant of people, the label of pioneer settlers (following Lugliè 2018: 286, 290) seems entirely appropriate.

In Sardinia, the dates from Filiestru and Su Coloru would place these initial Neolithic entries between ca. 5900 and 5700 BCE, and potentially contemporary with those in the northern Tyrrhenian (Manen 2007). As we have seen, the picture arising from the still patchy evidence of the initial phase of Neolithisation on the mainland is one of small, mobile groups occupying natural shelters and/or modest, undefended open locales (pastoral camps), probably each on a seasonal basis. Evident too is the adjustment of the inherited 'Neolithic package' to local conditions, resulting in a diverse array of agro-pastoral adaptations variously supplemented by hunting and gathering. For Sardinia and Corsica, there are still an insufficient number of Impressa finds to challenge this as the most likely initial mode of settling the islands as well. Clearly Neolithisation on both islands did involve the replacement of the typical Mesolithic flake- or debitage-based so-called undifferentiated industry by a blade-based microburin industry. And on Sardinia at least Filiestru cave documented the introduction of domestic caprines and swine, and probably the Red fox.

Still, when taken together, the evidence also suggests some interesting exceptions to the mainland adaptations. The most striking is the apparent absence of any irrefutable evidence for domestic plant use or of ground-stone tools suited to processing grain. While this may reflect no more than the very small sample of Impressa-deposits investigated, it would clearly be incautious to assume that the initial Neolithic pioneers to the islands were fully agricultural. Another potential divergence from the mainland evidence is suggested by the site locations. The clear attraction of near-coast or littoral settings on the mainland is not closely matched in the islands. Only Strette (Corsica) and Cala Corsara (Spargi, Sardinia) can be considered coastal, while Basi, Campu Stefanu and Albertini on Corsica and Filiestru and Su Coloru on Sardinia are more than 10 km from the sea today (Filiestru is indeed an inland location). Last, the apparent effects of hunter-gatherer coexistence with Neolithic settlers in the mainland, which perhaps included mutual avoidance in terms of settlement choices, is not evident in the islands. At Strette and Campu Stefanu in Corsica and at Su Coloru in Sardinia, Neolithic occupations overlay Mesolithic strata, albeit with radiometric and/or sedimentary evidence of a temporal gap between them.

As discussed in chapter two, the question of Mesolithic-Neolithic relationships in Corsica and Sardinia is complicated by contradictory evidence from archaeology and genetic studies. Current opinion based on radiometric and stratigraphic evidence supports the idea of a hiatus between the latest hunter-gatherers and the earliest farmer-pastoralists, and thus pictures the Neolithic pioneers finding a demographically and culturally empty environment (Lugliè 2018, 296). This apparent hiatus has been noted in Sardinia, Corsica, southern Italy and southern France (Berger and Guilaine 2009, 32) and might perhaps be tentatively explained as a product of environmental degradation brought on by the so-called 8.2 ka event which will have resulted in cooler and drier conditions no longer easily sustainable by Mesolithic hunter-gatherers (see Chaper 2). In Sardinia, the hiatus has been variously estimated to have lasted between three and six centuries (Fenu et al. 2002, 334; Sarti et al. 2012, 460; Lugliè 2018, 290; 2009, 35). Countering this, as noted, are genetic data indicating the preservation in Sardinia of pre-Neolithic, island-specific haplotypes suggesting some degree of Mesolithic-Neolithic admixture and thus some level of Mesolithic-Neolithic engagement. At present, it seems we must remain open to the probability that some Mesolithic refuges survived into the era of the first Neolithic pioneers, although no material evidence of the entanglements implied by the genetic data has as yet come to light archaeologically.

5

The Cardial Phase

Introduction

The first post-Impressa phase of the Tyrrhenian Early Neolithic has been variously labelled Cardial, Tyrrhenian Cardial, Geometric Cardial, Classic Cardial and Ancient Cardial. Over the entirety of its range it is dated roughly from 5700/5600 to 5300/5200 in calibrated years BC (e.g. Lugliè 2018; Manen 2007; Binder and Sénépart 2010). Considering the accumulated evidence for this relatively short span of time regarding Sardinia and Corsica, one impression is clear: that of a rapid demic infilling of both islands. The typically modest extent of the deposits suggest further that this infilling was effected by small groups – perhaps families – targeting lowland settings, each in command of a locally adaptable version of the inherited Neolithic package. Their signature: the shell-decorated pots with geometric motifs which will be referred to here simply as Cardial or Cardial-Impressed ware.

Although it seems likely that the new ceramic mode was derived from the earlier Impressa phase, chronometric data suggest that the rate of the demic infilling was far too rapid to have resulted from the natural growth and fissioning of those few pioneer Impressa implants already in place (see below and Lugliè 2018, table 1). The more likely scenario will have featured multiple waves of immigrants, probably from Tuscany by way of the intervening islands, if the similarities in pottery decorations are any clue (see further below). While it is the norm to picture Neolithic colonists as agriculturalists, direct evidence of domestic plants such as charred remains of cereals with clear Cardial associations is actually lacking so far. By contrast, more widespread finds of butchered domestic stock – sheep/goats primarily, and lesser amounts from swine and cattle – suggest that the main economic focus of Cardial-bearing colonists to the islands was herding, supplemented by hunted deer, boar and mouflon as well as by the endemic pika, *Prolagus sardus*, presumably trapped (see Fig. 22).

The diagnostic pottery

The Cardial ceramic repertory comprises a narrow range of simple forms, many of which carry impressed decoration (Fig. 24). Typical are small to medium-sized hemispherical, cylindrical and spherical cups and bowls with flattened bases, sometimes carrying lateral lug- or ledge handles, and simple rims (Paolini-Saez 2010).

Like the earlier Impressa ware, Tyrrhenian Cardial ware features impressed decorations effected with a marine shell – typically the cockle or *Cardium* (about 30 per cent of the sherds from Filiestru Cave; Trump 1983). But here, the decorative coverage is more extensive and the designs more clearly organised in recognisable geometric patterns. Common motifs include horizontal zig-zags, triangular fields or orthogonal strips filled with parallel diagonals, vertical parallel zig-zags, nested chevrons, sometimes with accompanying lines of punctations or strokes – all effected by pressing the broad, serrated edge of a shell or, in the case of punctations, the narrow umbo – into the soft clay vessel before firing. Very close parallels are shared especially among sites on Corsica and in Tuscany, supporting the label Filiestru-Basi-Pienza for this particular decorative styling. Limited archaeometric results imply, however, local manufacturing, for the most part by simple methods with low temperature firing (Bertorino et al. 2000). Notably rare are large decorated vases and/or necked vessels, although some large vases have been reported from Capo Sant'Elia in southern Sardinia (Taramelli 1904; see below).

On the mainland, the question remains whether Cardial expression represents a continuation of the Impressa tradition or a separate influx. In support of the latter possibility, some have recorded a gap of 50 to 200 years between the two phases in southern France (Manen and Guilaine 2010, fig. 2). The few well-stratified deposits at our disposal for the islands, however, do not indicate such a hiatus. At both Sardinian and Corsican sites, Cardial remains are stratified directly above Impressa with no apparent intervening accumulations. At Filiestru Cave and less clearly at Su Coloru, moreover, a gradual replacement of Impressa by Cardial wares is implied in the seriation (see above). At the same time, demographic trends do suggest the infilling of both islands by multiple waves of new Cardial-bearing immigrants.

Settlement and demics

There are by current counts some 44 Cardial-bearing deposits on Sardinia (Lugliè 2018), excluding a still unconfirmed number of aceramic sites (see Introduction). Both cave/rock-shelters and open-air deposits have been identified, in about equal numbers. Most of our evidence, however, comes from the former, while with the exception of a very few deposits, the open sites are known largely from surface finds: diagnostic sherds, sometimes associated with lithics. To these might also be added an unknown number of aceramic lithic scatters of uncertain association.

Caves/rock-shelters

Already described for their rare Impressa finds, the caves of Filiestru-Mara, Su Coloru-Laerru and Cala

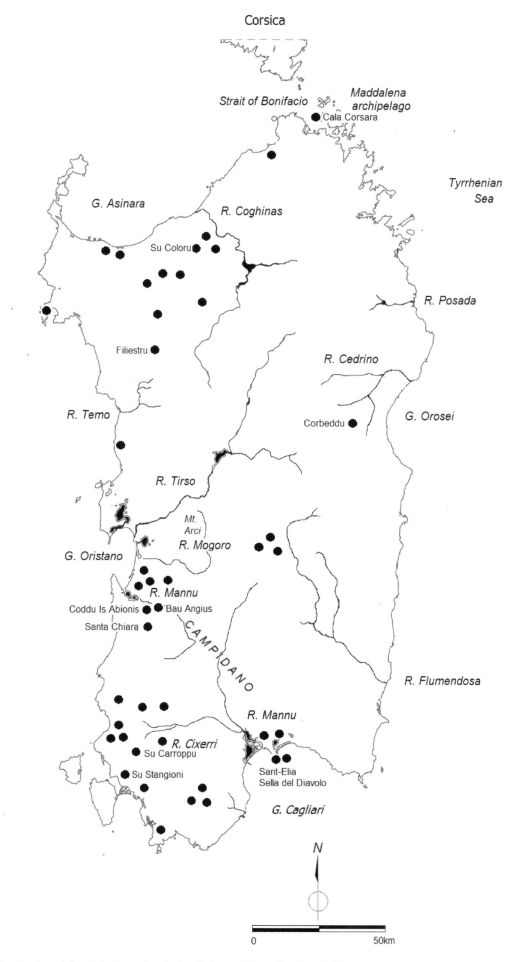

Fig. 22. Distribution of Cardial-phase sites in Sardinia (modified after Lugliè 2018, fig. 2).

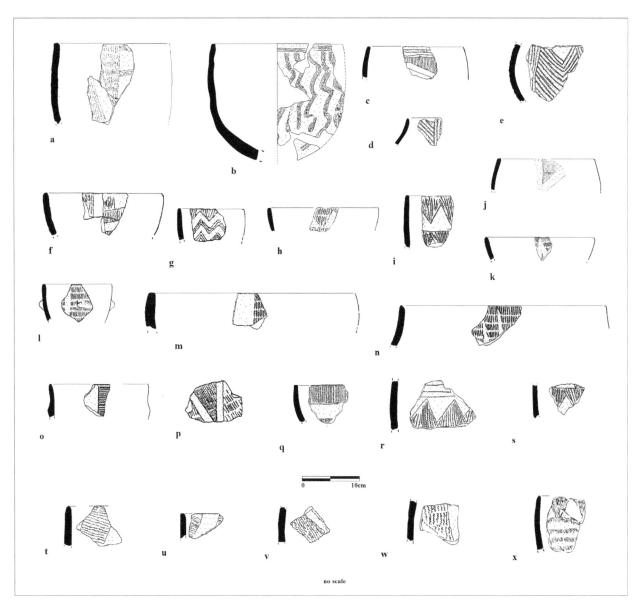

Fig. 23. Cardial pottery. Proveniences, a: Bau Angius (after Lugliè 2018, fig. 4), b-e: Su Stangioni (after Lugliè 2018, fig. 7; Usai, Migaleddu and Lugliè 2009, fig. 1), f-n: Filiestru (after Tanda 1995, figs. 3-4; Lugliè 2018, fig. 4), o-s: Santa Chiara (after Lugliè 2018, fig. 4), t-w: Su Coloru (after Fenu et al 2002, fig. 4), x: Cala Corsara (after Ferrarese Ceruti and Pitzalis 1987, fig. 3).

Corsara-Spargi also preserved important Cardial assemblages, comprising ceramics, lithics and, at Filiestru and Su Coloru, faunal remains as well. Based on internal dimensions and available living space at Filiestru (roughly 250 sqm), its investigator surmised that during the Cardial phase, 'a single community occupied the Grotta Filiestru, the largest inhabitable cave in the territory. Its size implies a population of up to 4-6 families, perhaps 25-30 people at most' (Trump 1990, 49). Although clearly debatable, the cave does seem to have served as a pastoral farmstead during its earliest phase of use. Similar remains from stratum H at Su Coloru that included some bones of boar (Masala 2008, Table 8) suggest that this cave more likely served as a seasonal hunting and pastoral camp. Cala Corsara on the northern islet of Spargi yielded Cardial ware, lithics and marine molluscs, and is felt by its investigators to have served as a way-station serving maritime traffic between

Corsica and Sardinia (Ferrarese Ceruti and Pitzalis 1987). Adding to these is the important rock-shelter deposit at Su Carroppu in the southwest.

Su Carroppu-Sirri

Su Carroppu represents another category of Early Neolithic cave-sites (Atzeni 1972; 1977; Lugliè et al. 2007), interpreted both as a refuge (possibly for groups of hunter-herders) and as a burial place. Already described in chapter two with regards to its important Mesolithic component, the site is located some 10 km inland from the southwest coast at an altitude of 350 m, in a zone of rocky hills overlooking a small valley. It is a small, deep limestone shelter. Its lowest deposits contained fragments of Cardial-Impressed Ware, remains of domestic and wild animal species, the latter including deer, boar, pika and fish, and chipped stone artefacts, including geometric

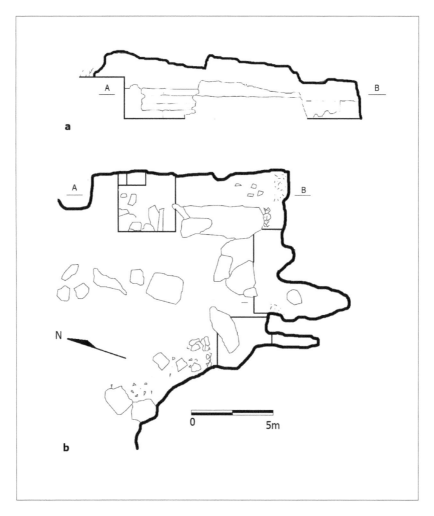

Fig. 24. The Su Carroppu rock-shelter, a: section, b: plan (after Lugliè et al. 2007, fig. 3).

microliths of local chert, quartzite and jasper, and of obsidian from Monte Arci farther afield (Fig. 24).

Open-air settlements

Su Stangioni-Portoscuso

Of the 20 or so open-air Sardinian sites with Cardial pottery, only two have provided detailed information. The open-air settlement in the far southwest at Portoscuso (Cagliari) dates to the latter end of the Tyrrhenian Cardial phase in the island, and bears evidence too of Epicardial material (Usai 2002; Usai et al. 2009; Lugliè 2017; 2018). Although lacking structural remains, a number of ash-filled pits may represent the vestiges of floor hearths. From these cavities, measuring 2-2.5 m in diameter by 30 cm in depth, were recovered Cardial ceramics and a flaked stone kit including geometric pieces suited to hafting as tranchet arrowpoints (Lugliè 2018, fig. 5). Apparently, food remains were not preserved. The location is not self-explanatory from an agricultural perspective, and it may well have served as a seasonal station, as suggested by its investigators (Usai et al. 2009, 12) – perhaps for hunting, given the lithics recovered. Today, the coast is less than a kilometre away, but in the mid-sixth millennium, it would have been several kilometres distant.

The Capo Sant'Elia complex

Capo Sant'Elia is calcareous promontory in the Gulf of Cagliari at the mouth of the Mannu river, now impounded as the Lagoon of Santa Gilla (Fig. 25). Archaeological deposits dating from Early Neolithic through Medieval periods were first discovered and investigated in the late nineteenth and early twentieth century (Orsoni 1879; Patroni 1901; Taramelli 1904) with subsequent analyses of the materials and site locations by Atzeni (1962) and most recently Ibba et al. (2017). Although these have yielded little detailed data, the locale is of interest for its evidence of intensive exploitation of marine shell-fish. At least two sites on the promontory have reported finds of impressed ware: Grotta di Sant'Elia and Sella del Diavolo. The former, located on the north slope below the peak of Sant'Elia just under 125 metres elevation is no longer traceable. It was excavated by Francesco Orsoni (1879), who reported remains of vases decorated with the edge of a cockle shell in designs comparable to those from Filiestru, Su Coloru and elsewhere (Alba and Canino 2005, 74), i.e. either Impressa or Cardial ware.

Some 300 m east and downslope of the cave was discovered the open-air site commonly called Sella del Diavolo but alternatively Marina Piccola A or, by the investigator,

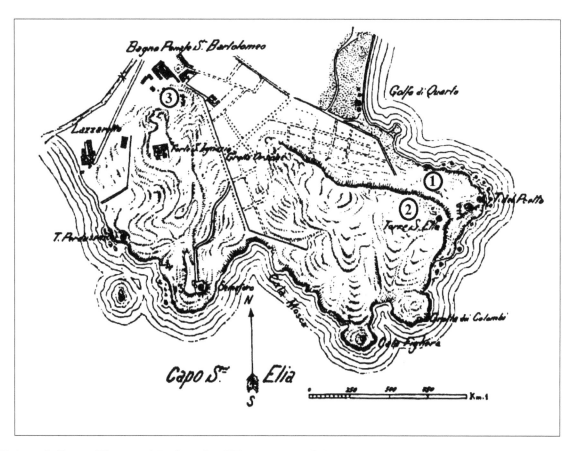

Fig. 25. Antonio Taramelli's map of the Capo Sant'Elia complex, 1. Sella del Diavolo, 2. Grotta di Sant'Elia, 3. Grotta del Bagno Penale (from Taramelli 1904, fig. 2).

i focolari di Poetto, the hearths of Poetto beach, for its prominent hearth features (Taramelli 1904). The deposit occupied a shelf above a small alluvial gulley or *burrone* currently about 20 metres above the Gulf of Poetto. Rich cultural deposits (up to two metres deep and six or seven metres wide) ran to some 15 metres in length. Within this site area, eight or ten charcoal- and ash-filled depressions identified as hearths were excavated. Surprisingly, given the date of the investigation, the contents of each were run through a mesh from which copious remains of mostly burnt marine shells, some bone, pottery including Cardial ware and numerous obsidian and flint tools were recovered. The excavator, Antonio Taramelli, attributed the hearths to an equal number of huts although he clearly showed that no evidence of floors, walling, foundations or post-holes had come to light. Unfortunately, we lack plan maps or detailed spatial information.

A lithic tool set mostly in obsidian presumably from Monte Arci comprised blades, geometric pieces, scrapers, points, but rarely arrowheads. Interestingly, Taramelli felt that 'certain knives with curved blades, sharp at the end and with large and sturdy grip at the base' (1904, fig. 4:8) had been designed for opening bi-valves, after trying them out for this purpose himself. Regarding the pottery – most of which was undecorated – a special note was made of sherds from very large jars possibly used for storage, which are otherwise rare in Cardial deposits. Food remains were dominated by marine molluscs that included both the types common or known to the area such as the *Cardium*

or cockle as well as non-local items such as *Mytilis edilis*. Some shells were perforated as if to serve for adornment; a single, large fish vertebra was similarly pierced. Mammal bones were fewer in number and showed signs of burning and butchering. They represented (in Taramelli's estimation) domestic sheep, goats and cattle, as well as the wild pika. A single, large diorite axe (*mazza* or *ascia*) from the surface could indicate that ground clearance had taken place but no remains of either plants or millstones were reported.

The finds taken together could represent the remnants of either a small hamlet, or deposits from repeated periodic visits by smaller groups, in any event featuring intensive shell collecting, herding, and possibly some fishing and hunting. But it is good to remember that the sea level was much lower in the mid-sixth millennium (by some 17 metres; Antonioli et al. 2007, fig. 8b), and the coastal landscape considerably different. A reconstruction based on bathymetric readings in the gulf shows the headland rising above a coastal plain up to 15 km wide at the mouth of the Mannu river just to the west, and the sea no closer than two kilometres to the south. The open-air Cardial-phase settlement just described would thus have sat over 35 metres above the sea which would have been some three km away. A coastal depression somewhat closer may have supported a saline marsh, however, and thus perhaps collectible marine foods, while the effluence of the Mannu river probably provided extensive arable alluvial terraces.

Site distribution and demic infilling

Regarding the distribution of the open Cardial-phase sites, within the limitations of what must be a very partial sample, the known locations seem generally to coincide with watered settings with prime pasture along the lower reaches of river- or stream valleys and near the gulfs. That such a correlation is less evident for natural shelters is perhaps to be expected, but it does raise the issue of their roles in local settlement regimes. A functional complementarity of open and sheltered sites has been argued for Corsica and the Languedoc (i.e. a combination of open farmsteads and seasonal pastoral cave-camps), and this is possibly applicable also to the Sardinia (Skeates 2012). But a lack of clear indications of Cardial-associated cultivation and for the juxtaposition of both types of deposits within a coastal setting as on Capo Sant'Elia described above cautions against drawing any general conclusions.

As noted, a conservative count of Cardial-bearing Sardinian deposits currently runs to some 44 sites. If at all representative, this implies a four-fold increase above the minimum three known Impressa locales over a period estimated to three to five centuries (ca. 5700/5600 to 5300/5200). In terms of annual growth rates, this translates to between 2.7 per cent yearly (over 500 years) and 4.6 per cent yearly (over 300 years). Such a rate is well in excess of common, archaeologically-based estimates for Neolithic population growth rates that converge around 0.1 per cent per year (Carneiro and Hilse 1966, 179; Hassan and Sengel 1973, 580; Bourgeois-Pichat 1967) and clearly well beyond that which can reasonably be accounted for by natural growth and fissioning of the original Impressa implants alone. A plausible conclusion is that the colonisation of Sardinia (and probably Corsica) by Cardial-bearing agro-pastoralists involved multiple waves of immigrants. Given the close affinity in decorative ceramics with Tuscany, the intervening islands of the archipelago would seem to be the most likely route of entry. This is given support by the similar decorative styles of ceramics from the sites along the possible route, Pianosa, Elba and Piombino, and, in some instances, finds of Sardinian obsidian (as on Pianosa; Tykot 1999, 71). Considering the limited number of radiocarbon dates available (Lugliè 2018, 291, table 1), it would furthermore seem likely that Corsica and northern Sardinia were colonised first, and southern Sardinia shortly after.

Burial deposit

Scattered human remains recovered at Su Coloru suggest little more than a casual deposition without signs of observance (Masala 2008, Table 8). No other burials of this phase have yet been reported in Sardinia. On the mainland too, Cardial-associated burials are rare (Starnini et al. 2018, 306), a fact which Manen (2007) has interpreted as implying customs that de-emphasised the dead, in contrast to Neolithic mortuary customs further east. The few known exceptions have amounted to scattered remains deposited in simple pits without offerings (at Cava Barbieri-Pienza, see Calvi Rezia and Sarti 2002) and a child's skull set in

a stone circle (at Settecannelle, see Ucelli Gnesutta 2002). The Su Coloru remains may represent similarly simple burials, subsequently disturbed.

Subsistence

Domesticates

The earliest botanical remains of cultivars have been recorded at Filiestru cave, in the predominantly Cardial deposits of trench D (Ucchesu et al. 2017, 6). The reports are ambiguous, however, and it seems more probable that they were associated to the earliest Epicardial remains from the upper cuts of this stratum; therefore, they will be considered in the following chapter. Cardial-associated faunal remains are better represented, notably in the caves of Filiestru, Su Coloru and also Corbeddu-Oliena. Filiestru preserved butchered remains of domestic stock – ovicaprines (over 80 per cent) but also swine (*Sus scrofa*) and cattle (*Bos taurus*). From the same levels came a large number of remains from very small animals too, e.g. bird, vole (*Microtidae*), tortoise, vertebrate microfauna, cockle and land snail (*Helicella sp.*). These probably entered the cave by both natural and human agencies, the marine molluscs – few in number – as collected foods and perhaps ornaments; the cockle used for decorating the characteristic pots (Levine 1983, 125). Masala's study of finds from combined Early Neolithic strata at Su Coloru (quadrant KL 22-32, levels 83-92) presents a range of wild species including bird, turtle, pika, fox and boar, as well as domestic dog, swine, cattle, sheep and goat (Masala 2008, Table 8). Bones of the domestic dog (*Canis familiaris*) are not uncommon in Neolithic contexts generally, and make a first appearance in Sardinia at Su Coloru), although not at Filiestru or Corbeddu. As elsewhere, the dog will have been a camp follower, herd protector, hunting companion and, in times of crisis, an emergency food source.

Shell-fish

Marine molluscs were not well represented at Filiestru, Su Coloru or Corbeddu – all of them interior upland caves. Excavated hearths at the open site of Sella del Diavolo on Capo Sant'Elia, within ca. three km of the south coast in the mid-sixth millennium, instead preserved large numbers of burned and presumably eaten remains (Taramelli 1904). A range of species were recognized: *Cardium tuberculatum, Cerastoderma, Cerythium vulgatum, Cerythium triviale, Pecten varius, Murex trunulus* (banded dye-murex, edible), *Arca Noae, Ostraea lamellosa, Ostraea edulis* (flat oyster), *Patella aspera, sitta, coerulea* and *barbara* (limpets), *Mytilus edulis* (black mussel), *Spondylus gaederopus* and *extensus, Tapes decussaius, Pinna squamosa* and *Pectunculus*. Some of these were perforated, perhaps to be worn.

Fox and Pika

The relatively abundant remains of fox (*Vulpes vulpes*) and the endemic pika (*Prolagus sardus*) at Filiestru and

Su Coloru would seem especially important for shedding light on questions raised in the Introduction, such as whether *Prolagus* posed a serious threat to early attempts at cultivation. That they were eaten is likely at Su Coloru (Masala 2008, 9-10), but less so at Filiestru (Levine 1983, 124). While we cannot assume that these animals were killed in direct proportion to their numbers in the wild, it is worth noting that at both sites, the ratio of pika to fox was high (19:1 at Su Coloru and 7:1 at Filiestru). For comparison, at the contemporary lake-shore village of Marmotta at Bracciano on the Italian peninsula the reverse was true: fox outnumbered hare by 2:1 (Tagliacozzo 2005-2006, 434). The fox, we are fairly certain, is not native to Sardinia (or Corsica) and must have been brought in by the earliest Neolithic colonists (Vigne 1988; Masala 2008, 5). While they may have been exploited for skins, there is nothing at least in the Filiestru bones to indicate skinning. It seems not implausible that they may have been imported to keep down the seemingly great numbers of potential garden pests like the pika (Wilkens 2010; Masala 2013, 69). Indeed, perhaps it was because of an inability to do so that cultivation appears not to have taken hold in the island until the later sixth millennium, among Epicardial-bearing farmers, perhaps after the *prolagus* numbers had been significantly reduced (see chapter six).

Mouflon and boar

A preliminary report from Corbeddu Cave of the mouflon (*Ovis musimon*) and from Filiestru and Su Coloru of the wild boar (*Sus scrofa meridionalis*) are of great interest. As both are considered to be feral varieties of previously introduced Neolithic domesticates, *Ovis aries* and *Sus scrofa,* it is notable that such escapees from domestic herds had already diverged enough, anatomically, to be recognisable in bone, tusk and horn remains. They must be considered potentially huntable game.

Red deer

Cardial-phase strata at Corbeddu Cave include what may be the first appearance of the red deer, *Cervus elaphus*, in the island (Sanges 1987). Unless local refuge populations from the ice-age have gone undetected archaeologically, this large, wild ungulate appears to have arrived in Sardinia with the first Neolithic colonists. Recent genetic studies have identified the Italian peninsula as its most likely origin (Doan et al. 2017). There remains the intriguing and unanswered question of the circumstances and mode of its arrival, however (Hmwe et al. 2006). The ancient translocation of deer into non-native habitats including islands has been widely documented in Europe (Nussey et al. 2006, 56; Stanton et al. 2016), and following Vigne's thesis (1993), Masseti has suggested that they were introduced and then released in a free-ranging state 'enabling man to keep the number of animals under control through occasional hunting as required' (2006, 88). This aligns with Vigne's proposal of *cynégétisation*, whereby deer were appropriated as much for their symbolic as their dietary value, and required the recreation of their status as

wild hunted game within the Neolithic setting (1993, 213). But the hypothesis remains debatable. More reasonable might be Jarmen's earlier suggestion that 'the Neolithic Italian husbanded his herds of deer in a way not dissimilar to that in which they are now treated in deer parks, or to the way in which neolithic man treated his sheep' (1972, 132).

Crafts

Bone and shell instruments and ornaments

In the Cardial-phase deposits at Filiestru, there was a small number of bone splinters from caprines which had been worked into awls, points or punches (Trump 1983, 67-69; Masala 2008, fig. 19). Perforated shells and one fish vertebra from Sant'Elia have already been noted; all are likely to represent ornaments such as necklace elements (Fig. 26). Perforated shells have been widely recorded within Cardial contexts outside the island especially in Liguria, but also in the Tuscan archipelago at La Scola-Pianosa (Micheli 2004, table 1; fig. 3).

Flaked stone

Stone tools were fashioned from local quartz, rhyolite and flint. The latter, mainly from the Perfugas quarries in northern Sardinia, was sometimes imported into Cardial contexts in Corsica (e.g. Strette, Renaghju) as it had been in the earlier Impressa site at Campu Stefanu (Lugliè 2012; Bressy-Leandri 2016). Lithic tool kits on Sardinia as well as Corsica appear to have expanded on earlier traditions that employed the microburin method whereby blades were further reduced and retouched to produce an array of geometric microliths including rectangles, trapezes, lunates, triangles, as well as larger scrapers, burins and transverse tranchet points (Fig. 27, e.g. Depalmas 1995; Trump 1983, 12; Weiss 2000; Brandaglia 1985; Binder 1987). Some tranchet points have, on close examination, revealed impact fractures (Gassin and Lugliè 2012), suggesting they were hafted as arrowheads of the kind seen in Impressa-contexts at Su Coloru, possibly Cala Corsara, Filiestru and also on the mainland (Guilaine and Manen 2007; Binder et al. 2003; Briois et al. 2009). Experimental studies have shown them to be quite effective on game,

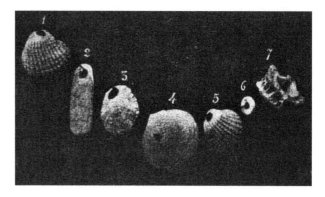

Fig. 26. Bone and shell ornaments from Capo Sant'Elia. (from Taramelli 1904, fig. 3).

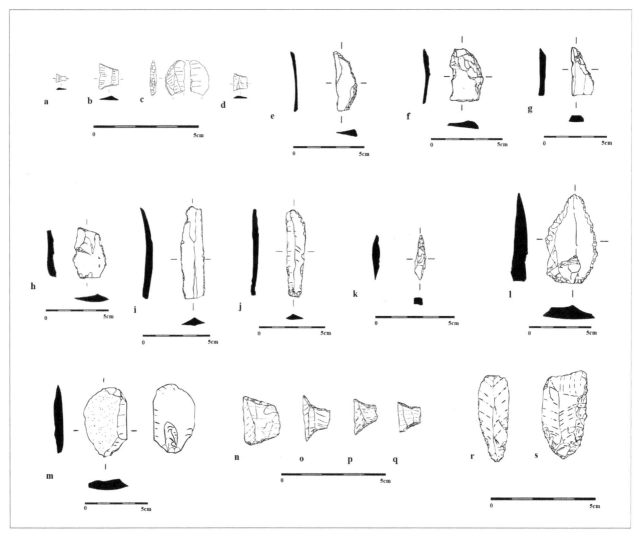

Fig. 27. Cardial-phase flaked stone. Proveniences, a-d: Su Coloru (flint, after Sarti et al. 2012, fig.1), e-m: Filiestru (f, h, i, j obsidian; e, g, k, l, m flint, after Trump 1983, figs. 27-29), n-s: Cala Corsara (after Ferrarese Ceruti and Pitzalis 1987, fig. 4).

inflicting wide, relatively shallow but highly debilitating wounds (e.g. Brizzi 2013; Ashby 2005). If they were indeed used for hunting, the targets are likely to have been red deer, mouflon and boar. Gassin and Luglié (2012) have suggested their use also for small animals like *prolagus* for archery training, for putting down domestic stock, or as weapons. Any and all seem reasonable in light of the faunal evidence noted above. Their use in offense/defence – well documented in oft-cited Egyptian pre-Dynastic warfare media (e.g. Clarke et al. 1974) – would also not be out of place in an Early Neolithic landscape of scattered, vulnerable stock-keeping homesteads. Possibly relevant too are finds of tranchet points in some Iberian Neolithic male burials, perhaps suggesting their potential value as a status marker (Gibaia and Palomo 2004). Tools clearly used in plant harvesting are, however, all but absent. A single lunate from Su Coloru with wear consistent with use as a sickle bit is a rare exception (Sarti et al. 2012, fig. 1B).

Perhaps the clearest differentiating feature of the Cardial lithic industry was the far greater use made of obsidian from Monte Arci in west-central Sardinia. Only rarely found in Impressa contexts, it is frequently found in Cardial contexts on both islands, although on Corsica clearly in fewer numbers (de Lanfranchi and Weiss 1973). It is also found in small amounts outside the islands in contemporary Impressa/Cardial contexts for example on Pianosa and probably Giglio in the Tuscan archipelago between Corsica and the mainland, as well as to the north at Peiro Signado in Languedoc, and at Arene Candide, Grotta Pollera and Pianaccia di Suvero in Liguria (Tykot 1999; Briois et al. 2009; Ammerman and Polglase 1997; Cesari et al. 2012a, 84-85; Vaquer 2007).

The agencies by which obsidian circulated remains an issue for further research, but there is some consensus that networks were probably unorganised, and that the find-circumstances reflect frequent episodes of marine mobility among Early Neolithic Cardial settlers (Bigazzi et al. 2005, 10; Luglié 2012 and 2018). At the same time, relative proximity and presumably access to the Monte Arci obsidian quarries appear to have affected differential patterns of lithic selection and reduction. Since the several volcanic glass deposits at Monte Arci have discrete geochemical signatures (see Tykot 1996;

Lugliè et al. 2006), it has been possible to observe that at sites nearer the source, the *chaîne operatoire* seems to have been oriented towards the production of more standardised bladelets and blades in the glassier variety (SA), by indirect percussion and pressure technique. The issue of differential access is interesting. It is uncertain whether, as Lugliè suggests (2018), resident groups nearest the sources asserted control over certain obsidian types, but such a scenario would complement the notion of weaponry as an element in the tool kits. It has been observed that obsidian leaving the island for Corsica and the Tyrrhenian mainland tended to come from the SB2 source, less locally favoured, worked into more general tools following opportunistic reduction by direct percussion techniques (Lugliè 2018, 294). As other suitable knapping stone was available in these regions too, the possibility that obsidian was valued as much for its symbolic as its practical qualities has been suggested (Vaquer 2007, Terradas et al. 2014) – another interesting proposition to be sure, but one that would benefit by evidence for its use in other than domestic contexts.

Artistic expression

Apart from widely used shell-impressed designs on pottery, several examples of intentionally embellished artefacts have been tentatively interpreted as representing artistic expressions. One is a pair of *Cardium* bi-valve shells from Filiestru (D7-1) bearing incised designs: irregular parallel lines on one, irregular orthogonal lines on the other (Trump 1983, fig. 27:65). In addition, eight or so flattish pebbles from three neighbouring sites near Terralba by the Gulf of Oristano (Bau Angius, Santa Chiara, Coddi Is Abionis), with probable Cardial association, bear deep incisions effecting crude geometric designs – similarly orthogonal (Lugliè and Pinna 2012). Taken together, Carlo Lugliè feels that these represent a 'taste for abstract geometric patterns' like that expressed in the Cardial Geometric ceramics (2017, 47) (see Fig. 28).

Corsican relations

By all accounts, the colonisation of Corsica by Cardial-bearing groups followed a similar trajectory and, if the adherence to a common Filiestru-Basi-Pienza stylistic 'canon' is any indication, was probably effected by migrants from the same mainland home via the Tuscan archipelago. Similar environments were favoured for settlement, mainly in the far north and far south where river- and stream valleys offered arable and pasture as well as access to littoral resources. It also seems that similar subsistence choices were made. Everywhere, herded caprines and hunted/trapped *prolagus* were important, followed by swine and cattle, with a further emphasis at some locales on marine molluscs, as at

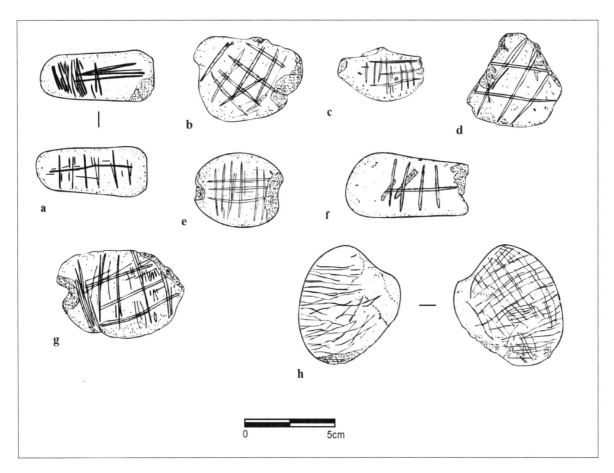

Fig. 28. Incised stone and shell. Proveniences, a-g: Bau Angius (stone, after Lugliè and Pinna 2012, fig. 2), h: Filiestru (shell, after Trump 1983, fig. 27).

Torre d'Aquila-Pietracorbara (Vigne 1995, table 2-3) and Strette-Barbaghju (Bressy-Leandri 2016). The red fox is also known from Strette (Vigne 2007, 260), while the red deer is not accounted for as yet. Lacking too are any cultivars, although finds of millstones at Strette and Petra A suggests that this may be due to preservational lacunae rather original absence (Costa et al. 2002, 767). Perhaps the clearest divergence between the two islands is seen in the lithic industries. While tool kits appear closely comparable, the apparent dependency on obsidian from the west-central Sardinian source and to a lesser degree good quality flint from the northern Sardinian quarries must have conditioned inter-island relations at this time.

Interpreting the Cardial modality

Two general observations emerge when considering the Cardial-phase record as a whole. The first is the stylistic evidence for the preservation of a Tyrrhenian reference sphere that is at once more restricted geographically than that of the former Impressa phase (with affiliations traceable eastward across the entire Mediterranean), but at the same time more canonical in its adherence to the so-called Filiestru-Basi-Pienza style. David Trump's early reflections from Filiestru underline the apparent importance to the first Cardial-bearing colonists to Sardinia of preserving a broader, non-local cultural identity: 'its people were never isolated. The Cardial Ware is found in identical form from the Iglesiente to Sassari, and barely distinguishable from that of Corsica or Provence. The use of cardial decoration at the Grotta Filiestru, over 20 km in a straight line from the nearest habitat of the cockle, makes the same point on a smaller scale' (1983, 16). The concept of a Tyrrhenian cultural *koiné* would thus seem to be applicable. The implied contraction of networks of affiliation compared to that of the Impressa phase might be explained in terms of a natural attenuation over time of earlier ties, real or reconstructed, with a common homeland, and the strengthening of ties less historically remote and more practically grounded in interactions serving immediate adaptive needs as expressed in material and social exchange, best exemplified in the movement of Monte Arci obsidian.

As noted, the cultural unity embraced in the Filiestru-Basi-Pienza decorative canon suggests the north-central Italian mainland as the most likely homeland of the Cardial-bearing colonists to Sardinia, arriving by way of the Tuscan archipelago. It is generally surmised that southern Corsica would have served as the last stepping stone into Sardinia's islets of La Maddalena in the northeast, and this scenario takes on additional weight in light of recent understandings that early Neolithic migrants seem to have moored more freely by boat along the coasts that previously realised (e.g. Manen and Sabatier 2003; Leppard 2014; Lugliè 2012).

The second observation is that the evidence at our disposal suggests that Cardial-bearing colonists mobilised a selective range of features adapted to local conditions with little commitment to any agricultural ideal, rather than transplanting any full version of the inherited so-called Neolithic package. This is evident when comparing Cardial contexts on the central Italian mainland – the most likely origin of the colonists. The picture there is one of small communities immersed in broad-based subsistence regimes combining an emphasis on cultivation and herding with active exploitation of diverse wild game and plants. Several different varieties of domestic wheat, barley, oats and pulses were supplemented with a diverse range of wild plants such as grapes, blackberry, elderberry, strawberry, sloe and cherry (Ucchesu et al. 2017), while the herding of domestic caprines, swine and cattle (and perhaps the red deer) was accompanied by the hunting/trapping of boar, deer, aurochs, fox, wildcat, hare, hedgehog and various birds, reptiles and fish, and the collection of marine molluscs (Tagliacozzo 2005-2006, Table 1). Technologies suited to these pursuits took the form of a basic microlithic tool kit in flint and obsidian adapted to scraping, cutting, piercing and shooting with bow and arrow, a ground-stone industry for axes, hoes, pestles and millstones, and a ceramic repertory of Cardial-impressed and plain utilitarian forms including hemispherical bowls, cups, globular cylinder-neck vases and jars sometimes accompanied by more finely made plates, bowls, mugs, cups, goblets and amphorae (e.g. Fugazzola Delpino 2002; Calvi Rezia and Sarti 2002; Volante 2007).

From this range of resources, tools, skills and expectations drawn from direct experience on the mainland or indirectly from traditions, Neolithic island colonists put into operation selective elements for their sustenance. If the current lack of any clearly Cardial-associated finds of cultivars and ground-stone tools for grain processing or land clearance is representative, then it seems that the traditional earmarks of agriculture were not part of the initial Sardinian Neolithic package. Nor do wild plants – well represented in the mainland sites – seem to have figured much in the island adaptations (Ucchesu et al. 2017, table 4). By contrast, in formulating solutions to animal exploitation, the mainland strategies were more closely replicated. The husbandry of domestic caprines took precedent, with swine and cattle secondary, while the indigenous pika perhaps offered an additional source of meat and skins (e.g. Masala 2013, 69). Notably, the fox was imported, perhaps for its meat and/or skin, as was the red deer, avidly hunted on the mainland. It may initially have been husbanded once introduced to Sardinia; in any event, with time, it seeded thoroughly wild, huntable herds. Similar attempts seem not to have been made to import other mainland game (e.g. aurochs, roe deer, fallow deer, hare) although, as seen at Sella del Diavolo, a taste for marine molluscs was in some places accommodated. As regards lithics, much of the mainland kit was replicated in Sardinia and Corsica, but the ceramic repertory appears to represent rather a selection of a few basic shapes, presumably suited to local needs.

6

The Epicardial Phase

Introduction

Cultural deposits dated to the second half of the sixth millennium BCE document a clear and significant discontinuity in material expressions: the pottery evinces new production standards and the lithics new retouch techniques. Settlement distributions suggest altered locational priorities too, and funerary practices evince some differentiated locales. Most notably, the new material repertory is accompanied at least at one site (Filiestru cave) by remains of the first introduced domestic plants in the island: wheat and pea (see Lugliè 2018 for a recent review). If we are to trust the evidence of seriation from Filiestru cave, our only well stratified and published deposit, it is evident that the new cultural mode, referred to as Epicardial, came on abruptly, less in the nature of a gradual influx of new styles, more in the nature of a new wave of settlers. Considering the geographical distribution of Epicardial remains, the new ceramic style if not its promoters appear to have entered the island at several points mainly along the west coast where there is evidence of replacements and to a lesser degree hybridisation with the Cardial tradition. As it stands today, the evidence suggests several possible scenarios involving alternatively more or less agonistic circumstances. The Cardial-to-Epicardial transition has been recorded in neighbouring Corsica, northern Italy and southern France, where stylistically similar ceramics support the idea of a common reference sphere – a Tyrrhenian Epicardial *koiné* (Paolini-Saez 2010).

The diagnostic pottery

The recognition of a distinctive post-Cardial ceramic facies was first recognised at the key sites of Filiestru (Trump 1982), Grotta Verde-Alghero (Tanda 1980) and Grotta di Monte Majore-Thiesi (Foschi 1982), and is today recorded at some 28 Sardinian locales. As elsewhere throughout its Tyrrhenian distribution (e.g. Tozzi and Weiss 2001), the new ceramic standard replaced that of the Cardial tradition rapidly – at Filiestru increasing from two to 99 per cent across one sedimentary horizon – while leaving very few examples of hybridity (at Grotta Verde and Monte Majore). This observation has been translated to a still widely accepted two-phase model that distinguishes the initial appearance of Epicardial ware within predominantly Cardial contexts also called Early Neolithic II or Filigosa-Grotta Verde from its established presence as the predominant if not exclusive ware type. The new mode is instead called Early Neolithic III, Epicardial/Tyrrhenian or Linear Carved/Linear phase (see Tanda 1987; Foschi Nieddu

1987; Lugliè et al. 2012). Despite considerable diversity subsumed within the Epicardial *koiné*, as a whole, the facies represents a strong divergence in its forms and decorative mode from previous expressions. Vessels are typically globular or piriform with round rather than flat bases in the form of jars with converging necks, deep hemispherical bowls and cups. Handles are far more frequent than previously, occurring in opposing sets of two or three with vertical elbows or lateral upturned loop types (see Fig. 30).

Some of the presumably earliest Epicardial vessels such as those from Grotta Verde appear to represent hybrid expressions comprising limited applications of Cardial impressions on unprecedented vase shapes (Tanda 1987). But generally, the new corpus is distinguished by its apparent avoidance of the marine shell as a decorative tool in favour of alternative instruments for effecting raised curvilinear and often notched cordons, punctations or various linear incisions/excisions. Very simple geometric motifs are the decorative norm, but occasionally more complex designs comprised fields of punctations within incised triangles. Epicardial fabrics are generally more refined than those of the Cardial ware, with surfaces often carefully polished and rarely carrying a red-ochre slip or wash (Trump 1983; Tanda 1992; 1987; 1998; 2008; Lugliè et al. 2012). Although Epicardial ware was unprecedented in the island, most of the new forms and designs would fit comfortably within the wider matrix of Epicardial expressions that appeared in the Tyrrhenian region during the second half of the sixth millennium and known as poinçonnée, linear incised/carved, and Linearbandkeramik. As with the earlier Cardial facies, however, the closest stylistic affinities are with more or less contemporary Epicardial wares in Corsica and Tuscany-Lazio where the new production standards and its carriers are likely to have come from (Lugliè 2018, 294, fig. 8; Tozzi and Weiss 2001; Caponi and Radi 2007; Paolini-Saez 2010; Grifoni Cremonesi 2001; Lorenzi 2007, 32-33).

Settlement and demics

As noted, Epicardial pottery is currently recorded at some 28 Sardinian locales, including 16 open-air sites and 12 cave- and rock-shelter deposits. Half of them represent re-occupations (7 open sites and 7 shelters). It is, however, difficult to judge whether this current inventory is representative of the original settlement landscape. Apart from the extensive coastal areas drowned by the rising sea-levels, it is doubtless the case that the commonly undecorated Epicardial sherds have often

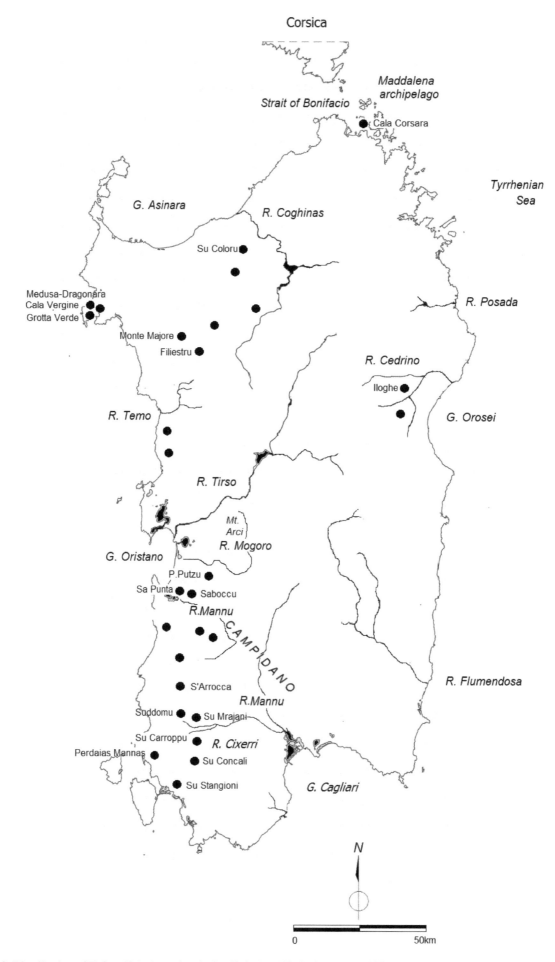

Fig. 29. Distribution of Epicardial-phase sites in Sardinia (modified after Tanda 1995 and Lugliè 2018).

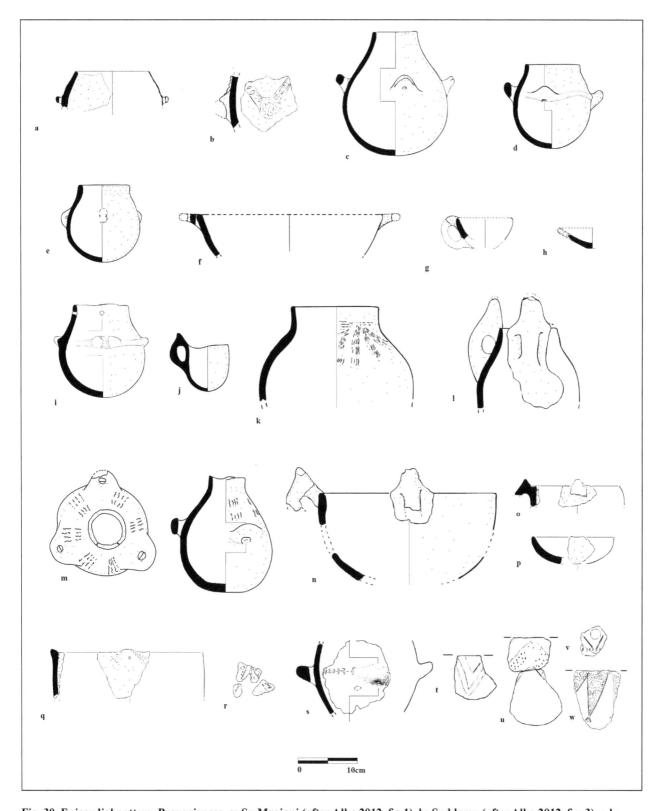

Fig. 30. Epicardial pottery. Proveniences, a: Su Mrajani (after Alba 2012, fig.1), b: Suddomu (after Alba 2012, fig. 3), c-h: Filiestru (after Trump 1983, figs. 11-12), i-n: Grotta Verde (after Lo Schiavo 1987, fig. 3; Cocchi Genick 1994, fig. 67), o-r: Sa Punta (after Lugliè et al. 2012, fig 3; Lugliè 2018, fig. 8), s: Su Stangioni (after Usai 2002, 448), t-v: Su Carroppu (after Lugliè 2018, fig. 8), w: Su Concali di Corongiu Acca-Villamassargia (after Lugliè 2018, fig. 8).

gone undetected compared to the more diagnostic Cardial wares. Nevertheless, several Epicardial deposits have supplied important evidence of the use of shelters and open-air locales for habitation.

Filiestru-Mara

Of the dozen cave/rock-shelter deposits reporting Epicardial finds, Filiestru provides the greatest detail. This large natural cavern, described earlier in relation to its Impressa and Cardial remains, also preserved evidence of subsequent, intensive use by Epicardial-bearing occupants. Epicardial ware (locally called Filiestru ware) appeared in the uppermost cut of stratum D7 (D7-1) as three complete, undecorated vessels in an otherwise Cardial-dominated stratum where they accounted for only two per cent of the total ceramic finds; in the overlying stratum D-6, the Epicardial ware increased sharply to account for 99 per cent of the ceramic finds. By Trump's calculations, this horizon change correlated with an abrupt increase in occupational intensity at the site as artefact density rose from 723 ceramic and lithic finds per cubic metre of deposit to 880 items per cubic metre (Trump 1983, Table 12). Significantly, it was also from strata D7-1 and D6 that the earliest (and sole) evidence of cultivars in the island was recovered, thus correlating with the appearance of Epicardial pottery (Ucchesu et al. 2017, 6; Lugliè 2018, 295). These amounted to a score of fragments (caryopses) of hulled emmer (*Triticum dicoccum*) and einkorn (*Triticum monococcum*) as well as of domestic peas (*Pisum sativum*) (Trump 1990, 21; Ucchesu 2013, Table 6).

The Epicardial flaked stone was dominated by flint (70 per cent, based on published numbers; Trump 1983, Table 4). The lithic kit was generally similar to that from Cardial levels, e.g. blade and flake scrapers, points and knives, some with an innovative steep inverse retouch (see Depalmas 1995) and, according to Trump (1983, table 4), 19 transverse arrowheads. The only changes detected in the lithic kit that would seem to reflect the incorporation of cereal-based cultivation near the cave is an increase of lunates possibly employed as sickle bits (Trump 1983, 12) and in finds of ground-stone tools – rare elsewhere in the island – some of which may have been used in processing grain. Two came from D7-1, one from stratum D6-3 (dated

to 5216-4859 cal BCE), and another from stratum B10 (with two associated dates of 5615-5344 and 5543-5316 cal BCE).

Adding to these observations, Hurcombe has identified five obsidian flakes with microwear and residues consistent with use as knives for cutting or slicing flesh or hide (1992, Table 2).

Faunal bone remains continued to document a focus on caprine herding in the Epicardial phase (82 per cent), but with a slight increase in cattle and fewer swine. There was also a significant reduction in numbers of pika and fox, and in the ratio of pika to fox (Levine 1983, Tables 12-27), a datum probably reflecting important implications for agricultural conditions. Regarding the use of the cave's interior space, the preponderance of ash, charcoal and burned cobbles in trench B during all Neolithic periods suggests that hearth-related activities clustered near the cave's north wall some 4-5 m from the mouth and presumably in the lee of prevailing northern winter winds. Although somewhat more intensively utilised by Epicardial-bearing occupants than previously, the cave appears as earlier to have supported a small farmstead, now engaged in cultivation (Trump 2000, 22).

Sa Punta-Marceddì

Two neighbouring sites have recently been discovered near the Gulf of Oristano on Sardinia's west coast, and provided rare data on Epicardial open-air habitations (Fig. 31). Sa Punta was identified on the shores of the Marceddì marine lagoon in 2004, although unfortunately only after having been all but removed by modern construction work. Nevertheless, the surviving deposits have preserved significant structural and sedimentary

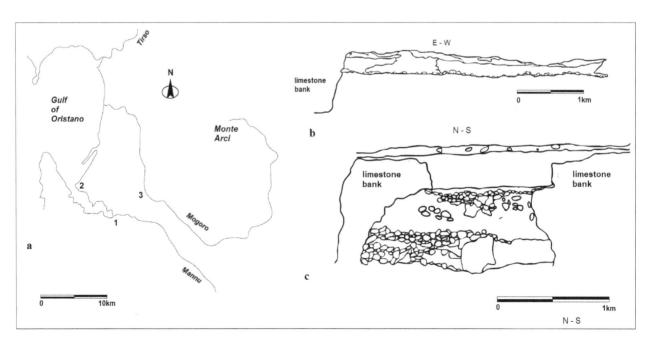

Fig. 31. Sa Punta-Marceddì, a: location (1. Rio Saboccu, 2. Sa Punta, 3. Pauli Putzu), b-c: profiles of the ditch (after Lugliè et al. 2008; Le Bourdonnec et al. 2009; Pittau et al. 2012).

remains of an open settlement which has since been under investigation (Lugliè 2014; et al. 2012, 264). The deposits are situated only 20 m from the present shoreline on the summit of a limestone plateau, near the lower Mannu and Sitzerri rivers – a freshwater lacustrine environment prone to periodic flooding. Apart from patches of anthropic residues probably from huts and storage, the site's main surviving feature is an unusual, ditch-like structure carved from the underlying limestone bank (currently at 2 m asl) to an average width of one metre and a minimum depth of 1.2 m. It has been traced running east-west for some nine metres. Its transverse section is irregularly bell-shaped, with a flaring base up to 1.75 m wide. Most of our information about the site comes from finds within the ditch fill, which comprised alternate layers of sandy alluvium and pebbles containing food remains (mainly marine shells), ceramic sherds with linear incised decorations and lithic cores, flakes, blades and some finished tools almost exclusively of obsidian from nearby Monte Arci. The accumulation presumably constituted a waste dump. At a depth of approximately 0.5 m, the trench was 'capped' by a cobbled pathway running its full length. Three radiocarbon assays date the sealing of the trench by this pathway at between 5476 and 5036 cal BCE. A tooth from a domestic sheep – the only mammalian remains recovered – supplied one of the dates, an unidentified bone another, and a shell of *Ostrea edulis* the third (Lugliè 2018, table 1). The original purpose of the bedrock ditch is unknown. Alluvial sediments indicate at least periodic inflows of freshwater and this is also supported by finds of dinoflagellates and algal spores. It has been suggested that it functioned as a drainage channel to protect huts and livestock from flooding, or as a canal to supply freshwater for irrigation, drinking and watering livestock (Pittau et al. 2012, 1268-69). In light of contemporary settlement modes in the mainland, we might add its possible use as a footing for a fence or wall (Cavulli 2008; Radina and Sarti 2002).

Regarding the local economy, pastoral activities are suggested by palynological analyses that identified spores of coprophilous fungi indicating the presence of dung (Pittau et al. 2012, 1267). Interestingly, the investigators have interpreted the large amount of charcoal derived from low herbaceous plants as possible evidence for purposeful burning of pasture to encourage regrowth of new forage plants – a practice common in the island today. Shells of *Mytilus*, *Tapes* and *Ostrea* imply periodic gathering ventures to the coast. Neither pollen nor macrobotanical residues have confirmed that cultivation took place at the site, however, but wild arboreal and non-arboreal plants suited to distant forest- and nearer brackish environments were attested (Pittau et al. 2012: Table 2).

Rio Saboccu-Guspini

Rio Saboccu was identified ca. eight km southeast of Sa Punta on a terrace at what is presently the mouth of the same Marceddì lagoon some five km from the Gulf of Oristano. During the later sixth millennium, when sea levels were much lower, it would have occupied the shores of the lower Mannu river. The deposits, which cover about a hectare, included two deep sunken features (S1 and S2) which had been exposed in profile by the progressive erosion of the terrace. Both features had been excavated into the gravelly surface to depths of 0.9 and 1.3 m respectively and preserved rich anthropogenic fill containing charcoal, faunal remains and artefacts, these last comprising a small collection of coarse, undecorated sherds from mainly simple hemispherical bowls with rounded rims, and ca. 1000 lithic tools and debitage (Lugliè et al. 2008). Both features appear to have been elliptical and probably represent the bases of sunken huts. The larger structure (S2), which measured 9.5 m, provided two radiocarbon dates on charcoal from *Arbutus unedo* of 5341-5066 and 5320-5027 cal BCE, implying an occupation more or less contemporary with neighbouring Sa Punta. Palaeontological and sediment data suggest the habitation occupied a lacustrine setting not unlike that at Sa Punta, on an alluvial terrace covered by xerophile Mediterranean woodland and maquis with *Juniperus* and *Buxus Sempervirens* bordering the nearby river. In terms of fauna, only domestic caprines were evinced. Like at Sa Punta, there was no clear evidence for cultivation, and the investigators believe subsistence will have been oriented toward ovicaprine rearing and hunting. As at Sa Punta too, very few finished tools were recognised in the lithic assemblage, dominated by cores and debitage (nearly all of local obsidian) reflecting expedient manufacture. The more standardised forms were limited to geometric pieces, some of which appear suited to hafting as transverse points (Lugliè et al. 2008, fig. 5).

Site distribution and demic patterns

Overall, Epicardial occupations followed the same placement strategy as Cardial occupations had, and at least half of those known constitute re-occupations of former locales. At the same time, there are notable and puzzling differences. Both on the north coast, inland from the Gulf of Asinara, and in the southeast, at the mouth of the Mannu in the Gulf of Cagliari, Epicardial deposits are lacking where Cardial sites had previously been supported. Whether this reflects patchy sampling or demographic hiatuses is uncertain. In any event, the new ceramic style (and probably new migrant groups) appears to have entered the island at several points along mainly the west coast and, to a lesser extent, the more treacherous east coast at the Gulf of Orosei (as seen in the newly founded open-air site of Iloghe-Sant'Arvara; Lugliè 2018, fig. 2:24). Considering stylistic affinities outside the island, Tuscany-Lazio seems the most likely cultural and demographic source, with the Tuscan archipelago and Corsica the most likely route into Sardinia's northeast probably via Cala Corsara in the Maddalena archipelago, as previously.

Mortuary practices

Human remains are somewhat better represented in Epicardial contexts than in previous phases, but the evidence is still very slight. It indicates, however, a designation of separate burial locales near habitations and the deposition of burial offerings. Two caves are of special interest in this regard, Grotta Suddomu in the southwest, and Grotta Verde in the northwest.

Grotta Suddomu-Iglesias

This is a small, natural cavity at the foot of the eastern slope of Monte Casula in the southwest, neighbouring the cave habitation of Su Mrajani (Fig. 32). Although highly disturbed by clandestine diggers, fragments of a human skull and long bones were recovered on the surface with two ceramic sherds, one of which bore notched-cord decorations diagnostic of the Epicardial phase. The small burial chamber, with triangular section, is reached by a short irregular corridor several metres from the cave's north-facing mouth (Alba 2012; Cicilloni et al. 2014). The apparent absence of hearths, faunal or lithic remains suggests that the shelter was designated for funerary use

only, perhaps by occupants of nearby Su Mrajani (Alba 2012, fig. 1).

Grotta Verde-Alghero

On the promontory of Capo Caccia in the northwest is the cave of Grotta Verde (Tanda 1980; 1987; 2002; Skeates 2012). This extraordinary grotto descends by narrow, branching tunnels from its current entrance at 88 m asl to a large chamber some 36 metres below the current sea level (Fig. 33). In a small, karstic chamber now submerged at 8.5 metres below the sea, underwater excavations recovered human skull fragments and partially articulated vertebrae along with three complete Epicardial (Filiestru style) vessels. This is the earliest evidence in the island of systematic burial with material accompaniments. The apparently primary inhumations had been placed in niches partly cut from the rock; other Epicardial vessels were found in both lower and higher chambers, and one cup contained a small greenstone axe head. As noted, these particular ceramic accompaniments portray hybrid qualities combining Epicardial forms and instrumental decorations with traditional Cardial impressions. One jar moreover bore a plastic rendition of a head in the crux of its peaked elbow handles, in the opinion of some scholars representing an image of a human face (Tanda 2002, 442; 1980, 54, figs. 4d, 9, 10e; cf. Lilliu 1999, figs. 106-107 and 344). If so, this would be the first Neolithic human depiction in the island and, so far, a Sardinian *unicum*, with no known close parallels among contemporary expressions in the mainland (Volante 2008, 116; Cocchi Genick 1994, fig. 46:11); it may, however, rather represent an animal such as a ram, given the horn-like design (Fig. 34).

Subsistence

Thus far, domestic plant evidence has come only from Filiestru cave, described above. Represented were hulled emmer and einkorn (*Triticum dicoccum* and *monococcum*) and the domestic pea, *Pisum sativum*, in association with local Epicardial ceramics and several milling stones (Trump 1990, 21; Ucchesu 2013, Table 6). Faunal remains are somewhat better represented. Caprines continued to dominate, accounting for over 80 per cent of domestic stock remains, while there is a slight increase in cow from less than one to five per cent, and a slight drop in pigs from 19 to 12 per cent. The slaughter patterns appear to have been non-selective: caprines were killed at all ages while the single ageable cow was killed at under three years of age – all presumably for meat. An over-representation of forelimbs was noted, as indeed in all Neolithic assemblages, and may imply the introduction of select parts for consumption into the shelter, while keeping places of slaughter and primary butchering elsewhere (Levine 1983, 120; Trump 1990). Possibly significant as a correlate to the appearance of domestic plants at Filiestru is the sharp decrease in numbers of both *prolagus* and fox remains from 203 and 24 in Cardial contexts to 7 and 8 in Epicardial respectively. It seems not unreasonable that this might reflect a long-term reduction of *prolagus* numbers

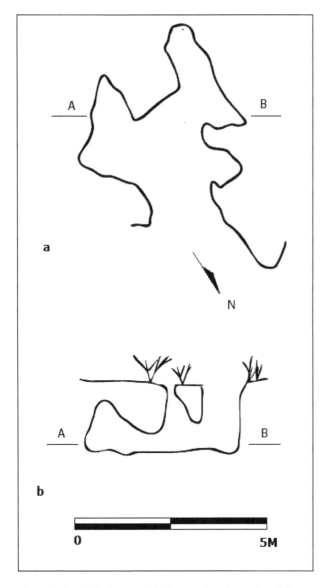

Fig. 32. Grotta Suddomu-Iglesias, a: plan, b: section (after Alba 2012, fig. 3).

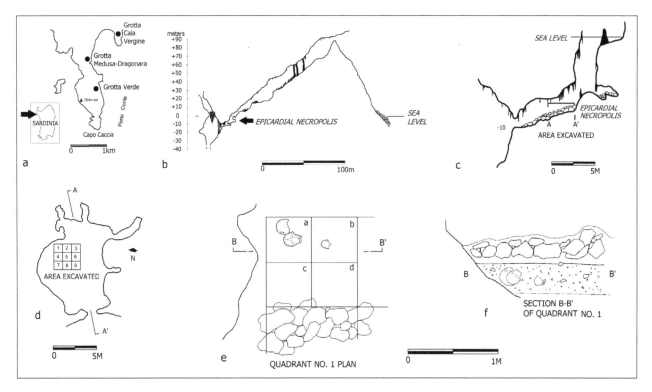

Fig. 33. Grotta Verde-Alghero, a: location on the promontory of Capo Caccia (after Antonioli, Ferranti and Lo Schiavo 1994, fig. 1), b: section of the cave (after Antonioli, Ferranti and Lo Schiavo 1994, fig. 3), c. section of necropolis deposits, d: plan of the excavated area, e-f: plan and section of quadrant no. 1 showing find-spots of burial accompaniments (c-f after Lo Schiavo 1987, fig. 2).

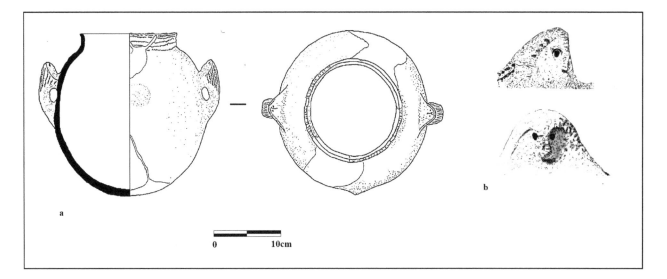

Fig. 34. The Cardial-Epicardial vase from Grotta Verde, a-b: vase; detail of figurative handles (after Lilliu 1999, figs. 106-107 and 344).

by the introduced fox, and in consequence the creation of conditions better suited to cultivation.

Evidence from two caves in the Porto Conte and Capo Caccia area (Alghero) have given some additional dietary indications. The small rock-shelter of Cala Vergine, which during the period in question would have been about a kilometre from the coast, preserved shells of marine molluscs (*Patella caerulea* and *Phorcus turbinatus*) bearing evidence of human consumption: one *Phorcus* had had its apex removed, presumably to ease flesh extraction.

One of the limpet shells (*Patella*) was C14-dated to 5450-5250 cal BCE (Palombo et al. 2017, table 16). From the neighbouring cave of Medusa-Dragonara, a human lower incisor gave a corresponding AMS date of 5510-5420 cal BCE (Palombo et al. 2016, Table 1). Notably, carbon and nitrogen isotope values suggest that the tooth belonged to an individual with a balanced, terrestrial-based diet, characterised by the consumption of both animal and vegetal foods but with no apparent indications of marine food consumption (Palombo et al. 2016). Scant remains from Sa Punta and Saboccu in the Gulf of Oristano, as

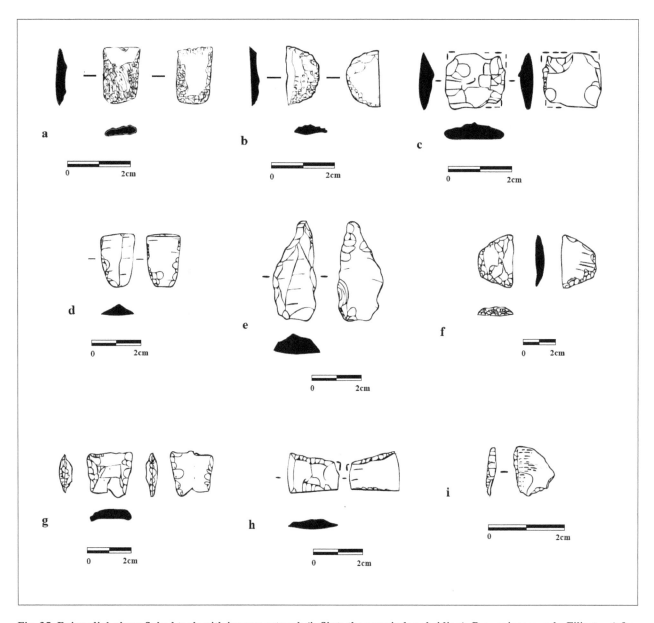

Fig. 35. Epicardial-phase flaked tools with inverse retouch (i: flint; the remainder obsidian). Proveniences, a-b: Filiestru (after Trump 1983, figs. 26, 28, 29), c: Pitzu 'e Pudda (after Alba 2015, fig. 4), d-e: Rio Saboccu (after Lugliè et al. 2009, fig. 21), f: Su Stangioni (after Usai 2002, fig. 14), g: Perdaias Mannas (after Alba and Canino 2005, tav. 2), h: S'Arrocca Abruxiada-Arbus (after Alba and Canino 2010, fig. 10), i: Su Coloru (after Sarti et al. 2012, fig. 1).

noted, appear to represent a local focus on ovicaprine herding, shell collecting and possibly hunting but not, it seems, cultivation.

Crafts

Flaked stone

The Epicardial lithic industry generally continued the production of most of the earlier forms with geometric items dominant (Fig. 35). There are, however, fewer blades relative to flake-tools, evidence of more expedient methods of core reduction, and smaller tools. With the apparent exception of Filiestru, there are also fewer tranchet points. As earlier, the choice of flint or obsidian appears to be related to proximity to the quarries (Depalmas 1995; Tanda 1998; Lugliè et al. 2008; 2012, 466). Potentially diagnostic, if rather subtle, is the apparent

implementation of alternative forms of steep-edge retouch – the introduction of so-called inverse truncation (Alba and Canino 2004, 216; 2010, 135; Alba and Canino 2005; Alba 2015). Distribution data indicate that obsidian from Monte Arci continued to find its way to Corsica, the Tuscan islands and the Italian mainland, especially Liguria (Vaquer 2007, 2; Tykot 1999). Notably, a first appearance of obsidian from Lipari in Corsica, moreover on the island's northern tip, might suggest a more competitive market (Le Bourdonnec et al. 2009).

Ground-stone tools

Ground-stone tools are rare in Early Neolithic contexts in Sardinia, but several millstones at Filiestru cave, both small and large, were found in Epicardial layers along with remains of cultivars (Trump 1983). Fragments of millstones are also recorded from Grotta di Monte

Majore-Thiesi along with an axe/hatchet (and, as noted, a greenstone axe was found in a vase in Grotta Verde; Tanda 2002, 442).

Bone implements

Tools fashioned from bone are well represented at the caves of Filiestru and Monte Majore (Trump 1983, 67-69). They have been studied by Laura Manca (2006), who identified them as mainly awls made from the long bones probably of domestic sheep/goats with the aid of stone points (Fig. 36). Six came from Filiestru along with a stone abrader featuring a groove (6 mm diameter) suited for making and sharpening such points (Trump 1983, 69). At Monte Majore, 16 awls were recorded (Lo Schiavo 1986; Foschi Nieddu 1998, 300, tav. II). Ten of these were apparently fashioned by splitting a long bone lengthwise, snapping it in two at a point demarked by double incisions, then grinding on points (Manca 2006, 935-37). Several pieces with blunt ends from both sites could not be positively identified, but one from Monte Majore preserved a partial perforation that suggests it may have served as a needle. Along with the awls from Filiestru, one might note also a single blunt instrument that Trump listed as a spatula (1983, fig. 28): a robust fragment of a long bone (58 mm long) with one end polished to the shape of a blade.

Corsican relations

Close ties with neighbouring Corsica as a customer of Sardinian obsidian, stepping-stone for incoming settlers and co-member in the Tyrrhenian cultural *koiné* are likely

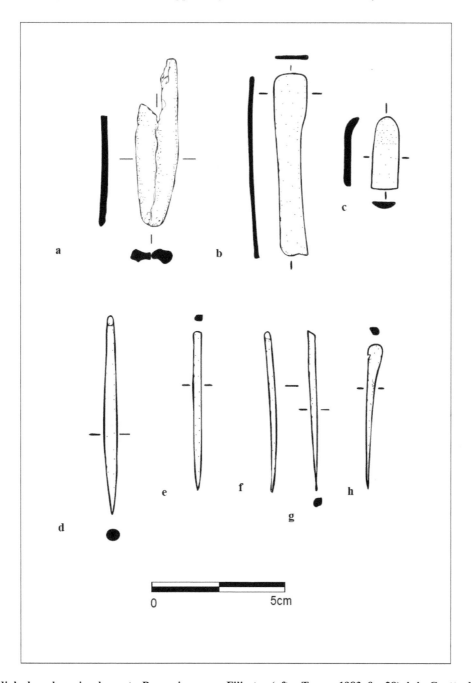

Fig. 36. Epicardial-phase bone implements. Proveniences, a: Filiestru (after Trump 1983, fig. 28), b-h: Grotta di Monte Majore (after Tanda 1987, figs. 2-3).

to have remained (cf. Paolini-Saez 2000; Costa 2001; Lugliè 2018; Tramoni and D'Anna 2016). Cultivars have not as yet come to light in Corsica but finds of milling stones at several sites suggests these are forthcoming, and that agro-pastoral adaptations supplemented by gathering and hunting was a main mode of subsistence in Epicardial Corsica as well as in Sardinia (Bonifay 1983; Lorenzi 2007; Weiss 2007; Tozzi and Weiss 2001; Costa et al. 2002).

Differentiating the Epicardial modality

The identification of a distinctive Epicardial phase in Sardinia is predicated on the recognition of discontinuities. Although it is uncertain to what degree our current data base represents the Epicardial landscape, a number of these discontinuities can still be enumerated and discussed:

1. The appearance of cultivars and ground-stone tools, a small decrease in pigs and small increase in cattle. The former is limited to the Bonu Ighinu valley at Filiestru Cave at least for now, where the only remains of domestic plants and rare examples of millstones have been found as yet.

2. The appearance of a ditched structure at Sa Punta in the Gulf of Oristano. As noted, ditched and palissaded settlements are attested in the mainland at this time (Starnini et al. 2018, 306; Skeates 2015) and may indicate conditions of insecurity or conflict – conditions increasingly attested in European Neolithic contexts elsewhere (Runnels 2007; Ivanova 2007; cf. Schulting and Fibiger 2012; Armit et al. 2007).

3. A retraction of settlements from previously occupied areas near the north coast and in the southeast, for reasons as yet obscure. As both areas are suitable for cultivation, as indicated by later prehistoric and historic records, especially in the Mannu river valley in the northwest and the homonymous drainage in the south, the new availability of domestic cultivars would seem unrelated. Alternatively, if the influx of Epicardial-bearing groups promoted an atmosphere of hostility, as one reading of the Sa Punta trench-works might suggest, then the coastal areas may have been perceived as excessively risky to settlement (as is well known, such a defensive pattern characterised island settlement during historical periods of heightened risks of piracy or attacks).

4. The evidence of built structures in the form of elliptical sunken huts. Although uncertain in terms of function, if they were indeed habitations, this would contrast those of contemporary northern Italian dwellings which are believed to have been 'short, rectangular, wooden framed and posted' (Starnini et al. 2018, 306) as well as that revealed at Epicardial Petra A on Corsica which appears to have been a small, oval, wood-framed building (Weiss 2007, 13).

5. The evidence of a rapid influx and replacement of Cardial by Epicardial ware representing a shift also in vessel design and decorative canons (see Paolini-Saez 2010). This would seem to counter recent assessments of the Cardial-Epicardial transition as a 'slow process of cultural drift occurring within the tradition of Cardial Ware (Impressed Ware) pottery in the Tyrrhenian area' (Lugliè 2014), and argue rather for rapid cultural replacement consistent with new arrivals probably from Tuscany-Lazio via Corsica.

6. Innovations in the stone industry involving the introduction of the inverse retouch.

7. The first unambiguous remains of purposeful burials with accompaniments in designated locales. Evidence for similar concerns regarding the treatment of the dead begin to appear also in the mainland at this time (cf. Malone 2003, 292-93, 297).

8. The appearance of what may be the first representation of a head. So far limited to a single jar with Cardial-Epicardial features from Grotta Verde, the small face rendered in relief may mark an important horizon in the island after which such depictions became a constant element in Sardinian Neolithic expressions.

Taken together, such differences from established Cardial adaptations make a strong case for considering the Cardial to Epicardial transition in terms of an influx of new colonists. The material remains dating to subsequent centuries, from the late sixth to early fifth millennium BCE, in turn document modifications to the Epicardial cultural profile. These are taken to demark the beginning of the Sardinian Middle Neolithic, recognised locally as the Bonu Ighinu phase.

7

The Bonu Ighinu Phase

Introduction

The cultural profile that emerged on Sardinia during the early centuries of the fifth millennium is referred to as Bonu Ighinu, after the eponymous upland valley where the distinctive pottery that defines this phase was first revealed, in basal levels of the cave of Sa Ucca de su Tintirriolu in Mara (Loria and Trump 1978). Bonu Ighinu is taken to signal the beginning of the Middle Neolithic. It is also, sometimes, regarded as the first distinctively Sardinian culture, but this last perspective is misleading. Apart from a common ceramic style, the island supported a diverse range of local adaptations at this time. It is true that in some regions of the island, material expressions unprecedented in the Sardinian record and also unique for the Tyrrhenian region as a whole appeared at this point: shaft-accessed hypogeal tombs, open-air necropoli, skilfully carved statuettes, a rich array of utensils, ornaments and accoutrements in bone, shell, teeth and greenstone, and carved and moulded ovine protomes. But in many other locales, adaptations changed little from Epicardial times, save in the restyling of pottery. Subsistence regimes seem to have varied from largely pastoral-hunting to 'classic' Neolithic farming-herding. Interestingly, some of the diversity can probably be accounted for by developments in the lithics industry. It seems likely that the obsidian resources came under some degree of control now, by settlements in the Gulf of Oristano, and that their privileged access, at least temporarily, lead to differentiation, as indicated by status insignia such as exceptional tombs, relatively rich mortuary accompaniments and distinctive artistic expressions presumably on the part of an elite (Fig. 37).

The diagnostic pottery

Bonu Ighinu pottery represents a significant break from that of the previous phase. However, unlike the Cardial-Epicardial interface, the new forms share enough attributes with those preceding them to suggest an indigenous development (Fig. 38). Most notable is the characteristic raised-elbow handle, sometimes appointed with figurative mouldings depicting stylised ovine reliefs or, rarely, anthropomorphic images recalling that seen on the Epicardial jar from Grotta Verde (see Lilliu 1999, figs. 103, 106-110, 338-41, 344-48 and below). If one can take the available radiocarbon data at face value, some considerable overlap of dates on Bonu Ighinu remains from Cuccuru S'Arriu-Cabras and Grotta del Rifugio-Oliena with dates on Epicardial remains elsewhere suggests an extended period of transition during which both facies coexisted in the island.

Although ranging in quality, the best fine-ware Bonu Ighinu vessels represent a high level of achievement. The fabric is refined and compact, the vessel walls thin, the surfaces highly polished in shiny brown or black-grey. The most common forms are bowls including innovative hemispherical and carinated types with either simple or flared collars. Not uncommon too are collared jars with elbow handles, often with the decorative buttressing noted above, while new forms include single-handled carinated and cylindrical cups and ladles (cf. Usai 2009, fig. 7). Many vases were distinctively decorated using, apart from mouldings, thin engravings, excisions and most commonly very fine micro-point impressions. Rims and carinations usually carry rows of thin notches or engraved lines with notches, while vessel bodies might be so decorated with schemes of festoons, concentric circles, semicircles, spirals and triangles forming solar, zoomorphic, checkerboard or triangular motifs, in some cases including the distinctive hanging triangle (cf. Loria and Trump 1978, figs. 7-11; Lilliu 1999, figs. 110, 124, 126, 345).

Bonu Ighinu pottery has been identified at over 45 locations across the island. Its earliest dated occurrences come from Grotta del Rifugio in the eastern highlands of Oliena, where AMS dates of 5315-5071 and 5295-5046 cal BCE were derived from burial remains with rich accompaniments including diagnostic decorated pottery and shell- and stone ornaments. The remaining available dates come from the caves of Filiestru and Sa Ucca de su Tintirriolu, the shelter of Su Carroppu, and Cuccuru S'Arriu (see below), and fall into the early to mid-fifth millennium (Lugliè 2018, table 1). Although distinctively Sardinian, Bonu Ighinu wares find similarities with productions of the Serra D'Alto and Ripoli facies on the Italian mainland (cf. Laviano and Muntoni 2009, fig.1; Radina 2003, figs. 5, 6, and 9; Gravina 1988, fig. 8) and, more closely still, those of the Curasien-poinçonné facies on neighbouring Corsica (cf. Tramoni and D'Anna 2016, 2-3).

Settlement and demics

As a very rough and necessarily preliminary measure of population changes, and without attempting to differentiate habitation from mortuary deposits, one might – as earlier – compare site numbers between Epicardial (28) and Bonu Ighinu (45) phases, a period of some five centuries (ca. 5000-4500 BCE). The increase amounts to some 0.12 per cent per year, a rate in keeping with traditional archaeologically-based estimates for Neolithic population growth (Carneiro and Hilse 1966, 179; Hassan and Sengel 1973, 580; Bourgeois-Pichat 1967) and reasonably

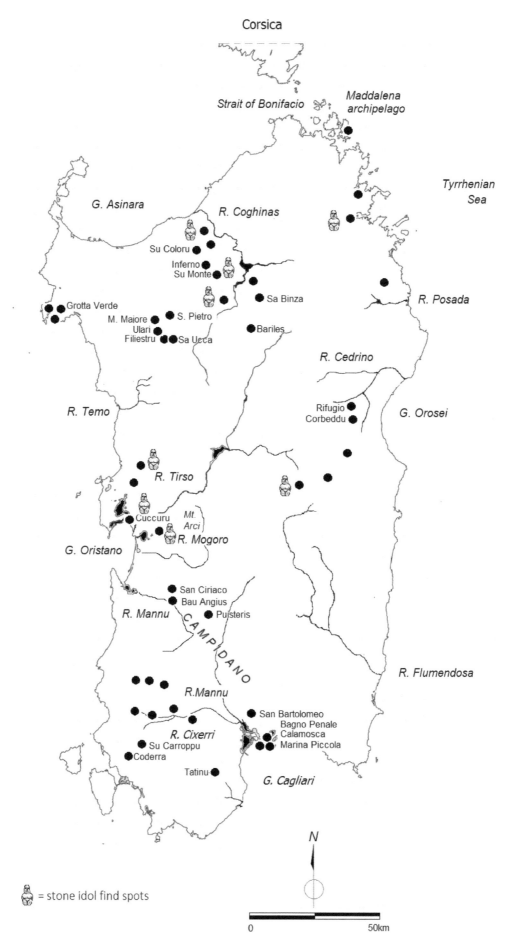

Fig. 37. Distribution of Bonu Ighinu sites including find-spots of stone idols (modified after Lugliè 2017, fig. 14; Paglietti 2017, fig. 3).

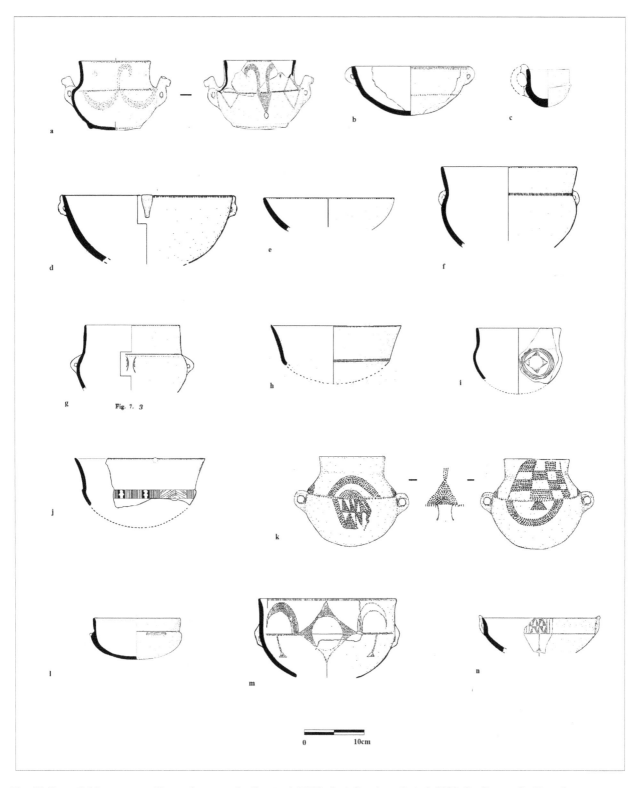

Fig. 38. Bonu Ighinu pottery. Proveniences, a-b: Grotta del Rifugio (after Agosti et al. 1980, fig. 8), c-g: Sa Ucca de su Tintirriolu (after Loria and Trump 1978, figs. 6, 7, 8, 9), h: Cuccuru S'Arriu (after Atzeni 1978, fig. 17), i: Grotta di Monte Majore (after Soro 2013, tav.1), j: Tatinu-Santadì (after Lilliu 1999, fig. 349), k: Grotta del Bagno Penale (after Lilliu 1999, 364), l: Grotta Bariles (after Tanda 1977, fig. 2), m-n: Grotta dell'Inferno (after Loria and Trump 1978, fig. 11).

accounted for by natural growth and fissioning of existing groups.

Habitation remains of the Bonu Ighinu phase have come from both natural shelters and open-air locales. Previously inhabited caves (e.g. Filiestru, Corbeddu, Su Carroppu, Su Coloru, Grotta Verde) continued to serve as dwellings or were re-occupied, while others saw use for the first time for habitation and/or for funerary deposits. Of the latter, the cave of Bagno Penale on the cape of Sant'Elia at Cagliari in the south is noteworthy. Remains of Bonu Ighinu pottery here, as well as in the nearby cave of San Bartolomeo and probably at the open-air locales at Calamosca and Marina Piccola (Ibba et al. 2017, 360),

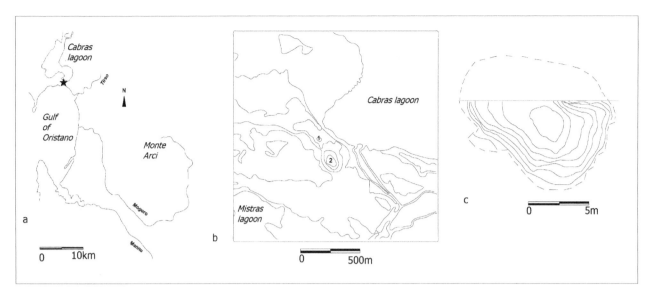

Fig. 39. Cuccuru S'Arriu, a: general location, b: location of necropolis (1) and settlement (2), c: plan of structure 422 (after Sebis, Lugliè and Santoni 2012, fig. 3).

would appear to signal a modest repopulation of the Gulf of Cagliari area, following an apparent hiatus. The most informative of the open-air settlements is Cuccuru S'Arriu on the western Gulf of Oristano.

Cuccuru S'Arriu-Cabras

This open-air deposit on the west coast was excavated in the late 1970s, but the results have only been partially published (Santoni 1982; Sebis et al. 2012). As this is currently the only data available from controlled excavations of an open-air Bonu Ighinu settlement, its significance is immeasurable, particularly so since the site was directly associated with a necropolis, also excavated and in part published (described below). The settlement is situated some 100 metres east of the necropolis on a low sandy relief or *cuccuru* (Fig. 39). A number of structures have been identified, although only one – structure 422 – has been excavated to any greater extent. It is a large, roughly oval, sunken feature which appears to have measured ca. 12 x 6 metres. It may represent a sunken hut like those revealed in Epicardial deposits at Riu Saboccu to the southeast (see above), or perhaps an unroofed commons: within, several large fire features suggested hearths. Material remains included lithics and pottery as well as abundant faunal remains here dominated by domestic cattle, with lesser numbers of caprines and swine, and a not insignificant quantity of marine molluscs with signs of human consumption. As yet, neither plant foods nor millstones have been reported. The lithic assemblage is similar to that from the adjacent necropolis, especially graves 386 and 415 – geometric microliths primarily made of obsidian from the nearby SA flow at Monte Arci (Lugliè et al. 2011). The site appears to have been re-occupied in the subsequent San Ciriaco phase (see below).

Tombs and mortuary practices

With the appearance of Bonu Ighinu, it becomes possible to distinguish at least three distinct modes of disposing

of the dead. Caves such as Su Coloru (Masala 2008) and Filiestru (Levine 1983, table 27) have yielded isolated skeletal remains in otherwise domestic contexts, without evidence of accompaniments or special treatment that might be interpreted as burial rites. Other caves, such as Grotta del Rifugio-Oliena, Grotta del Bagno Penale-Cagliari and Sa Ucca de su Tintirriolu-Mara, by contrast, appear to represent designated mortuary sites, bearing larger skeletal assemblages with associated grave goods, and in some cases evidence of mortuary feasts. A similar mode was observed, although not clearly, in Epicardial contexts such as Grotta Verde (see above). Investigations at Grotta del Rifugio and Grotta del Bagno Penale have provided interesting details.

Grotta del Rifugio-Oliena

This limestone cave in the east-central highlands near Oliena presents an irregular interior extending less than 20 metress in from the mouth (Fig. 40). The evidence for habitation (hearths, middens, living floors) is ambiguous, but a deep, natural cavity in the rear wall was found to contain human burial remains (Biagi and Cremaschi 1980; Agosti et al. 1980; see also M.G. Melis 2014, 7 and Skeates 2012). By Germanà's estimate (Agosti et al. 1980), the disarticulated skeletons of no fewer than 11 individuals were represented: five men, three women and three infants. The adults were of robust stature with healthy dentition consistent with isotope evidence of a high-protein diet (discussed below). Most notably, the bone assemblage appears to have been thrown *en masse* into the cavity along with a wealth of accompaniments. Although no selection of skeletal parts seems indicated, the remains probably represent the removal of burial remains from graves elsewhere, i.e. a secondary burial. The bones were found within a distinctive matrix of dark sediments containing large amounts of ash and charcoal along with a rich array of items including diagnostic ceramics – some elaborately decorated – as well as over 2000 stone-, bone-

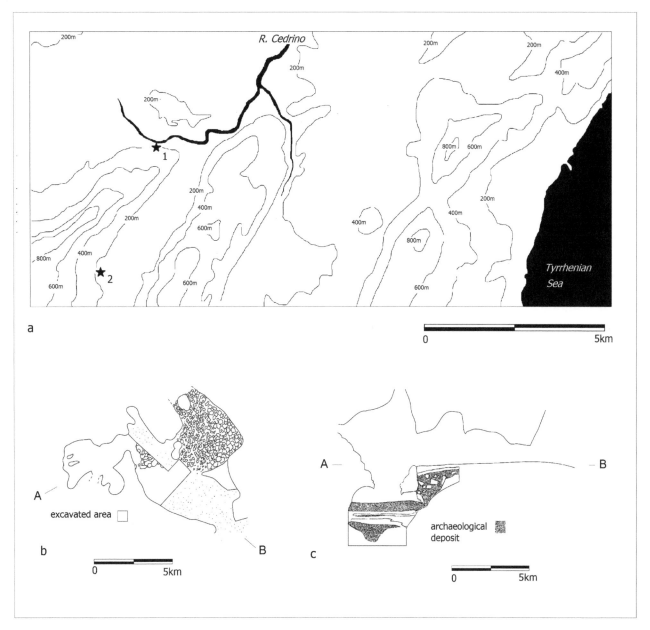

Fig. 40. Grotta del Rifugio. a: location of Grotta Rifugio (1) and Grotta Corbeddu (2), b-c: plan and section of Grotta Rifugio (after Biagi and Cremaschi 1980, figs. 3 & 5).

and shell tools and ornaments (Agosti et al. 1980, figs. 10-14).

The ceramic vessels include an often-reproduced carinated necked vase with stylised zoomorphic (ovine?) handles and punctate decorations featuring a ram with high arched horns (Biagi and Cremaschi 1980, fig. 5). Faunal remains representing food debris possible from funerary feasts were from wild game, especially *prolagus* and smaller mammals, but also species newly introduced into the island – the wildcat and the marten – as well as the domestic dog, some butchered domestic sheep/goats, swine and cattle and some molluscs (Agosti et al. 1980; Lai et al. 2015: table 1; see also below). Also recovered and recently studied by Ucchesu (2013) were the remains of carbonised plants perhaps representing hearth fuel or animal fodder, acorns and pine nuts. Neither domestic plants nor ground-stone tools were reported (see also Agosti et al. 1980,

88-89 and below). AMS dates of three samples of human bone ranged from 5475 to 5046 cal BCE (Lugliè 2018, table 1). If the material association is correct, this signals the earliest example of the Bonu Ighinu phase.

Grotta del Bagno Penale-Cagliari

As noted above, this natural cave is located on the cape of Sant'Elia in the Gulf of Cagliari near at least two open-air sites, Calamosca and Marina Piccola, with likely Bonu Ighinu associations (Ibba et al. 2017, 360). When the site was discovered in the early twentieth century, it had been largely destroyed but for small segment of surviving deposits – more of less intact – including the skeletal remains of one or two individuals along with marine shells, bone ornaments, an obsidian 'knife' and flakes and ceramics of dense paste and well-polished reddish surface in the form of bowls and handled jars.

At least one shallow bowl with red finish bore diagnostic narrow notches around the rim, nearly identical to one from the cave of San Bartolomeo a short distance to the northwest. Another fine-ware vase – a necked jar with opposing vertical loop handles (Taramelli 1904, fig. 7) – is notable for its fine, punctate designs on three faces, and also has apparent parallels at San Bartolomeo. Between the handles on one side, there is a composite design with a checkerboard motif in the upper register, and an up-turned semi-circle enclosing a triangle in the lower. On the opposite side of the vessel, two concentric down-turned semicircles occupy the upper register, while below there is a complex design with opposing triangles, nearly identical to that on a fine-ware bowl from Inferno Cave-Muros in north-west Sardinia (see Loria and Trump 1978, Tav. X). On one side of the vase above the handle, there is another triangle with short vertical suspension – an example of the hanging triangle-design also found at the caves of Inferno and Monte Majore in the northwest (Canino et al. 2017, nos. 48-49). Some of the shells were identified by the investigator as food remains, possible from funeral feasts. Others were perforated, as were two carved bone pieces (one disk and one elliptical), probably to constitute jewellery components (Taramelli 1904, 33, fig. 3; see also Manca 2006, 940).

The necropolis of Cuccuru S'Arriu-Cabras

In addition to cave burials, the Bonu Ighinu phase comprises burials in built tombs within open-air necropoli (Fig. 41). At present, only Cuccuru S'Arriu, described above, presents this mode. The necropolis is situated on a small rise of land, and apparently served the funerary needs of the Bonu Ighinu settlement some 100 metres to the west (Sebis et al. 2012, fig.1). Under the general direction of Vincenzo Santoni, 13 hypogea and nine simple pit graves have been located, investigated and partially published (Santoni 1976; 1977; 1982; 1988; 1995; 1999; 2000; Germanà and Santoni 1992; Sebis et al. 2012; Lugliè and Santoni, forthcoming). The tombs are distributed in two distinct areas separated by ca. 20 m. Based on ceramic attributes, these zones appear to be roughly contemporary. The northern area held eight tombs roughly aligned N-S with five hypogea to the north and three pit graves to the south. The southern area held 14 tombs clustered irregularly with six pit graves toward the SE and eight hypogea toward the NE.

The two tomb types, considering the relative investments embodied in the architecture and the contents, clearly reflect status distinctions. The pit graves (four cut from the bedrock, five from the soil), held individual, primary burials with the skeletons found on their left flank in semi-fetal position. A modest array of accompaniments included stone beads (chlorite?), bone points and geometric microliths (Santoni 1982, 106). The hypogea – all similar in construction and contents – comprised instead single, elliptical chambers with vaulted ceilings (ca. 2.5 x 2.0 m), referred to as oven-like (*a forno*). Access was via a vertical shaft cut into the sandstone to a depth of about a metre or

slightly less. The chambers were in some instances sealed by a wall of irregular stones (ca. 75 cm), against one or more a *breccia* slab was set edgewise as a 'door'; the floors of the chambers were paved with *breccia* as well (Contu 2000, fig. 3:1). Each tomb had a primary inhumation laid on the left flank facing the opening; in several tombs (nos. 384, 386, 416) there were also the remains of a second, and probably secondary, burial (Germanà and Santoni 1992).

Each of the hypogea contained an array of accompaniments that included fine-ware vessels, numerous bone points, beads of shell and stone (chlorite?), geometric microliths and, notably, one or more finely carved stone idols or statuettes (discussed below). The idols were positioned as if held in the right hand of the deceased, near the chest (see Fig. 42 and Santoni 1982, 106, figs. 4-5). Tomb 386 – perhaps the wealthiest – held, along with items such as those noted above, three idols, a greenstone axe and numerous shell beads found concentrated about the head and chest of the primary skeleton, suggesting the remnants of jewellery. In most tombs, the entire burial assemblage was furthermore covered in red ochre (Germanà and Santoni 1992).

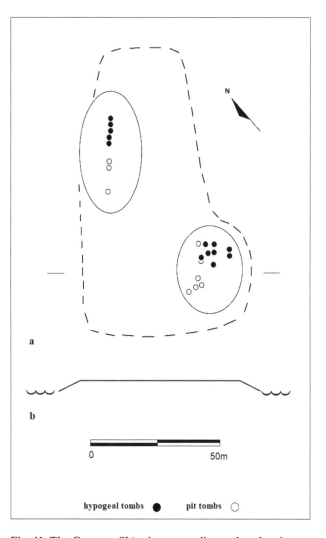

Fig. 41. The Cuccuru S'Arriu necropolis, a: plan showing locations of hypogeal and pit tombs, b: site elevation (after Santoni et al. 1982, fig. 3).

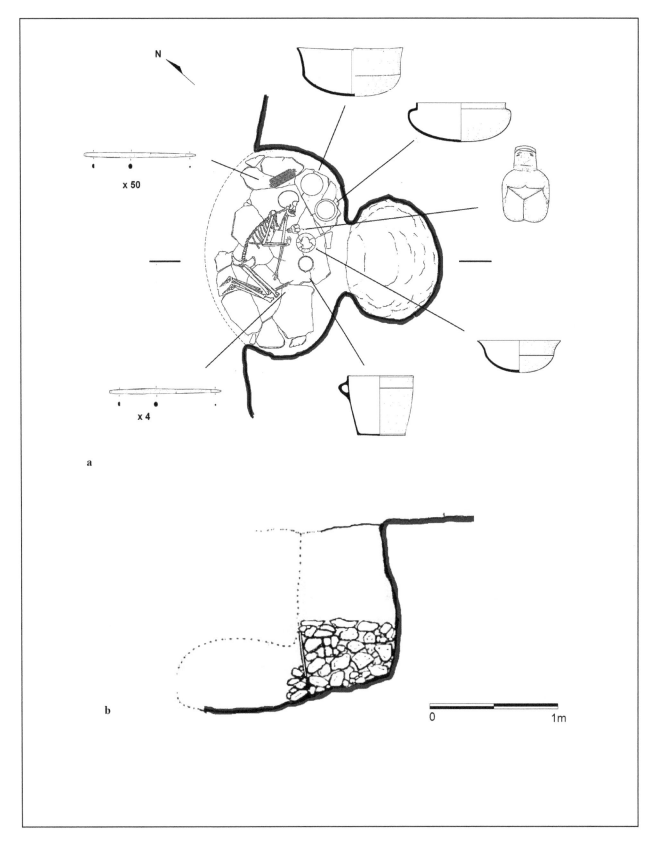

Fig. 42. Tomb 387 at Cuccuru S'Arriu. a: plan of the hypogeum with contents, b: section (after Santoni et al. 1982, figs. 3-4).

Anatomical analysis of four skeletons (two from tomb 386, one each from tombs 384 and 387), suggests that the inhumed individuals were adult or nearly adult males and, in the case of tomb 386, accompanied by the partial remains of a child, probably female (Germanà 1992, 139). The male in Tomb 384 was of very short stature, possibly resulting from a congenital pathology, while the other two were of normal height or just above. It was noted too that the teeth were free from caries and showed little use-wear, especially so in the young male in tomb 386 (Germanà 1992, 19). Skeletal samples from two burials (385 and 386) have recently provided radiocarbon dates falling into the second quarter of the fifth millennium cal BCE (Lugliè 2017, 56).

The significance of these finds is considerable, but the fact that the results are only partially published limits our understanding of them. Still, some regularity can be noted in the left-flank disposition of the primary inhumations in both hypogeal and pit tombs, as well as the similar range of accompaniments in both – apart from the idols, which differentiate the hypogea. They are also distinguished by the presence of secondary remains (cf. Lugliè 2018). The phenomenon of hypogeal burial as such was not unique to Sardinia at this time. Similar customs appeared across much of the Mediterranean during the fifth millennium, including the southern Italian peninsula, but curiously not in Corsica. It has been proposed that the very wide incorporation of this new custom came about through the circulation of obsidian from various sources and with it ideas and people in interlocking networks of exchange that bound these regions together within a cultural *koiné* (Tykot 2003; Vaquer 2007; Freund 2014; Walter 2000, 607-20 and below). The appearance of hypogea in Sardinia's western gulf, as will be discussed more fully below, is certainly likely to reflect social changes relating to the obsidian industry specific to this area. In this regard, it is perhaps useful to recognise that apart from their more obvious manifestations of status distinctions, hypogeal tombs were in effect artificial caves (cf. Melis 2014, 8). As such, they might be seen as the products of decisions to re-locate traditional burial locales (caves naturally bound in space) to locales favoured and chosen for settlement. As monuments, they might even be viewed as strategic, in so far as they may have contributed to legitimising residential claims on the basis of the presence of ancestral remains (Saxe 1970; Renfrew 1976).

Subsistence

A number of Bonu Ighinu deposits have yielded plant remains of varying quality. From Filiestru cave, where both wheat and pea were recorded in Early Neolithic (Epicardial) levels, the Bonu Ighinu strata also yielded *Triticum* and *Pisum* but in reduced numbers, and without recorded millstones (Trump 1990, 21; Ucchesu et al. 2013, 1). In the nearby cave of Sa Ucca de su Tintirriolu, in deposits bearing Bonu Ighinu ceramics, there are recorded instances of hulled barley (*Hordeum vulgare*), lentil (*Lens culinaris*) and broad bean (*Vicia faba*), but apparently no millstones (Loria and Trump 1978, 133 [incorrectly attributed to Filiestru by Bakels 2002, Table 3]). As the cave of Sa Ucca appears to have served mainly mortuary use, the food remains may represent grave offerings. Hulled barley, lentil and broad bean had already come under cultivation in the mainland by the bearers of Impressa-ware (Early Neolithic), but appear here for the first time in the Bonu Ighinu (Middle Neolithic) phase (Ucchesu 2013, table 3).

Note can be made also of carbonised remains from Grotta del Rifugio, representing wild plants: maple (*Acer sp.*),

strawberry tree (*Arbutus unedo*), juniper (*Juniperus sp.*), olive (*Olea europaea*), mock privet (*Phyllirea sp.*), black pine (*Pinus cf. niger*), terebinth (*Pistacia terebintus*), holm oak (*Quercu ilex*) and buckthorn (*Rhammus alaternus*) (Ucchesu 2013, table 6). These probably represent remains of hearth fuel and/or animal fodder. The olive (for its fruit), the oak (for its acorns) and the pine (for its small nuts) may also represent human consumption remains, but this must remain entirely hypothetical (see Agosti et al. 88-89). Faunal materials are, as expected, far better represented with remains reported from five caves (Filiestru, Su Coloru, Sa Ucca, Corbeddu and Rifugio) and one open site (Cuccuru S'Arriu). The most noteworthy discontinuity with the preceding Epicardial phase is the generally greater number of cattle represented.

At Filiestru, the Bonu Ighinu assemblage is similar to that from underlying Epicardial deposits, but with some notable differences: an increase in marine and terrestrial molluscs, a similar increase in pika and, perhaps not unrelated, an absence of fox remains, as well as an increase of cattle remains relative to caprines and swine from five to 17 per cent. As in earlier assemblages, caprines appear to have been randomly slaughtered (all age groups are represented), while the few ageable cattle were slaughtered when young (five to 30 months) rather than as over-aged draft- or milk animals (Levine 1983). Regarding consumption at Filiestru, the over-representation of forelimbs of stock (similar in all Neolithic strata) implies that butchering was conducted elsewhere while only selected parts where brought into the shelter for consumption (Levine 1983, 120). At Su Coloru in the north, cattle remains also show an increase, here from 10 to 31 per cent of all finds, while pika account for only eight per cent (down from 33 per cent). There are also marginally more dog remains, while boar is lacking altogether. Notable here is also an appearance of the red deer (*Cervus elaphus*), an imported species documented in Cardial levels at Corbeddu Cave (Masala 2008, fig. 8). At Sa Ucca de su Tintirriolu, a small bone sample from deposits dominated by Bonu Ighinu ceramics and possibly representing mortuary feasts came mainly from domestic caprines (54), followed by swine (seven) and cattle (three), along with pika (six; Wilkens 2003, table 2).

The evidence from Grotta del Rifugio is especially informative. Along with remains of a few domestic sheep/goats, cattle, swine and domestic dog, gathered molluscs and numerous pika, bones of marten (*Martes martes*) and wildcat (*Felis sylvestris*) as well as several very small mammals (*Sorex Araneus, Pitimys Subterraneus and Apodemus flavicollis*) are recorded for the first time. These were all extraneous to the island and apparently imported (Agosti et al. 1980; Lai et al. 2015, table 1). As at Sa Ucca, the Rifugio remains may represent mortuary feasts or perhaps offerings. The data have recently been complimented by results from stable isotope readings on human skeletal samples which suggest a heavily meat-based diet as well as significant intragroup variation (Lai et al. 2015, table 1). Such findings are not contradicted by the apparent lack of caries in the human teeth, an observation also made at Cuccuru S'Arriu and felt to indicate little consumption of stone-processed plant foods (see Germanà 1981 and below).

The single assemblage available from an open settlement, that of Cuccuru S'Arriu, is notable for the elevated representation of cattle remains accounting for 71 per cent of the stock animals. Also noted was the complete skull of a domestic dog (*Canis familiaris*) (Bignon et al. 2008, tabs. 2-3). The high number of mollusc shells of primarily marine species with signs of human consumption is understandable: even with the much lower sea levels (ca. -10 m), the site would have been within a few kilometres of the coast. The remains, along with ceramics and lithics, came from a number of features representing perhaps a sunken hut or plaza (str. 422) and large, perhaps communal hearths (Sebis et al. 2012). The absence of evidence of either plant remains or millstones is probably not due to sampling- or preservational lacunae. As hinted above, Germanà's observation (1992) of the absence of caries and only minor degrees of tooth wear among the necropolis remains (hypogea 386, 387) would be incompatible with diets based on cereals or other plant foods processed with stone grinders (cf. Smith 1984; Formicola 1987; Lanfranco and Eggers 2012, 7), but fit well with a pastoral, meat-based diet (as suggested in the faunal evidence at Rifugio and perhaps Su Coloru). Unfortunately, we currently lack human osteological data from sites with clear evidence of cultivation, such as Filiestru, for comparison.

Faunal introductions

Regarding the introduction of non-indigenous species, one might envision the larger stock animals, even the deer (perhaps as fawns) and the fox (perhaps as tamed kits) accompanying Neolithic colonists to the island in their boats, with the small rodents travelling along undetected (cf. Clutton-Brock 1981; Masseti 1998, 8-9). Less easily envisioned are the means by which the marten and the wildcat arrived here. Both are represented in mainland sites (Tagliacozzo 2005-2006; Vigne 2007), and the populations in Sardinia and Corsica as well as those in Crete and on Cyprus appear, on genetic grounds, to have been initially introduced from the Near East, and thus to have made similar marine voyages (Driscoll et al. 2007, fig. 1A), but how and why is unclear.

Crafts

Flaked stone

The flaked-stone industry seems generally to have continued in the Epicardial tradition of knapping. It features retouched (normal and inverse) flakes and blades, crescents, burins, scrapers, as well as transverse or tranchet points. As earlier, local obsidian dominates the assemblages close to the Monte Arci source, and the use of local flint – especially that from Perfugas – is increasingly common in the north Fig. 43). Similarly, the reduction of

small cores by direct percussion and the infrequency of finished tools bespeak a general opportunism. At the same time, certain contexts, possibly with elevated status such as Bau Angius-Terralba and Cuccuru S'Arriu, document a more systematic production of blades by indirect percussion and pressure flaking, as well as the making of more standardised tools such as bi-truncated geometric items (Lugliè and Lo Schiavo 2009; Lugliè 2004; 2012; 2017, fig. 13; Sebis et al. 2012). As regards Filiestru in particular, Hurcombe's study of four obsidian flakes from stratum 5 revealed microwear and residues consistent with use as butchery implements for cutting flesh and hide (1992, Table 2).

On the basis of the scant distribution data for the early fifth millennium, it seems that obsidian from Monte Arci continued to leave the island for sites in northern Italy, southern France and neighbouring Corsica (Lugliè 2012). Sardinian obsidian was used exclusively on Corsica, while mainland sites drew heavily also on southern sources at Palmarola and Lipari (Binder et al. 2012: tab. 2; Vaquer 2007, fig. 4), and while the rare piece of Sardinian obsidian found its way into the southern Italian peninsula (Acquafredda and Muntoni 2008), the principal area of distribution remained the north. There is some interesting evidence of a shift in use criteria at the Monte Arci source at this time: whereas SA (southern slopes) and SC (western) varieties had been favoured for local use and the SB varieties rather for export during the Early Neolithic (Tykot 1996; Lugliè et al. 2007; 2008), this appears to have been reversed during the Middle Neolithic, when SA and SC varieties more often made it abroad, while SB was reserved for local use (Lugliè 2017). Very limited data suggest that this may be reflected in the reduced quantities of SA at Filiestru (Tykot 1996, fig. 5), and on Corsica (Orange et al. 2018, fig. 7), and its proportional increase in mainland sites (Binder et al. 2012, fig. 2 and tab. 3; Freund 2014, figs. 3 and 5). One important exception is apparently Cuccuru S'Arriu, near Monte Arci, where SA obsidian continued to be favoured. As will be taken up below, this may evince some local control over access. Regarding trade in flint, the Early Neolithic pattern of occasional exports of the Perfugas stone to Corsica is by contrast little evinced for the early fifth millennium (see Bressy-Leandri 2016).

Ground-stone tools

An increase in the production of ground- and polished stone tools is reported generally for the Bonu Ighinu phase (cf. Tykot 1999, 72), but millstones and similar grinding tools suited to processing cereals – never common in earlier deposits – remain scarce in Bonu Ighinu contexts as well, with a single example from structure 422 at Cuccuru S'Arriu (Sebis et al. 2012, 500). Polished greenstone axes – an earmark of the Neolithic elsewhere and a favoured object of long-distance trade in the Tyrrhenian region and beyond (Garibaldi et al. 2013) – are similarly scarce, with single examples reported from tomb 386 at Cuccuru S'Arriu (Germanà and Santoni 1992, 79),

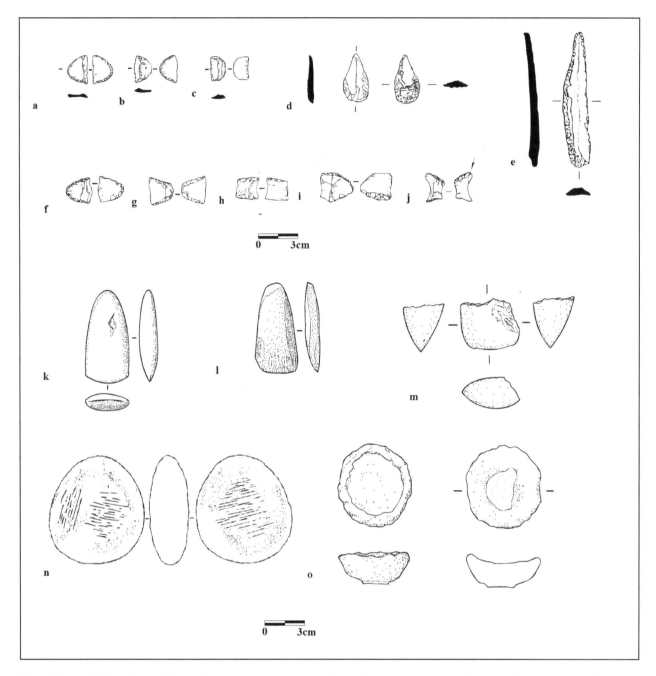

Fig. 43. Bonu Ighinu-phase lithics (a-j, flaked stone; k-o, ground stone). Proveniences, a-c: Cuccuru S'Arriu, tomb 415 (obsidian, after Luglié 2017, fig. 13), d-e: Filiestru (flint, after Trump 1983, figs. 26-27), f-j: Grotta del Rifugio (obsidian, after Biagi and Cremaschi 1980, fig. 7), k: Sa Ucca (after Loria and Trump 1978, fig. 16), l: Grotta del Rifugio (after Agosti et al. 1980, fig. 11), m: Filiestru (after Trump 1983, fig. 26), n: Grotta del Rifugio (after Agosti et al. 1980, fig. 11), o: Filiestru (after Trump 1983, fig. 27).

Grotta del Rifugio (Agosti et al. 1980, figs. 10-12); Sa Ucca de su Tintirriolu (Loria and Trump 1978, XXXVII); Monte Majore (Foschi Nieddu 1987, 865); and probably Corbeddu (Sanges 1987, 827). There are also, however, finds of hand-stones, pestles, grinding stones, abraders and bone-point sharpeners from various Bonu Ighinu contexts.

Bone implements

Objects carved from animal bone were rare in Early Neolithic contexts but comparatively common in Middle Neolithic Bonu Ighinu deposits, numbering some 150 specimens in total. The vast majority has come from the

necropolis at Cuccuri S'Arriu (over 100), while smaller collections have come from other sites across the island, including Su Coloru, Sa Ucca, Filiestru, Corbeddu, Rifugio, Coderra-Iglesias, Tatinu-Santadi, Monte Majore and Bagno Penale (cf. Manca 2006; Loria and Trump 1978, 128; Biagi and Cremaschi 1980, figs. 4-6; Santoni 1982, fig. 5; Foschi Nieddu 1987, 465; Masala 2008, 12). The study by Manca (2006) has provided some insights on this industry. By far the most common items are pointed bone implements. Manca's observation of these under magnification suggested a range of possible applications: awls from carved bone splinters (a few retaining epiphyses), various points with or without alterations for hafting or mounting, and pins with perforations – possibly used as needles. Points with single or double lateral incised divisions of basal and proximal parts as well as longitudinal incised slots may have been hafted or mounted onto shafts as projectile points. The points from the Cuccuru S'Arriu tombs are so far unique in having been worked full-length to more or less uniform shapes (tapered to both ends) and dimensions (20 cm in length; medial thickness 0.7 cm). Medial sections are ovoid, and the distal ends sub-rectangular, plano-convex and, rarely, bevelled (Manca 2006: fig. 2B). Notable too is the so-called spatula with incised decorations and perhaps a stylised human face from the cave of Sa Ucca (Loria and Trump 1978, 128, fig. 10:1 and Tav. IX:4). A similar but undecorated tool from Su Coloru may be contemporary (Masala 2008, 12).

Bone, shell and stone ornaments

As implied in the above site descriptions, ornaments made of stone and shell as well as bone and teeth became standard additions to Bonu Ighinu funerary assemblages (cf. Manca 2006; Usai 2009). Most common are rings, disks and/or necklace beads in stone and shell; boar's tooth pendants and bracelets of shell are also known (Fig. 44). A bone ring with a carved volute from the burial deposit at Grotta del Rifugio is a notable *unicum* (Fig. 44g and Agosti et al. 1980, fig. 12:7).

Deserving special consideration are finds of what are probably bracelets or armlets made from various polished greenstones (Fig 45 and Tanda 1977; Soro 2009, 105-6). Ten or so are known from six find-spots in the north of the island, and outside Sardinia similar items are not infrequently found in Early- and Middle Neolithic contexts in the central and northern Italian mainland (Pessina and Tiné 2008; Micheli 2012; 2017), in southern France (Courtin and Gutherz 1976), and in rare instances also in Corsica (Tramoni et al. 2007). Unfortunately, none of the Sardinian specimens have been recovered in situ, but come instead as casual finds in caves and open deposits. On contextual grounds and loose ceramic association, eight can probably be assigned to Bonu Ighinu contexts: four from Sa Binza Manna-Ploaghe and one each from Grotta Bariles-Ozieri, Monte Majore and Grotta Sa Rocca Ulari-Borutta. Both the Bariles and Ulari caves contained funerary deposits, while the cave at Monte Majore held mainly habitation remains, and little is known of the other find-spots. In terms of morphology, the Sardinian stone rings vary comparably to mainland examples (Tanda 1977). About half have triangular/sub-triangular sections, while the four from Sa Binza Manna have distinctly plano-convex sections – the internal diameters ranging from 9.5 to 4.7 cm. As on the mainland, a range of hard, green-hued stones were favoured for these presumably ornamental rings including jadeite (Sa Binza Manna), nephrite jade (Grotta Bariles) and olivine (San Pietro di Sorres). All but the nephrite, which must have been imported, occur naturally on the island (Bertorino et al. 2002, 92).

Imagery

The 'volumetric' statuettes

The Middle Neolithic in Sardinia, as elsewhere, features a relatively large production of stone-, terracotta- and generally believed to reflect cultural/chronological bone statuettes in a range of morphological stylesvariation (Tanda 1977, 25-29; Atzeni 1978, 58-64; Antona Ruju 1980, 115-39; Lilliu 1988, 50; Atzeni and Santoni 1989, 36). For Sardinia, Giacomo Paglietti has convincingly argued for a stylistic distinction between the so-called volumetric statuettes of the early Middle Neolithic Bonu Ighinu phase and the folded-arm statuettes of the subsequent Late Neolithic San Ciriaco phase. Following his scheme (2008, 12; 2017), the volumetric statuettes will be considered here, and those of the folded-arm variety in the next chapter.

The volumetric statuettes (Fig. 46) are typically referred to as mother-goddess idols in the literature (Santoni 1982; Germanà and Santoni 1992) and constitute a distinctive and prominent feature of the Bonu Ighinu repertory about which relatively little is understood with any certainty. There are currently 21 known examples from nine sites distributed in the central and northern parts of the island. However, only those from the necropolis of Cuccuru S'Arriu have provided meaningful contextual information. They are made from a variety of local stones (limestone, sandstone, marble, kaolinite, trachyte, granite, alabaster) and in one case, fired clay. Many are well preserved, with sizes ranging from 3.15 to 18 cm in height (Paglietti 2006, tab. 1).

A common three-part design is evident as idols of different sizes tend to have similarly proportioned heads, torsos and lower extremities. At the same time, individual idols vary in specific details. Most appear to wear a head-dress, commonly a habit-like hood, although one from Muros carries a radiating concentric design on the top of the head. Another fragmentary piece, from Perfugas, is unique in its apparent depiction of a nursing mother with intricately braided tresses resting on her shoulders and nape in groups of four or five long plaits, possibly adorned with terminal weights (Fig. 46e). While most statuettes depict hands held down at the sides, the idol from Tomb 410 at Cuccuru S'Arriu shows them on the breasts, while that from Muros shows one held on the thigh. Another, the largest in the corpus from Cuccuru S'Arriu (tomb 386), wears an elaborate headdress with hangings over the shoulders and back. The absence of any phallus argues for the female body as the intended reference; otherwise uniformly lacking are any indications of nipples or navels.

Although figurines have been recorded in contemporary mainland sites (the single, possibly unfinished idol of a later type from Corsica will be discussed in the following chapter), Bonu Ighinu statuettes are stylistically unparalleled in adjacent regions (Skeates 2017; Holmes and Whitehouse 1998).

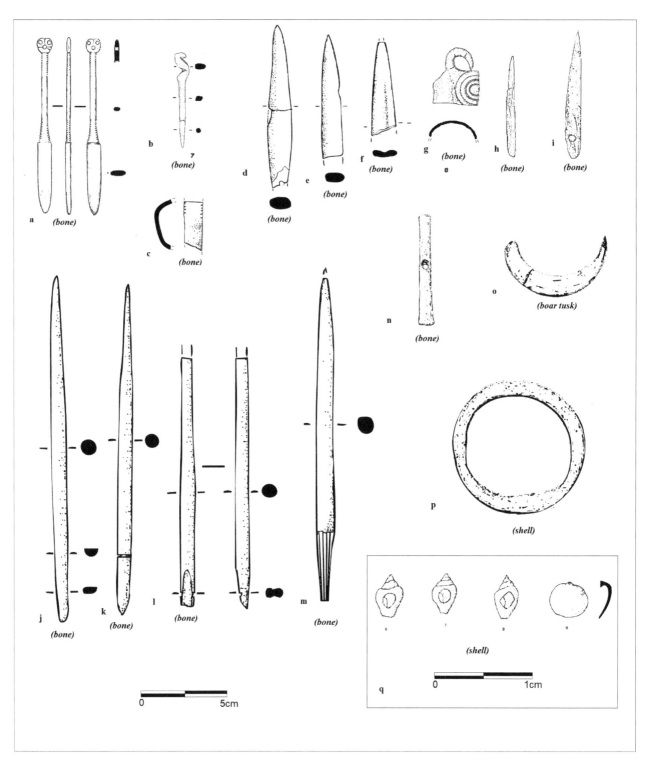

Fig. 44. Bonu Ighinu-phase implements and ornaments of bone, shell, teeth. Proveniences, a, c, i: Sa Ucca (after Loria and Trump 1978, fig. 10; Canino et al. 2017, no. 66), b-h, n-q: Grotta del Rifugio (after Biagi and Cremaschi 1980, figs. 8 and 11; Canino et al. 2017, nos. 65, 67, 68, 72), j-l: Cuccuru S'Arriu (after Manca 2006, fig. 2), m: Coderra (after Manca 2006, fig. 3).

The characteristically rotund, voluptuous, corpulent or indeed 'volumetric' proportions and sometimes 'oriental' attributes have suggested comparisons with Anatolian idols especially from Catal Huyuk, Hacilar and Can Hassan I, but the much earlier dating of the eastern examples makes any direct association unlikely (cf. Lilliu 1999). Much in keeping with traditional approaches to the eastern figurines (Mellaart 1967; Gimbutas 1989), these highly skilled products have been regarded as stylised depictions of corpulent female bodies representing a fertility deity (Usai 2009; Atzeni 1978). Viewed as naturalistic representations, they have often been read in terms of symbolic references for example to conception, birth, motherhood, milk, eroticism and, when veiled in ochre, with life-sustaining blood (Santoni 1982, 107; Lilliu 1975; 1999). When placed with the deceased, in Alberto Moravetti's words, 'The Mother Goddess could also relieve the traumatic event of death and ensure a life

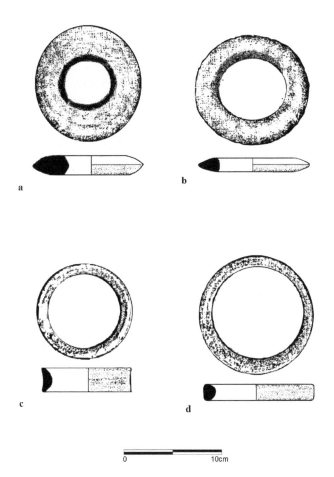

Fig. 45. Sardinian stone rings. Proveniences, a: San Pietro di Sorres-Sassari, b: Grotta Bariles, c-d: Sa Binza Manna (after Tanda 1977, figs. 1-2).

that the figurines were not modelled from life, as humans simply do not put on weight or excess adipose fat in the way depicted in the idols (cf. Tchernov 2009, fig. 1; Liebermeister 1995, Abb. 143). It can be noted in this regard that the often cited Neolithic Anatolian 'venuses' are far truer to life, in their often clear rendering of pendulous breasts, sagging thighs and belly, dilated navels, dimpled elbows and knees, and overall proportions consistent with gynoid obesity (see Shah 2007 for an inventory). The Bonu Ighinu idols appear by comparison more like disproportionally exaggerated and inflated, taut forms.

In the same way, it seems doubtful that the idols reflect any experience-based understanding of the relationship between excess body weight and fertility. Obesity to the degree depicted in the Bonu Ighinu statuettes could only have had deleterious effects on reproduction, e.g. higher incidence of amenorrhea and anovulation, low conception rates, high miscarriage rates and increased risk of pregnancy complications – in short, lowered reproductive potential (Dag and Dilbaz 2015, 111). Unless we are to grant pronounced stylisation as the aim of the sculptors, the Bonu Ighinu figurines cannot, it seems, be assumed to reflect experience with human anatomical responses to excessive caloric intake, nor yet with its effects on fertility. Instead, we might with greater confidence propose that these depictions represent hypothetical extensions of the doubtlessly experienced relation between dietary health and fertility within the less than secure Neolithic subsistence regimes in which they were embedded, and that they may embody some positive (if ideal) notion of diverting disproportionate quantities of food from the local economy toward consumption. A similar reading has recently been proposed even for the rotund female depictions in the Catal Huyuk corpus that are felt to have 'tangibly rendered an ideal metaphor for abundance', if not necessarily biological fertility (Pearson and Meskell 2014, 240).

Phallic depiction

A carved stone phallus from the open-air site of Bau Angius in Terralba has been attributed to the Bonu Ighinu phase and, if correctly so, this would represent the first such representation in the island (and a clear divergence from the so-called mother-goddess repertory). Studied by Carlo Lugliè (2008), the item is carved from local crystalline porphyry of very fine grain, shaped and polished on one side only. Its dimensions are roughly 6 cm in length by 3.2/2.4 cm in diameter, and it is appointed with multiple concentric ridges. It bears evidence of wear, and a probable break at the base. Without knowledge of its original associations, there is little to be said regarding its function or perhaps symbolic significance. However, based on the ridges, Lugliè has brought attention to the possibility of a realistic depiction of genital tattooing, mutilation or circumcision, perhaps in the context of rites of passage or cult performances (2008, 56-57, 59). In either case, in Bonu Ighinu contexts it is a *unicum*, and contemporary parallels from outside the island are very

beyond, in a cyclical re-elaboration of birth as a cultural and symbolic model of rebirth' (1999, 6; transl.).

But alternative readings have been proposed. In keeping with current research (e.g. Nakamura and Meskell 2009; Insoll 2017), some view artefacts such as these in terms of their social significance including their active role in the construction of identities (Losi 2012; Vella Gregory 2006; 2007; 2017; Lugliè 2017). In an early example of this approach to the Sardinian evidence, Dolores Turchi drew analogies with traditional but quite recent mortuary customs of placing dolls with the deceased, suggesting that Neolithic idols may have functioned similarly as companion dolls serving to appease the otherwise lonely and potentially dangerous spirit of the dead (1992, 2-4). More recently, Vella Gregory (2006; 2007; 2017) has taken another non-generative approach which foregrounds the potential significance of such objects as secondary social agents. In her model, the figurines represent particular body types and embody lived experiences relevant to individuals' relation to society and to the formation of identity (2007, 30).

It would seem that the single point around which all readings of the Bonu Ighinu figurines converge is the apparent significance of depicting corpulent bodies. A cursory comparison of the anatomy portrayed in the idols with that of living obese individuals suggest, however,

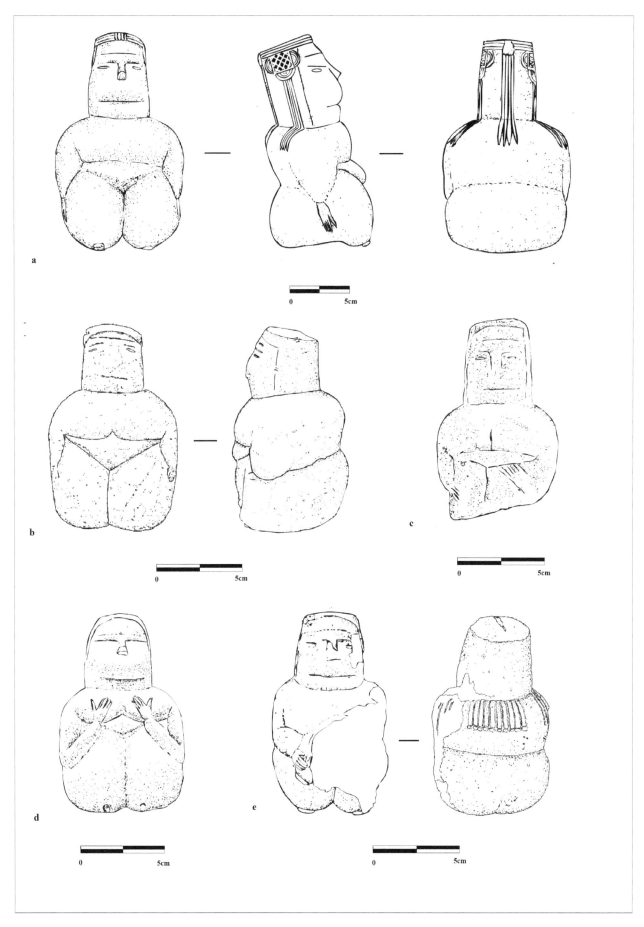

Fig. 46. Bonu Ighinu 'volumetric' statuettes. Proveniences, a: Cuccuru S'Arriu, tomb 386 (after Lilliu 1999, figs. 196-198), b: Cuccuru S'Arriu, tomb 387 (after Lilliu 1999, fig. 195), c: Su Monte-Muros (after Paglietti 2008, fig. 2.9), d: Cuccuru S'Arriu, tomb 410 (after Paglietti 2008, fig. 2.8), e: Sos Badulesos-Perfugas (after Lilliu 1999, fig. 204).

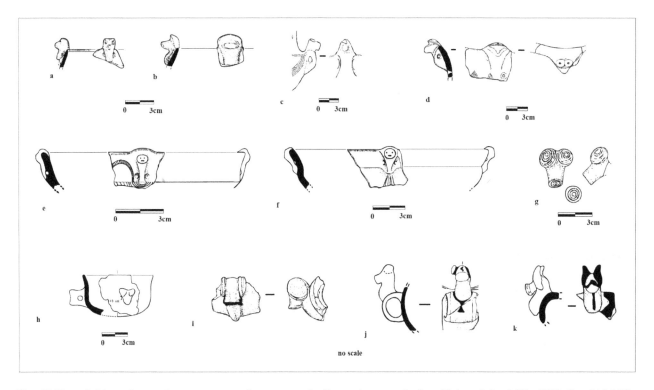

Fig. 47. Bonu Ighinu-phase ovine protomes and comparanda. Proveniences, a-b: San Ciriaco (after Lilliu 1999, figs. 340-341), c: Grotta del Rifugio (after Biagi and Cremaschi 1980, fig. 5), d: Grotta di Monte Majore (Lilliu 1999, fig. 345), e-f: Sa Ucca (after Lilliu 1999, figs. 346-347), g: Puisteris-Mogoro (after Lilliu 1999, fig. 339), h: Cileca, Corsica (Tramoni and D'Anna 2016, fig. 3), i: Masseria Mischitelli, Italy (after Gravina 1988, fig. 8), j-k: Scamuso-Mola di Bari, Italy (after Laviano and Muntoni 2009, fig. 1).

few. But reference has been made to a single example made on a tooth from a probably slightly later context on Malta (Red-Skorba, 4400-4100 BC; Lugliè 2008, 58; cf. Vella Gregory 2005, 29, 166-70).

Ovine protomes

Ceramic Bonu Ighinu vase handles were not infrequently embellished with animal protomes (Fig. 47). These vary considerably in realism/stylisation, but despite their occasional attribution as taurine (cf. Tanda 2007, 479) or phallic (Lilliu 1999, figs. 126, 363), they seem likely to depict the heads of horned sheep (cf. Lilliu 1999, figs. 339-41). One of two examples from the open-air site of San Ciriaco-Terralba clearly shows horns with growth rings curling back from the head in a single arch (Moravetti 2017, fig. 1), while what are likely to represent more stylised depictions of tightly curled horns are found on vase handles from the cave of Monte Majore (Lilliu 1999, figs. 124, 126, 354, 363) and the open site of Puisteris-Mogoro (Lilliu 1999, fig. 399). As ewes in early domestic breeds as well as feral mouflons were generally polled or carried small horns, heavily-horned animals shown here are clearly rams (cf. Tagliacozzo 2005-2006, 436; Zohary et al. 1998, 130).

Although such depictions are rare in the Tyrrhenian Middle Neolithic, at least one highly stylised but otherwise comparable example is known from Cileca in Corsica, on a contemporary Curasien vase (Tramoni and D'Anna 2016, fig. 3). Elsewhere, such mouldings are found in

greater number on contemporary vases of the Serra d'Alto phase in the central-southern Italian peninsula where the horned ovine head – in some examples clearly a ram - are often realistically depicted (Gravina 1991, fig. 6:8; 1988, fig. 8:6; Laviano and Muntoni 2009, fig. 1; Radina 2003, figs. 5, 6, 9).

Images of the human face?

The already mentioned bone spatula from Sa Ucca de su Tintirriolu, with its perforated handles possibly alluding to the human face, is a tantalising item to interpret. Similarly cryptic images can be seen on some vase handles otherwise akin to the stylised ovine protomes, and one example from Monte Majore would actually seem to represent a hybrid expression, where 'eyes' have been added to the tops of the curled horns (Fig. 47d). Similar examples from Sa Ucca and Filiestru have eyes and mouths while the zoomorphic features are reduced to an ovine profile (Fig. 47e-f; Trump 1983, fig. 15A; Lilliu 1999, fig. 348).

Interpreting the Bonu Ighinu modality

Discontinuities and persistence

With the Bonu Ighinu phase, one recognises the appearance, elaboration or expansion of features that seem to describe a discontinuity with the preceding Epicardial phase. The Bonu Ighinu pottery is better made in a wider range of forms and often carefully decorated with time-consuming techniques of micro-punctation and zoomorphic/ anthropomorphic mouldings. Craft industries turned out an array of utensils, ornaments and accoutrements in bone, shell, teeth and polished greenstone, and skilfully carved stone statuettes.

One also registers a more gradual transformation through the Bonu Ighinu phase in a lithic industry dominated by simple percussion-made microlithic tools in obsidian and flint but now augmented by rare occurrences of pressure-flaked obsidian blades; in a subsistence economy expanded by the addition of cultivated barley, lentils and broad beans; by the increasing popularity of the domestic dog; by the curious introductions of the martin and the wildcat; and in the appearance of new sites in most island regions, presumably due to fission and dispersion of a slowly growing population with an increasingly well-adapted economy.

Finally, there is the evidence of continuities: the persistence of open-air settlements with sunken features, the use of caves/rock-shelters as habitations and/or mortuary sites, the export of obsidian to Corsica, Tuscany, Liguria, the French Midi and, more rarely, to the southern Italian peninsula, as well as the persistent references to a wider cultural *koiné* seen in the ceramics.

Bonu Ighinu has been considered to be the first distinctly Sardinian culture (e.g. Lugliè 2017), but the insular-level homogeneity/integration implied in the notion of an island-wide Bonu Ighinu culture may be the product of too wide a gaze. It is apparent, on closer inspection, that the Bonu Ighinu phase subsumed considerable intra-insular diversity. At the very least, one can draw a rather clear distinction between the Gulf of Oristano with its hinterland, and the rest of the island.

The Oristano Gulf and the rest of the island

It is among the sites fringing the western Gulf of Oristano that overt expressions of innovation and 'Sardinian distinctiveness' cluster – the open-air necropolis, the hypogea, the carved statuettes, the rare examples of pressure-flaked obsidian. The sites here moreover reveal the first strong evidence of a status hierarchy, expressed in the asymmetries of the burial treatments. In architecture and accompaniments, those interred in built necropoli with novel rites were set apart spatially, materially and symbolically from those interred with traditional observances in caves. At the same time, burial rites further distinguished those with the evident privilege of hypogeal burial with accompanying idols from everyone else.

This raises the question of what circumstances made this area diverge as one of cultural distinction during the early Middle Neolithic. There might be some remote possibility that exogenous factors were at play: as noted, the striking similarity between some Sardinian and Anatolian idols is suggestive, although any direct entanglements would appear impossible on chronological grounds alone. There is firmer ground, however, to consider the possible effects

of relations with Serra d'Alto modalities in the southern Italian peninsula (cf. Melis 2014, 8). In this regard, Bonu Ighinu developments are paralleled by more or less contemporary shaft-accessed hypogea (Tiberi and Dell'Anna 2014), vases with ovine handle mouldings (Laviano and Muntoni 2009) and the rare import of Sardinian obsidian (Acquafredda and Muntoni 2008, 947-55).

But existing evidence still points more strongly to the unfolding of circumstances in Sardinia and the northern Tyrrhenian in contributing to Bonu Ighinu developments in the Oristano Gulf. First, it is not difficult to see that if demands for high-quality obsidian increased, f.ex. with population numbers throughout the region, Oristano settlements would have become increasingly advantaged by their location, situated as they were near the island's and indeed the region's sole obsidian source, and to potential trade routes, both marine-based from the Gulf, and riverine via the Tirso (cf. Melis 2014, 8). With this framework in mind, one might tentatively juxtapose a number of observations/queries:

- Local consumption of select varieties of obsidian and redirection elsewhere
- Hypogea as sepulchres of privilege; ancestral claims to territory?
- Abundant cattle remains; accumulated wealth? Privileged consumption?
- Carved idols; symbols of affiliation? Of abundance, privilege/status?

It is tempting to subsume all these observations and impressions within a hypothetical model of socio-economic relations specific to the Gulf of Oristano and predicated on the obsidian trade. About the means and agencies involved, and the geography they encompassed in terms of routes and networks, one can only speculate. But the distribution of idols beyond the Gulf of Oristano – none of which unfortunately have provided contextual data – may hold some clues. The find-spots describe a rough course between the Gulf of Oristano and the Gulf of Olbia on the opposite, eastern coast, the traditional embarkation point for off-shore islets of the archipelago and for Corsica. Could this be the vague outline of a geography of overland commerce in obsidian based in the Gulf of Oristano and invested along its way with clients, allies, kin, customers, middlemen? If so, then what of returns? Non-perishables seem unlikely, at least in the form of readily recognisable exotica. Perishables seem more likely, e.g. textiles, skins, livestock. As noted, cattle remains are especially well represented at Cuccuru S'Arriu (cultivated foods like cereals are also candidates, but the paucity of millstones in the Gulf sites would suggest otherwise). In any event, an organised trade of obsidian for consumables and livestock would be consistent with readings of the sculptural evidence as expressions of an elite.

The role, if any, played by Corsica in such a scenario in unclear. On the one hand, engagement with Sardinia was sufficient to support shared ceramic standards and some access to Monte Arci obsidian. At the same time, this closely neighbouring island remained culturally distinctive by its lack of hypogeal burial customs, volumetric figurines or polished stone rings.

In the rest of Sardinia, more traditional adaptations predominated. But here too, local diversity is evident. Subsistence regimes varied according to relative emphases on cultivation, herding, hunting and gathering. It is significant in this regard that it is only in the Bonu Ighinu valley, as evinced in remains from the caves of Filiestru and Sa Ucca, that any 'classic' Neolithic agro-pastoral economy prevailed. Elsewhere, it rather seems that pastoralism augmented by hunting and gathering was the norm. In any event, as will be taken up in the next chapter, cultural adaptations characteristic of the Bonu Ighinu phase persisted in part and in part were radically modified during the later centuries of the fifth millennium, with the mode called San Ciriaco.

The San Ciriaco Phase

Introduction

The material remains of the so-called San Ciriaco culture of the later fifth millennium have sometimes been described as 'sober' and 'austere' (cf. Falchi et al. 2012, 407). The impression is understandable when compared to earlier, Bonu Ighinu production: the pottery is darker and generally unembellished, the shapes are more canonical, and the expressive upturned elbow-handles with zoomorphic protomes are all but absent. Figurines carved in stone and now also bone present a curious slimming of the torso to appear more rigid, and the exceptionality expressed in the Bonu Ighinu-phase hypogea at Cuccuru S'Arriu has been diffused among multi-chambered tombs newly cut from the rock in various locations across the island.

San Ciriaco remains have been identified at some 75 locales across Sardinia, and what follows is given over to foregrounding the diversity perceived among these (Fig. 48). Much of the evidence relies on cross-dating from but a few more or less 'pure' San Ciriaco contexts, some of which have also supplied radiocarbon dates ranging from 4336 to 4073 cal BCE (Melis 2011, 210). Period schemes refer to the San Ciriaco phase variously as Middle Neolithic 2, Recent or Late Neolithic. Here, Late Neolithic is given preference following Maria Grazia Melis' work (2011), which situates it between the Middle Neolithic/Bonu Ighinu phase and the Final Neolithic-Initial Eneolithic/Ozieri phase. As with the concept of a Bonu Ighinu culture, that of a San Ciriaco phase masks what on closer inspection is an archaeological landscape with significant and no doubt socially meaningful diversity in the craft industries, in subsistence regimes and in mortuary customs. Of the last, attention is drawn especially to the evidence of a uniquely joint inter-insular burial cult featuring megalithic cist tombs centered in northern Sardinia and southern Corsica.

The diagnostic pottery

San Ciriaco pottery, along with its similar Corsican counterpart Présien ware, is easily distinguishable from Bonu Ighinu (and Corsican Curasien) by its generally superior quality and overall adherence to more standardised production methods. The corpus is dominated by a limited range of fine-ware vessels in refined, compact, well-fired pastes with thin walls, accurately finished with polished surfaces in beige to shiny black (Fig. 49). A series of often rigid, angular shapes – all handmade – include cups and bowls in simple, handle-less open and carinated forms, some with innovative and distinctive inflected or stepped walls, deeper carinated pots with opposing vertical loop-, tubular or more rarely spool-handles, interspersed with knobs or bosses, single loop-handled ladles or scoops, and jars with or without handles, some of them collared. Embellishments are generally lacking, save single engraved horizontal encircling lines which tend to give an overall impression of austerity (Lugliè 2017; Fanti et al. 2018, 114, fig. 3; Molinari 2002). Some coarser, sand-tempered ware was also produced, most commonly as larger vessels; in particular jars with opposing handles and bosses (Fanti et al. 2018).

When embellished, decorative techniques and motifs varied widely: engraved concentric circles, lines arranged in oblique, radial or zig-zag patterns and, less commonly, parallel sets of minute comb-impressions or incised, vertical branching/dendritic motifs. Particularly diagnostic are the engraved spiral-with-meander designs, sometimes further filled-in with white clay. These find close extra-insular parallels in the so-called *vasi a bocca quadrata* (VBQ2) *meandro-spiralica* styles of the northern Italian peninsula (Ferrarese Ceruti 1965; Usai 2009; Banchieri et al. 1999, fig. 8) with more remote origins in southern Italy and along the Adriatic coast (Lugliè 2017, 63).

More generally, the San Ciriaco ceramic corpus taken along with that of Présien in Corsica seems to refer to stylistic standards of a broader, extra-insular *koiné* subsuming contemporaneous mainland industries, namely Diana-Bellavista to the south and Chassey-Lagozzo to the north, including the so-called VBQ styles. The Corsican vases were rarely decorated, however (Tramoni and D'Anna 2016; Lugliè and LoSchiavo 2009, 256). Note should made of a late, 'transitional' form featuring punctations within incised triangles usually referred to as *pointillée*. This is also found on Corsica, (see de Lanfranchi 1967; Melis 2011, 209-10), and sometimes considered part of the San Ciriaco-Présien corpus.

It would seem better, however, following Melis (2011, 210) to consider this a formative phase of the post-San Ciriaco Ozieri phase (Final Neolithic-Initial Chalcolithic; treated in detail f.ex. in Webster and Webster 2017, 6-31).

Settlement and demics

Apart from the locations of presumed habitation deposits, we have limited details regarding the structure and organisation of San Ciriaco settlements. What is certain from field data is that both natural shelters and open-air settlements continued in use or were newly founded. Among the former are Grotta Verde, Monte Majore, Filiestru, Sa Ucca, Rifugio, Corbeddu, San Bartolomeo

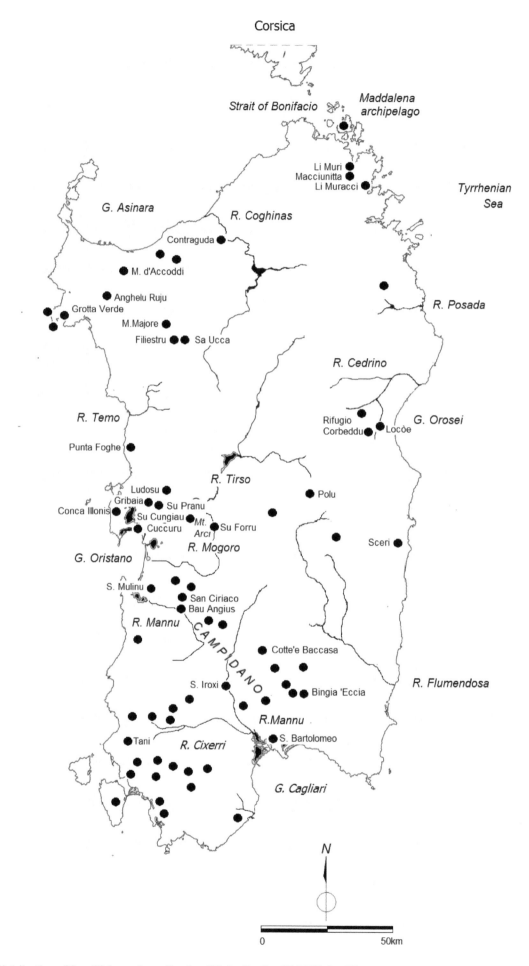

Fig. 48. Distribution of San Ciriaco-phase sites (modified after Lugliè 2017, fig. 22).

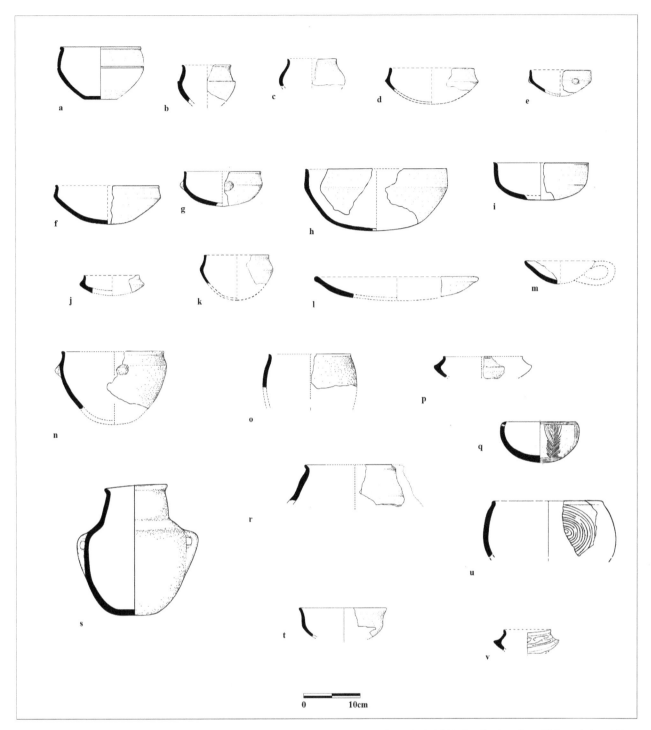

Fig. 49. San Ciriaco-phase pottery. Proveniences, a-c: Monte d'Accoddi (after Melis 2011, fig. 3), d-o: San Ciriaco (after Alba 1999, figs. 2-9), p: Contraguda (Boschian et al. 2001, fig. 16.1), q-u: Cuccuru S'Arriu (after Santoni et al. 1982, figs. 6, 10; Santoni, Bacco and Sabatini 1997, figs. 7 and 11), v: Tanì-Carbonia (after Ferrarese Ceruti and Fonzo 1995, fig. 15).

and Su Carroppu, while some long-frequented caves such as Su Coloru and Grotta dell'Inferno fell out of use. Among the open-air sites, Cuccuru S'Arriu, San Ciriaco and Bau Angius have yielded notable remains. In all, something like a florescence of open settlements in lowland alluvial settings can be noted during this phase. Partial evidence from a number of deposits in the Oristano gulf (e.g. Su Mulinu Mannu, Gribaia, San Ciriaco, Su Pranu Mannu, Bau Angius, Cuccuru S'Arriu) and at Monte d'Accoddi-Sassari suggest the perpetuation of the sunken hut as a mode for residential architecture, now accompanied by a

great diversity of auxiliary features representing seemingly communal hearths, probable trash dumps, clay-pits, silos, drainage ditches etc. (Pittau et al. 2012; Lugliè 2012; Fanti et al. 2017). A few sites have also yielded what are thought to represent cult deposits or *bothroi*, as at Gribaia-Nurachi and Bau Angius-Terralba (see below).

Considering demic changes between the Bonu Ighinu and San Ciriaco phases, taking as roughly representative the increases in site numbers from 45 to 75 over approximately five centuries (c. 4500 to 4000 BCE), we arrive at an estimated annual growth rate of 0.11 per cent, comparable to that for the Epicardial-Bonu Ighinu period (0.12 per cent per year) and to that generally assumed as normal increase among Neolithic groups (0.1 per cent per year, see above).

Monte d'Accoddi

Perhaps the best documented of the San Ciriaco settlements is Monte d'Accoddi, situated inland from the Gulf of Asinara in the northwest. This is also the site of the unique, Ozieri-phase temple-mound (see Epilogue, Webster and Webster 2017, 21-23; 67-73 and Webster 2019), beneath which lay the remains of the pre-existing San Ciriaco settlement. Diagnostic ceramics came both from the structural fill used in the construction of the temple platform (Traverso 2005-2007) and from remnants of underlying sunken huts (Tiné and Traverso 1992, xxxi). Excavations in the 1950s by Ercole Contu had, according to M.G. Melis' re-assessment (2011), uncovered a range of ceramic forms typical of the San Ciriaco phase including bowls, cups, pedestal-based vessels and spoons or ladles, all of high quality with well-fired fabrics and highly polished surfaces (Melis 2011, 210, fig. 3, 1-6; Tiné and Traverso 1992, tav. XXXIIIb). The size of the San Ciriaco settlement at Monte D'Accoddi can, however, only be very roughly gauged, from the several soundings made around the imposing temple-mound. Tiné and Traverso (1999, 14) pictured a modest habitation with perhaps half a dozen round-oval thatched and wood-framed houses that they likened to contemporary Ripoli-Vhò houses in the central Italian mainland (ca. 4-5 m in diameter; see also Bagolini and Biagi 1975, fig. 38). However, reports of diagnostic ceramics in soundings some 200 m east of the temple-mound suggests that the San Ciriaco settlement may have been much larger (Melis 2010, 210).

Subsistence

The increase in the island population registered with San Ciriaco, and in particular the florescence of open settlements in lowland settings such as the lower Campidano plain, have been felt to imply an expansion of cereal cultivation (Lugliè 2017: Ucchesu et al. 2017). While this may be reasonable assessment, it must be noted that direct evidence of agriculture is still quite limited. The site of Su Mulinu Mannu-Terralba has returned remains of cultivars in reliable association to San Ciriaco remains, including charred cereals – *Hordeum vulgare* and *var. nudum* and *Triticum aestivum/durum* – notably with ground-stone tools, along with a range of wild edible plants, such as *Ficus carica, Olea europaea var. sylvestris* and *Pinus sp.* (Ucchesu 2013, tav. 5; Ucchesu et al. 2017, tab. 4). Also noted were butchered remains of domestic stock (caprines, swine, cattle; Ucchesu et al. 2017). Similar remains have been reported from the rock-shelter of Su Forru de is Sinzurreddus in Pau some 10 km to the northeast on Monte Arci at 500 m elevation. Here were identified seeds of free-threshing wheats, legumes (*Genista sp., Medicago sp. Vicia/Lathyrus/Pisum*) and some wild fruits probably collected for human consumption (*Ficus carica, Pistacia*

lentiscus, Rubus sp. and *Sambucus sp.*; Ucchesu et al. 2013). At the same time, it is uncertain whether cultivation continued in the Bonu Ighinu valley (at Filiestru and Sa Ucca, see above), as San Ciriaco contexts have not been isolated in those deposits.

These otherwise quite limited subsistence data have recently been augmented with results from a study by Fanti et al. (2018) of San Ciriaco vessels from three neighbouring open-air sites in the Oristano gulf: Bau Angius, Gribaia and Su Mulinu Mannu. A novel integrated methodology was employed, combining the study of vessel morphology and morphometry, use-wear analysis, biomolecular and compound-specific carbon isotope analyses of residues preserved on the vessel interiors aimed at revealing modes of food consumption, preparation and storage. The results, based on the examination of 198 vessels, are both informative and enigmatic. Unexpected was the clear prevalence of residues of dairy fat registered at Bau Angius and Su Mulinu. This was found in both deeper vessels with signs of heating and smaller vessels without signs of heating, which together seem to document phases of preparing/cooking and serving/consuming milk products. Curiously absent were large vessels with unheated dairy residues which might have identified them as reserved for collecting milk/milking. Whether milk had been processed into cheese is uncertain, although the absence of specialised vessels such as sieves/strainers or double-boilers might suggest not (cf. Salque et al. 2013). In either event, these data document dairy use in Sardinia earlier than previously expected (cf. Lewthwaite 1986), and in keeping with evidence from surrounding regions (Halstead and Isaakidou 2011, 67).

Fat residues from ruminants (from meat and blood) were also common both from heated, larger vessels and seemingly unheated smaller ones. The species consumed were likely domestic caprines and cattle, represented also in butchered bone remains. More surprising is the absence of fat residues from non-ruminants – pigs/boar – since these too have left macro-faunal remains. The authors suggest that perhaps swine were prepared and consumed without using pottery (i.e. by roasting, smoking, salting), or by using perishable containers (Fanti et al. 2018, 125).

Residues from plants (not identifiable) were little detected in the Bau Angius and Su Mulinu pots, although more commonly in vessels from Gribaia, where they were mixed with animal residues (as noted, macrobotanical remains of cereals and pulses were also found at Su Mulinu). Unfortunately, the residues of such low-fat foodstuffs are not reliably detectable by the methods employed in the study (cf. Hammann and Cramp 2018). It is of course possible, as Fanti et al. suggest (2018, 124), that such foods were stored in some of the largest necked jars in which no animal fat residues were detected (2018, fig. 10).

Whether aquatic resources were much exploited is unclear. The investigations found no marine evidence in any of the vessels examined, again despite the finds of fish remains at least at Su Mulinu (Luglié et al., forthcoming), and the piles of shells from pits at Gribaia (see below and Fanti et al. 2017; Soro and Usai 2009).

Tombs and mortuary practices

The diversification of mortuary practice first evinced in the Bonu Ighinu phase continued with San Ciriaco. Natural caves and rock-shelters continued to serve as burial sites, and there is some evidence from Cuccuru S'Arriu that simple pit burials were sometimes made within domestic settings (Santoni 1982, 80). In addition, hypogeal rites probably derived from the oven-tombs of Cuccuru S'Arriu appeared in several island regions, while the locally unprecedented custom of interment in slab-built cist tombs with covering mound or cairn was adopted in the far northeast.

Hypogea

It seems likely that the hypogeal burial customs first documented in the Bonu Ighinu phase at Cuccuru S'Arriu were sustained during the subsequent San Ciriaco phase (Melis 2014; Santoni et al. 1997), but the evidence is problematic (P. Melis 2009; Ugas 2000; Tanda 2017, 111-14). Two multi-chambered rock-cut tombs (known as *domus de janas*, fairy houses, see Fig. 50) have yielded San Ciriaco ceramics: Sant'Iroxi-Decimoputzu in the lower Campidano plain (Ugas 1990) and Tomb X at Santu Pedru-Alghero in the northwest (P. Melis 2009). In both cases, the finds amount to a small number of sherds recovered near or just inside the entrance corridors or *dromoi*, a fact which has fostered concerns that these materials may have entered the tombs as secondary fill taken from deposits that actually predate the tombs (P. Melis 2009; Ugas 2000; Tanda 2017, 111-14). Three other tombs have recorded San Ciriaco materials in more secure interior contexts: at the necropolis of Anghelu Ruju-Alghero, a fragment of a marble San Ciriaco-type idol from tomb XXIII (Taramelli

1909; Paglietti 2008, 16-18, fig. 6); from Bingia Eccia-Dolianova in the lower Campidano, a carved stone polypod platter with zoomorphic protome and a carinated stone bowl with a spool handle (Lilliu 1999, figs. 97 and 99), and from the boulder-tomb at Sceri-Ilbonu near the east coast, fragments of San Ciriaco-type idols (Fadda 2006, 23, fig. 13; Nieddu 2006).

Unfortunately, little can be gleaned regarding possible cultic or social implications of these finds since the tombs in question evince long periods of re-use, some well into the Bronze Age, during which episodes of renovations, expansions, periodic clearing and filling have resulted in extremely complex and typically heavily mixed cultural remains. In consequence, it has so far been impossible to relate the sparse San Ciriaco finds either to specific burial assemblages or to architectural phases. At the least, however, one might conclude that some form of hypogeal custom was in use during the San Ciriaco phase in several island regions, and that it represents architectural and cultic norms probably rooted in the earlier Bonu Ighinu oven-tomb tradition.

Megalithic cist tombs

In addition to hypogeal burial customs, a parallel mortuary tradition established itself in parts of the island with close extra-insular parallels especially on neighbouring Corsica. The tombs are generally referred to as megalithic or proto-megalithic burials and featured the interment of the deceased in a rectangular cist or *coffre* built from stone slabs set on edge. Most often, cists are found within concentric rings of retaining boulders (so-called megalithic or peristaltic circles), felt to have originally supported a covering mound of earth and rubble. Also associated might be one or more aniconic monolithic uprights variously referred to as stelai, menhirs or baetyls. The Megalithic cist tombs have been found singly or in necropolis-groupings at about a dozen locations between

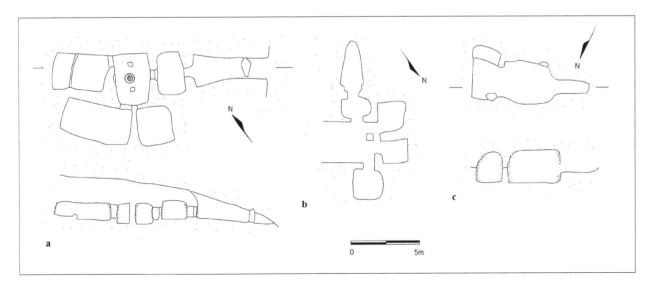

Fig. 50. San Ciriaco-phase hypogea, a: plan and section of Tomb X at Santu Pedru (after P. Melis 2009, fig. 5), b: plan of Tomb XXIII at Anghelu Ruju (after Taramelli 1909, fig. 60), c: plan and section of the tomb of Sant'Iroxi (after Contu 2000, fig. 18).

Fig. 51. Li Muri-Arzachena (Photo: ptj56 for WikiMedia Commons).

Arzachena and Olbia in the northeast. Excavations have allowed the more or less secure dating of several of these to the San Ciriaco phase: Li Muri and Macciunitta in Arzachena, and Li Muracci near Olbia (Lilliu 1963, 27; Santoni et al. 1997, 251). Recently, a fourth has been tentatively identified within the rock-shelter of Su Forru de is Sinzurreddus-Pau on Monte Arci near the Gulf of Oristano (Lugliè 2010; 2017, 61).

Li Muri-Arzachena

The best known of the Sardinian megalithic tombs are those of the necropolis of Li Muri in Arzachena (Fig. 51). It was excavated in the late 1930s and published to standards of the time (Puglisi 1941) with results frequently re-examined since (cf. Puglisi and Castaldi 1964; Castaldi 1984; Antona Ruju and Ferrarese Ceruti 1992; Antona 2003, 358-73). The site is situated on a rise of land (elevation c. 140 m asl) approximately 10 km from the present coastline, and includes the tightly spaced remains of five cist graves, four of which (I-IV) have encircling stone 'cairn' settings with outer diameters ranging between 5.30 and 8.50 m (Fig. 52). All the burial cists are similarly constructed of orthostatic slabs to roughly rectangular dimensions ranging from 2 x 2 m in the largest cairn (IV) to 1.6 x 1.2 m in the smallest (III). Unfortunately, only fragments of human long bones have been found, leaving no further clues as to the nature of the interments, whether single, multiple, primary or secondary. But traces of red ochre were noted that suggest its use in preparing the remains for burial. All the cists appear to have contained undecorated ceramics, accompanied by various adornments and tools, some with exotic references (Castaldi 1984, 32-33):

From Tomb IV, the largest, came five shaped and perforated spheroids (c. 7.5 cm in diameter) of green chlorite, four polished greenstone hatchet/axe heads (flat-triangular, 5-7.7 cm) and numerous elongated, spherical and discoid necklace beads of green and blue steatite (Lilliu 1999, fig. 172).

Tomb I (the second largest) contained a single perforated greenstone spheroid, two polished stone hatchet/axe or adze heads (one very small, 4.6 cm, of whiteish stone; a second fragmentary in serpentine stone), a pink stone smoother, a fragmentary bone point, and numerous green steatite necklace beads. Especially noteworthy are a finely made thin-walled stone cup (9 cm diameter at the mouth) in light steatite with two spool handles typical of the Diana culture vessels in the mainland, and four sections of pressure-knapped flint blades.

Tomb II contained another polished greenstone flat-triangular hatchet/axe or adze head (6.5 cm), a perforated stone spheroid (6.5 cm) and various necklace beads of andesite, while Tomb III, the smallest of the cairns, was found apparently empty of artifacts. Tomb V, located off the SW flank of Tomb IV, with a more trapezoidal cist (c. 2 x 1 m) but no evidence of a cairn, contained two sections of pressure-knapped flint blades, and various stone necklace elements.

Situated among the cairns were also three small stone orthostatic slabs. Empty when found, these were perhaps intended for offerings (Antona 2003). Also distributed among the works in no apparent pattern were a number of unworked monoliths in local granite standing to a height of some two metres, one set within a simple stone curbing next to Tomb V.

Interestingly, the blades found in several tombs have been identified as knapped from exogenous flint, probably coming from Gargano-Puglia in the southern Italian mainland (Lugliè 2017, 61; Lilliu 1999, 340). The perforated chlorite (possibly local) spheroids, interpreted as perhaps representing insignia of rank, sceptres or symbolic weapons (Lilliu 1999, 415; Lugliè 2017, 61), find at least one Sardinian parallel in a specimen from Su Cungiau de Marcu-Decimoputzu where there was also a stone idol (Lugliè 2017, figs. 13.6; 24, and below). Subsequent studies of the finds by Robert Tykot (1995, table H2) identified obsidian remains coming from tombs III, IV and unspecified spots, all derived from three sources on Monte Arci showing a preference for types SC and SA (Tomb III: 19 SA, 5 SB2; 17 SC; Tomb IV: 3 SA, 5 SC; unspecified 10 SA, 9 SB2, 121 SC) (see Fig. 53).

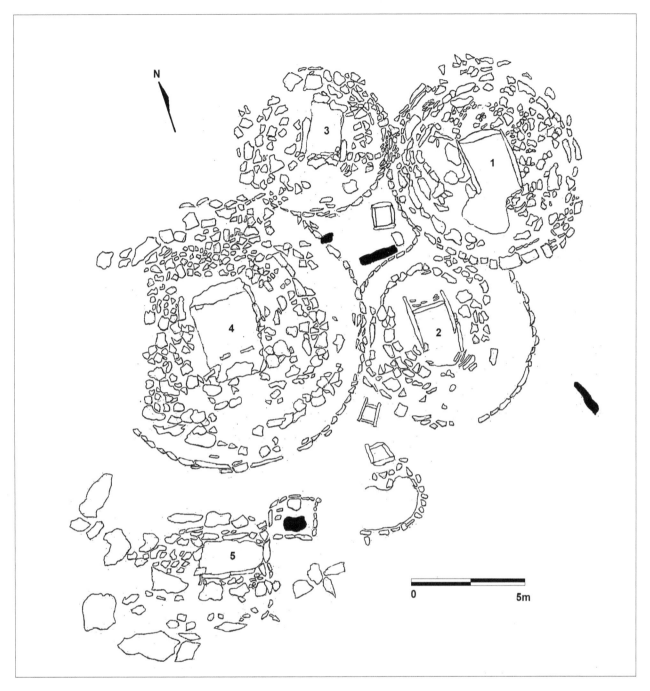

Fig. 52. The Li Muri necropolis, with menhirs marked in black (after Castaldi 1984, fig. 13; Moravetti 2012, fig. 6).

Macciunitta-Arzachena

This site comprises a large, well-preserved megalithic cairn (11 m in diameter) and traces of two more. It is situated about a kilometre nothwest of Li Muri in a similar setting (Antona Ruju and Ferrarese Ceruti 1992, 31-32; Paglietti 2009, fig. 4). Unlike the Li Muri remains, Macciunitta has preserved its artificial earth- and rubble mound to a height of ca. two metres. It is retained by a double ring of stones, the outermost forming a curbing of single and double rows of stone slabs set on edge. The centrally located, slab-built cist retains only the west and south walls, but also what has been identified as a stone cover slab, found overturned. Human remains were absent, but grave goods were recorded. These included undecorated ceramics similar to those from Li

Muri, a flat axe head in jadeite, blades and flakes in obsidian but not in flint, and numerous beads of elongated and spherical shape in white and green steatite, quartzite and porphyry (Puglisi and Castaldi 1964). An oblong boulder was found lying within the inner retaining circuit which would have stood to 2.5 m height near the outer east edge of the cairn (Puglisi and Castaldi 1965, fig. 1; Antona Ruju and Ferrarese Ceruti 1992, 31) (see Fig. 54).

Contemporary settlements that might locate the patrons of the Arzachena tombs have not so far been confirmed. Several rock-shelters reporting San Ciriaco ceramic remains occur locally, however (Monte Incappiddatu, Monte Pilastu and Cala di Villamarina-Santo Stefano), and may have supported contemporaneous occupations

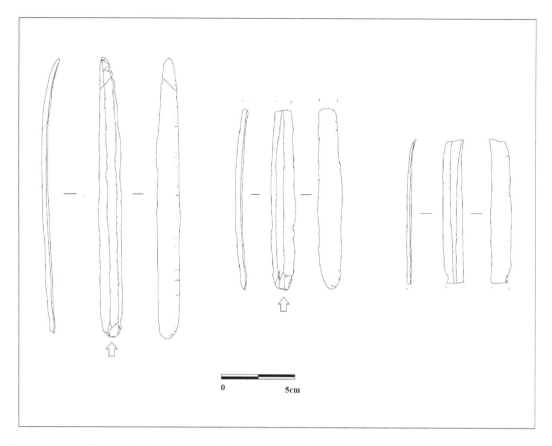

Fig. 53. Pressure-flaked flint blades from the Li Muri necropolis (after Guilbeau 2010, Vol. 3, figs. 90-92).

(Antona Ruju and Ferrarese Ceruti 1992; Antona 2003, 358-73).

Su Forru de is Sinzurreddus-Pau

Representing a so far unique 'outlier' to the Arzachena tombs, brief note should be made of the lithic cist burials recently uncovered in the rock-shelter of Su Forru de is Sinzurreddus at Pau on the eastern slopes of Monte Arci (c. 500 m asl) near extensive obsidian works. The deposit is still under investigation and largely unpublished, and excavations so far have revealed a large number of human bones belonging to a wide range of individuals male and female including infants, sub-adults and adults (Lugliè 2010; 2017, 61). Some of these showed clear traces of burning, tentatively interpreted as representing rites of secondary burial following cremation. Found in close proximity were stone slabs identified as remnants of a cist tomb of still unknown dimensions, completely destroyed by fallen ceiling rocks. Also associated were sherds of undecorated San Ciriaco pottery and a high concentration of obsidian flakes as well as several tanged, bifacial projectile points, the earliest examples so far in the island (Lugliè 2010; 2017, 61). Flotation processing of the sediments revealed traces of domestic wheats and legumes as well as edible wild fruits (Ucchesu et al. 2013 and below).

The northern Sardinian-southern Corsican commonality

The mortuary rites implied in these locally unprecedented remains were not unique to Sardinia. Very similar architectural expressions have been documented in more or less contemporary contexts across the mainland regions to the north from Catalonia to Liguria, including Corsica, in great numbers (Guilaine 1996; see also Paglietti 2008). It is clearly with the more numerous Corsican megalithic expressions that the northern Sardinian tombs find their closest parallels, both in terms of architecture and accompaniments (cf. Tramoni et al. 2004; 2007). This has led to the notion of a joint Sardinian-Corsican burial cult within the San Ciriaco-Présien *koiné* (cf. Guilaine 2003; Antona Ruju and Ferrarese Ceruti 1992; Tramoni et al. 2007, 271-72), and the evidence is compelling. Parallels are seen among southern Corsican necropoli for example in the incorporation of monoliths within and among tomb works and in the placing of some within small, individual stone settings or curbs (Paglietti 2009, 99). Speculation on the cultic significance of the monoliths have included notions of their housing divine spirits as in baetyls (from the Hebrew *beth-el* for seat or house of god), or once having carried painted symbols, or having been conceived as refuges for the souls of the interred (Antona Ruju and Ferrarese Ceruti 1992, 28). At the very least, they will have served as grave markers by virtue of their height. Variation in cairn size and accompaniments, with their attendant implications of differentiation among the deceased as at Li Muri, are also documented in Corsican necropoli (Paglietti 2009, 99; Lugliè 2017, 61). In terms of accompaniments, apart from closely comparable ceramics, some Corsican tombs have also reported perforated stone spheroids (Tramoni and D'Anna 2016, 61), stone necklace beads and axe heads (Tramoni et al. 2007; Leandri et al. 2007).

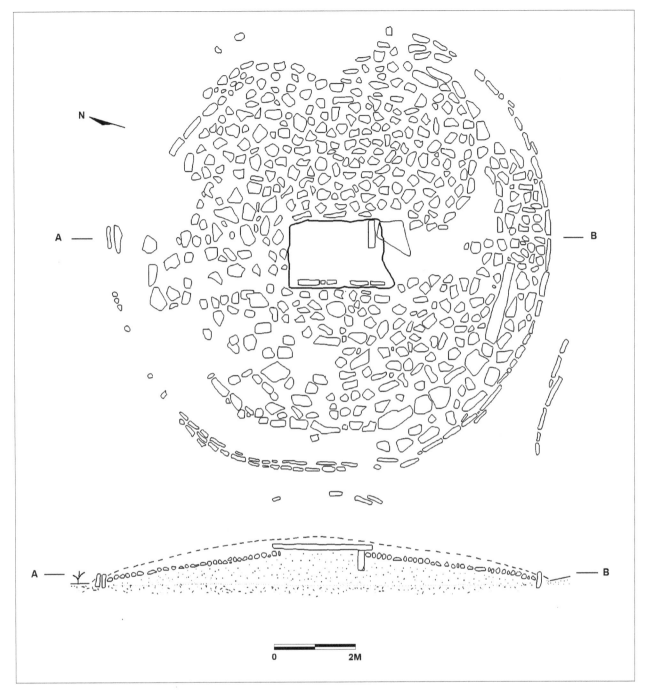

Fig. 54. The Macciunitta necropolis (after Antona 2003, fig. 1).

Non-funerary cult remains

At least two open-air deposits of the San Ciriaco phase have revealed features without any apparent domestic or mortuary associations which are interpreted as 'structured depositions' of objects representing symbolically invested practices (Fanti 2015; Fanti et al. 2017). These are unusual deposits, distinct from the larger domestic refuse pits found for example at San Ciriaco, Su Mulinu and Cuccuru S'Arriu (Santoni et al. 1997; Sebis et al. 2012, 498), and revealed instead as small pits (20-40 cm in diameter and depth) with subcircular-subelliptic plans containing selected and sorted objects of pottery, stone, bone and shell. About 30 such pits have been found distributed in discrete areas at two lowland sites near the Oristano gulf,

Gribaia-Nurachi and (to a lesser extent) Bau Angius-Terralba (Fanti et al. 2017; Soro and Usai 2009; Lugliè 2003).

Thus far, three types of these pit-deposits have been tentatively identified based on the recurrent association of artifact types that are felt to constitute sets (Fanti et al. 2018, 112): Type 1 contained groups of whole or in large part preserved pottery vessels. In these pits, the vessels had been stacked upright or overturned one inside the other. In some instances, there were sporadic bone or shell remains in close association, as well as nearly complete bone- and/ or ground stone tools (millstones, handstones, smoothers). One pit at Gribaia also contained a clay idol, and another idol came from the surface (Soro and Usai 2009, 4, fig. 2;

Lilliu 1999, 255). Type 2 pits (only at Gribaia) contained molluscs, and Type 3 pits obsidian and/or flint tools. It was further noted that despite thorough examination of the sediments by flotation and sieving, no macrobotanical evidence was found (Fanti et al. 2018, 119).

About the wider contexts in which these evidently symbolically charged pit-deposits or *bothroi* occurred, precious little is known. Both sites appear to have supported settlements, at Bau Angius from the Early Neolithic on (Soro and Usai 2009; Lugliè 2008, 55). As already noted, a study of residues from vessel interiors suggest some differences between the two sites: at Bau Angius an emphasis on dairy products, at Gribaia plant-foods along with dairy (Fanti et al. 2018, 125 and above). Various small pits of undefinable function are a common feature of Neolithic habitation and funerary sites in peninsular Italy and Sicily (see Lugliè et al. 2017), but parallels to the Gribaia-Bau Angius *bothroi* are so far seemingly not known.

Lithic industries

Information about San Ciriaco lithic industries is limited to the very few assemblages with secure associations and/or dating. Three contexts have provided reasonably reliable data: Contraguda, a lithics workshop situated near the Perfugas flint outcroppings in the north (Boschian et al. 2001; Falchi et al. 2012), Cuccuru S'Arriu-Cabras near the Monte Arci obsidian quarries (Santoni et al. 1997, 239), and Punta Foghe north of Monte Arci on the west coast at Tres Nuraghes (Fiori 1999 and 2000; Dini 2007). These together suggest that much of the former Bonu Ighinu range of tools continued to be produced from blades using traditional procedures of direct percussion. Generally, an opportunistic, expedient approach to core reduction with little technical investment is evinced, toward producing tools for immediate local use (Usai 2009) (see Fig. 55).

To these observations can be added the still unique occurrence of bifacial, tanged projectile points reported from Su Forru de is Sinzurreddus-Pau (Lugliè 2010; 2017, 61). These represent a significant break from the traditional transverse/trenchant point, not only in design but also in the greater production investment that they represent (cf. Inizan et al. 1999, 44-48). Although possibly an autochthonous development, influences from the Corsican industries would seem likely given the closeness of inter-insular relations indicated in ceramics and burial customs. Corsican Présien contexts have in fact yielded bifacial projectile points both of losenge and tanged types, from Monte Revincu (Gilabert et al. 2011: fig. 9:8-9), Guaita and Caldeira di Cintu, with at least one losenge point from Guaita knapped from Sardinian Perfugas flint (Lorenzi 2018, Pl. II:6-7).

Trade in obsidian and flint

The San Ciriaco phase presents rare evidence of importations of lithics from abroad. These come from the

Li Muri necropolis at Arzachena where, as noted, the flint of the large pressure-knapped blades from cist-grave I has been traced to sources in the southern Italian peninsula, probably Gargano (Guilbeau 2010; Lugliè 2017, 61). Reconstructing trade patterns specific to the San Ciriaco phase is otherwise limited by the small number of dated samples on and off the island. Some have read in the meagre San Ciriaco finds the outlines of a nascent insular-wide export industry integrating large workshops on Monte Arci with displaced specialised shops such as that at Punta Foghe (Lugliè 2012, 177; Lugliè and Lo Schiavo 2009), but evidence for this abroad (i.e. the exclusive use of the select SA variety of Monte Arci obsidian among the French Chassey sites) appears to date to the very end of the fifth millennium and the early fourth (cf. Binder et al. 2012; Freund and Batist 2014), placing such developments in the post-San Ciriaco Ozieri phase (Webster and Webster 2017, 10-11).

What can be said with some certainty is that obsidian continued to leave the island to northern destinations in Corsica, Tuscany, Liguria and southern France (Binder et al. 2012, 194; cf. Lugliè 2012). Not surprisingly, given the close affiliations with Corsica seen in pottery styles and burial customs, analyses have identified flint (mainly as debitage) from the Sardinian Perfugas sources in at least four late fifth-millennium Présien sites – Vasculacciu, Stantari and Tivulaghju in the south and, in the north, Monte Revincu – all of which also report Sardinian obsidian (Tramoni et al. 2007). More surprisingly, some of the flint found in Corsica originated from the lesser-known Sardinian deposits of the Montiferru massif near the west-central coast (Bressy-Leandri 2016). While Perfugas quarries had supplied flint to Corsica since the Mesolithic, exportation from the Montiferru source appears to have begun only with the San Ciriaco phase. Notably, Tivulaghju in Corsica features two lithic cist graves comparable to those at Li Muri in Sardinia, and also revealed areas with extensive workings of Sardinian obsidian including some raw blocks from the Monte Arci quarries (Tramoni et al. 2007).

Fig. 55. Punta Foghe on the west coast (Photo: D.A. Fadda for WikiMedia Commons).

Ground-stone tools

Apart from the grave goods from the Arzachena necropoli (greenstone and jadeite axe heads, perforated chlorite spheroids), utilitarian ground-stone implements such as pestles and milling stones are rarely reported from San Ciriaco contexts. The few finds have come from open-air sites in the Gulf of Oristano at Su Mulinu Mannu (also reporting cultivars), Gribaia-Nurachi, Bau Angius-Terralba and Cuccuru S'Arriu-Cabras (Fanti et al. 2017, 31; 2018, 112).

Ornaments

Personal ornaments such as necklaces, pendants etc. were not uncommon during the Bonu Ighinu phase, but are rare in San Ciriaco contexts. Finds are so far limited to those from the cist burials at Arzachena, with parallels in their Corsican counterparts such as Tivulaghju (Lugliè 2017, 61; Tramoni et al. 2007).

Stone vases

A small series of carved stone vessels are tentatively assigned to the San Ciriaco phase: a spiral-decorated steatite plate from Locoe-Orgosolo (Lilliu 1999, figs. 101-102; no. 148), a very fine carinated dish/cup also in steatite with opposing spindle-handles and 'bud' feet from the grave assemblage of Tomb I at Li Muri (Lilliu 1999, fig. 100, no. 147), with two additional specimens from the hypogea of Bingia Eccia-Dolianova (Fig. 56). One is a calcite bowl with a single spindle-handle, another a polypod plate with a zoomorphic protome carved from calcareous stone (Lilliu 1999, figs. 99 and 97). The latter is paralleled by a very similar vessel from Stantari in southern Corsica (which may in fact be Sardinian; see Lanfranchi 2000, 383). In addition, a fragment of a similar polypod plate in marl from an open-air deposit at Ludosu-Riola Sardo preserves a foot carved as a stylised zoomorphic protome (Lilliu 1999, no. 145; figs. 96a and 335).

Imagery

Depictions of animal forms are less frequent in San Ciriaco contexts than they had been in Bonu Ighinu settings. Only two examples are known: the stone vessels from Bingia Eccia and Ludosu noted above, with horned protomes seemingly depicting sheep (Lilliu 1999, figs. 97 and 99). Regarding the human form, however, a number of statuettes or idols are dated to the San Ciriaco phase.

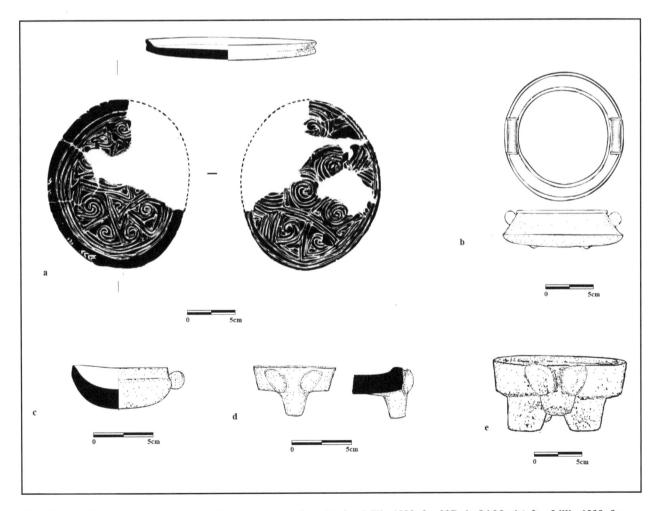

Fig. 56. San Ciriaco-phase stone vases. Proveniences, a: Locoè (after Lilliu 1999, fig. 337), b: Li Muri (after Lilliu 1999, fig. 336), c: Bingia 'Eccia (after Ferrarese Ceruti and Fonzo 1995, no. 18), d: Ludosu (after Lilliu 1999, fig. 335), e: Bingia 'Eccia (after Lilliu 1999, fig. 97).

The idols

The anthropomorphic statuettes assigned to the San Ciriaco phase (Paglietti 2008) signal significant changes in the portrayal of the human form, the material media chosen for their imaging and the loci considered suited to their use (Fig. 57). Regarding distribution, in contrast to the Bonu Ighinu idols, San Ciriaco specimens are found in the southern half of the island, with but a few exceptions. They have moreover been recovered in domestic contexts as well as mortuary and non-mortuary cult contexts (e.g. Vella Gregory 2007, table 2). Also contrasting the earlier productions, San Ciriaco idols are fashioned from bone as well as stone and clay. They are generally considered as representing female forms.

Potentially most informative for us, the San Ciriaco portrayals transgress the bounds of the earlier Bonu Ighinu repertory and range from more or less voluminous figurines to linear, rigid items. It is tempting to view this variation as denoting a temporal change in the way the female form was represented. In overall terms, as already noted, they seem to represent a gradual slimming-down of the human anatomy, particularly above the waist. This impression is strengthened when comparing them also to the strictly geometric, slim and stylised design of the subsequent Ozieri-phase idols. In consequence, San Ciriaco statuettes are often viewed as representing a transitional form, and as such sometimes referred to as 'elongated geometric' in terms of style (Vella Gregory 2006, 14; Cicilloni 2009, 220; Usai details such as eyes, fingers, nose and mouth, there is a 2009; Paglietti 2008, 12). In the rendering of anatomical variation which some have perceived as a similar trend toward rigid schematisation in facial expressions as well (Vella Gregory 2006, 14). The figures are depicted as sitting or standing, with exaggeratedly elongated head, narrow waist and disproportionately enlarged buttocks and thighs, warranting the concept of a steatopygeous rendition (cf. Contu 2000, 312) – a term used here in a descriptive rather than a medical sense.

That the corpus is of local derivation is not in question. The close likenesses with earlier volumetric idols particularly in the head and face, and in head coverings, leave little doubt of a Bonu Ighinu heritage. As a group, the San Ciriaco figurines are nevertheless considered distinguishable from both Bonu Ighinu and subsequent Ozieri idols by the position of the arms, which are shown folded under the breast, *a braccia conserte*. In dimension, they are generally smaller than their volumetric counterparts, ranging in height between 3 and 7.35 cm (Vella Gregory 2006, 14). Vella Gregory has interpreted them as material illustrations of a transition in social dynamics. In her words, 'the body was now used to convey a different message, with a lesser emphasis on difference and more on conformity' (2006, 20). If, as suggested in the foregoing chapter, the corpulent Bonu Ighinu sculptures rendered some notion of abundance symbolically or metaphorically, then that message was altered in the re-proportioned anatomies of the San Ciriaco production. Clearly, the social environment

was different, not least as seen in the presence of an exotic Corsican-Sardinian mortuary cult, with its increases in inter-insular relations (see Vella Gregory 2006, table 2 and below). In this regard, the single example of a San Ciriaco-style idol in serpentine from the megalithic deposit at Campo Fiorello-Grosso in southern Corsica is probably significant (Lanfranchi 2000; Grosjean 1963, 5-17), as is the greater sympathy to mainland styles seen in some San Ciriaco idols. Striking parallels are found in the more rounded forms of Serra d'Alto figurines, especially those from Matteo-Chiantinelle (Gravina 2008, fig. 3) and Fonti di San Callisto (Skeates 2017, fig. 1:2). Perhaps, as Vella Gregory implies, the exceptionality of Bonu Ighinu sculptures was gradually exchanged for the integrative (and commercial?) benefits of artistic expressions more in keeping with wider standards.

Interpreting the San Ciriaco modality

Taking in the island's Late Neolithic landscape in single gaze leaves contrasting impressions: one of unity, one of contrast. The first comes when considering the formal aspects of material expression. San Ciriaco pottery, even more than Bonu Ighinu ware, speaks of a conformity to high standards of production and styling that applied not only across the island but beyond to inform parallel Présien production in Corsica, and in part those on the mainland (Diana-Bellavista, Chassey-Lagozzo, VBQ). The same appears true of figurine art. The Sardinian uniqueness of the volumetric Bonu Ighinu idols has meanwhile given way to less unique stylings more in sympathy with those in Corsica and the southern Italian mainland, a phenomenon meriting the label of an extra-insular *koiné*. Within the island, under this common cultural umbrella, other continuities inhered in the perpetuation of the lithic industry and subsistence economies, in the use of caves and shelters, and in the gradual expansion and filling-in of the island's niches with new open-air settlements.

The second impression – that of contrast – comes when considering the evidence of cult expressions. On the one hand, the diffusion through the island of hypogea appears to extend old customs that linked burial to caves and shelters, originally accepting these loci as they occurred naturally, but beginning with Bonu Ighinu increasingly as artificial constructions made in the service of settlement and territorial priorities. It is moreover significant that these expressions of mortuary custom (which become the dominant mode during the subsequent Copper Age) remained within insular boundaries. It is therefore tempting to read them as contributing to embryonic developments of a Sardinian cultural identity more clearly outlined in the remains of the subsequent Ozieri phase (see Epilogue and Webster and Webster 2017, 128-29).

But during the San Ciriaco phase, these expressions found starkly divergent counterparts in the megalithic cist tombs of northern Sardinia and neighbouring Corsica. Parallels in architecture and accompaniments signal unprecedentedly intimate cultural ties between the islands

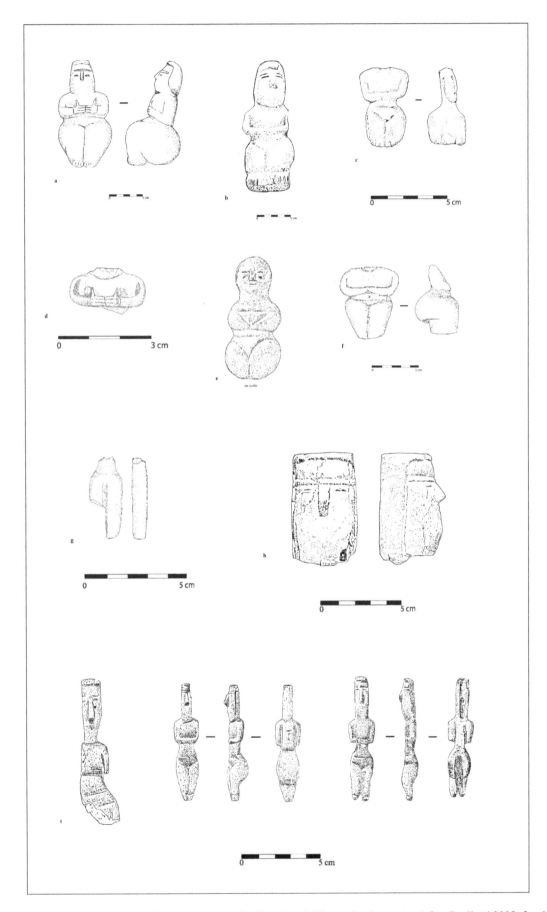

Fig. 57. San Ciriaco-phase statuettes. Proveniences, a: Su Cungiau de Marcu-Decimoputzu (after Paglietti 2008, fig. 6.9), b: Cotte'e Baccasa-Segariu (after Paglietti 2008, fig. 6.10), c: Conca Illonis-Cabras (after Paglietti 2008, fig. 6.2), d: San Ciriaco (after Paglietti 2008, fig. 6.1), e: Campo Fiorella-Grossa (Corsica, after De Lanfranchi 2000, 383), f: San Matteo-Chiantinelle (Italy, after Gravina 2008, fig. 4), g: Tomb XXIII at Anghelu Ruju (after Lilliu 1999, fig. 216), h: Polu-Meana Sardo (after Paglietti 2008, fig. 6.8), i: Monte Meana-Santadi (Paglietti 2008, fig. 6.4).

seemingly reflecting a joint Sardinian-Corsican burial cult. Like the hypogea, these tombs too probably served territorial interests (Tramoni et al 2007, 271-72), and their distribution has suggested the outline of a new social geography with controlling interest in the management of Sardinia's obsidian resources (Luglié 2009b, 219; 2017, 61). In contrast to Bonu Ighinu circumstances, spatial relations are not hinted at in the distribution of figurines, but rather in the placement of megalithic cists. Two nodes: one an isolated outlier on the obsidian-bearing Monte Arci itself (Sinzurreddus-Pau), the other strategically placed astride the Straits of Bonifacio – a traditional inter-insular transit point. Between them lithics will have moved among agents with common affiliations to cult and *koiné* (Melis 2011, 207). Such a geography might even accommodate the still rare appearances of enigmatic offering pits or *bothroi* at some Oristano settlements as counterparts to those placed among the tumuli of Li Muri-Arzachena. The social significance of these relationships has so far been little explored, but it would not exceed the evidence to suggest that the relative levels of wealth displayed among the megalithic burial cists signalled privilege and distinctions, if not structured hierarchies (cf. Tramoni et al. 2007, 251, 271; Melis 2014, 11).

Regarding questions of migration and diffusion, the high number of megalithic tombs in Corsica and the north Tyrrhenian mainland relative to Sardinia would seem to suggest that the new mortuary customs arrived in the islands from the north by 'upstream' transmissions along obsidian trade routes (Melis 2014, 9). At the same time, uncertainties in their relative dating allow for alternative scenarios (cf. Malone 2015, 182), namely one engendering diffusion from the southern Italian mainland. As M.G. Melis has reminded us, although megalithic burial was not the predominant funerary mode in southern mainland Italy, simple slab-built cist burials were sometimes made during the period in question (cf. Manfredini 2001; Ciancio and Radina 1979; Mazzieri et al. 2012, 352). A south-to-north scenario involving information, material and possibly demic transfers (see Luglié 2009b, 219) is also not without material support, as discussed: the flint blades from Li Muri made of Gargano stone, the rare finds of Monte Arci obsidian found in that same region, and the similarities between San Ciriaco and Serra D'Alto idols. It is tempting to add to this the generally disparate distributions of cist tombs mainly in the north of the island and idols mainly in the south.

9

Summation and Impressions

The Sardinian colonisation

It is only with difficulty that the breadth of the Sardinia Neolithic evidence submits itself to a brief summation; nevertheless, the main features might be sketched out as follows: first, both Sardinia and its neighbour island Corsica supported a meagre human presence from at least the seventh millennium BCE (if not considerably earlier). Apart from the still much debated upper Palaeolithic evidence, a modest number of Mesolithic deposits including habitations and burials are well confirmed. The initial appearance of Neolithic groups can be dated on both islands to the early centuries of the sixth millennium. This is roughly equivalent to datings from the northern Tyrrhenian mainland and only slightly later than those in the southern Italian peninsula, and would seem to document rather clearly the rapidity with which Neolithic groups arrived into the northern regions from the south, and to account moreover for the wide distribution of nearly identical impressa ceramic stylings across the entire area.

This demic progression northward was maritime-based; it followed a near-coast leap-frog pattern probably generated by specific social contexts characterised by periodic and frequent settlement fissioning (see Leppard 2014). The most likely entry route into the islands was via the Tuscan archipelago, with transit to Sardinia by the Straits of Bonifacio and the near-shore islets of La Maddalena. The initial pioneers or scouts probably comprised small groups, perhaps families, armed with a trimmed-down version of the mainland Neolithic package comprising domestic caprines and swine, a few selected ceramic vessel forms (bowls, cups, jars), and a simple, blade-based microburin industry distinct from the undifferentiated industry of the foregoing Mesolithic, and clearly locally oriented in terms of stone selection. Obsidian was little used, although some from Monte Arci did find its way to the mainland. Both natural shelters and open camps were inhabited, probably less as permanent settlements than as seasonal encampments.

Full colonisation appears to have commenced directly on the heels of the impressa presence and before the mid-sixth millennium. A jump in site numbers suggests new migrant groups, bearing a northern Tyrrhenian variety of Cardial-impressed pottery with close parallels in Tuscany that might suggest a homeland there. Natural shelters and open-air sites have been identified, the former used apparently for both habitation and casual burials. The modest extent of the habitation deposits suggest colonisation was carried out by small groups that targeted settings with prime pasture and arable along the lower reaches of river- or stream valleys near the gulfs as well some upland valleys. Importantly, however, there is no certain evidence that cultivation was practiced: the Sardinian Cardial-phase adaptations appear rather to have expanded on the caprine-focused economy to include cattle. Curiously, along with the red fox, which may have arrived with the first pioneers, the red deer also appears as an import from the mainland during the Cardial phase, as does (less surprisingly) the domestic dog. It is also during this phase that escapees from domestic stock formed feral populations of boar and mouflons. The lithic industry was broadened to include geometric microliths, scrapers, burins and transverse tranchet points in flint as well as local obsidian, adapted to scraping, cutting, piercing and shooting with bow and arrow and, more rarely, ground-stone axes, hoes, pestles and millstones. Expanded too was the ceramic repertory to include Cardial-impressed and plain utilitarian forms (bowls, cups, globular cylinder-neck vases and jars) and at times more finely made plates, bowls, mugs, cups, goblets and amphorae.

It is important to note that the first Neolithic pioneers would have found both islands impoverished in terms of huntable game, unlike the Italian mainland – apart from the small pika, whose value as a meat source must have been off-set by its potential threat to sown crops. Such contrasts between island and mainland faunas underline the work still to be done toward understanding the circumstances under which new lands lacking obvious natural benefits – like Corsica and Sardinia – were initially settled. Applying a traditional push-pull/cost-benefit model (cf. Anthony 1990) to the problem must surely place emphasis on the presumably high cost of remaining in the mainland, for those who left.

It is perhaps here that the twin notions of pre-adaptation and targeted-niche colonisation (see Leppard 2014; Anthony 1990; 1997; Fiedel and Anthony 2003) can shed some light by providing links with the otherwise enigmatic evidence of wild animals imported from the mainland. It is not unthinkable that the fox was brought in to reduce populations of the crop-threatening pika (see Wilkens 2010; Masala 2013, 69), and the red deer – avidly hunted by Neolithic folk on the mainland – to provide huntable game (Masseti 2006). This scenario requires that we seriously entertain the notion that the Neolithic colonisation of Corsica and Sardinia involved planning, and that the pioneer impressa sites represent actual scouting ventures (as Lugliè has implied; 2018) during which resources were assessed, pasture and arable located and evaluated, game and wild foods noted. It implies too some operational island-mainland information network through which knowledge acquired by scouting groups became part of the colonisers' pre-adapted Neolithic package.

We are not yet privy to whether such scouting assessments found the island unpopulated, nor whether that would have been counted as an asset. The evidence is equivocal: the material record suggests a hiatus between the last Mesolithic hunter-gatherers and the first Neolithic presence, while genetic studies suggest enough entanglement to have instilled the pre-Neolithic genetic markers traceable today. The potential value placed on the Monte Arci obsidian sources is also an issue here: although Sardinia was a regional supplier of this basic Neolithic commodity from the Cardial phase onward, its very minor occurrences in impressa-contexts bring into question its relevance to initial assessments of the island's suitability for colonisation.

In all events, a potentially pre-adapted Neolithic package comprising an informed selection of tools and resources will certainly have brought some added 'pull-value' to the choice to colonise the islands by allowing early settlers a more discriminating approach toward making the most of the insular niches. Perhaps the Bonu Ighinu valley is a prime example of one such first destination that proved capable of sustaining a permanent agro-pastoral population for the whole of the Neolithic period. On the mainland 'push' side, relative population pressure and its attendant social frictions within fission-prone communities may have been sufficient to tip the scale toward the emigration option (Fiedel and Anthony 2003, 157-58).

The Epicardial phase

During the second half of the sixth millennium, the archaeological landscape of Sardinia (and probably that of Corsica) reflect important changes. So-called Epicardial ceramics evince production standards in forms and decorations that are clearly divergent from the Cardial tradition. It also appeared abruptly, replacing the former wares (in the better stratified contexts), leaving few signs of hybridity, suggesting less a diffusion of a new style than a fresh influx of settlers. They appear to have entered the island at several points along mainly the west coast, and to a lesser extent the more treacherous east coast at the Gulf of Orosei. The Cardial-Epicardial transition is registered across the Northern Tyrrhenian region at this time, including Corsica, but close stylistic parallels suggest Tuscany-Lazio as the most likely cultural and demographic source of the Sardinian Epicardial.

The lithic industry appears to have altered little, however, apart from the incorporation of the inverse retouch. The limited evidence of burials suggests, however, the new practice of reserving some caves for mortuary use only, and involving burial rites that included ceramic accompaniments. Significantly, at least at one Epicardial deposit (at Filiestru Cave) reports remains of the first domestic plants in the island: those of hulled emmer and einkorn wheats and pea, in association with millstones

and lunates possibly used as sickle bits. That this has been correlated with a sharp decrease in numbers of both the pika and the fox could support the notion of a pre-adaptation in relation to conditions supporting cultivation. Elsewhere, pastoralism supplemented by hunting-gathering persisted, seemingly without cultivation.

Epicardial settlement remains are difficult to interpret. On the one hand, the frequent re-use of previously inhabited sites – especially natural shelters – seems to reflect cultural continuity. At the same time, if our sample is at all representative, there is a puzzling absence of Epicardial sites in areas previously supporting open-air settlements, specifically near the north coast, inland from the Gulf of Asinara, in the southeast, and at the mouth of the Mannu river in the Cagliari gulf. A possible clue to this circumstance comes from the ditched structure at Sa Punta in the Gulf of Oristano which may represent a palissade of the kind detected among contemporary mainland settlements and implying some level of insecurity or conflict. If future research finds additional examples more clearly identifiable as defence works, the retraction of settlements from some near-coast locales might justifiably be linked to an atmosphere of heightened insecurity associated to the new influx of Epicardial-bearing groups.

The Bonu Ighinu phase

The subsequent Middle Neolithic Bonu Ighinu phase of the early fifth millennium was one combining elaborated traditional features with unprecedented, even unique, socio-economic developments. Of the former, out of Epicardial ceramic traditions, there appeared a more costly industry producing better-crafted wares in a wider range of forms, decorated most notably with zoomorphic/anthropomorphic mouldings that find their closest parallels among Serra D'Alto repertories of the southern Italian peninsula. To the traditional percussion-based lithic toolkit was now added the rarer pressure-knapped obsidian blade, and the Bonu Ighinu valley added to its locally unique agricultural economy hulled barley, lentils and broad beans. Elsewhere, the herding of caprines, swine and cattle was augmented with the hunting of deer, boar, mouflon and pika, while the Grotta Rifugio near the east coast registers new – and curious – imports of wild species that included the marten and the wildcat. Natural shelters continued to serve residential and funerary functions, the latter represented now by richer accompaniments of pottery and ornaments. Lowland areas seemingly abandoned during the Epicardial phase saw a modest recovery of settlement at a rate consistent with indigenous population growth.

It would seem that a similar cultural profile including closely comparable ceramic norms developed on Corsica at this time. But it is also to the Bonu Ighinu phase that developments unique to Sardinia took form, despite the continued formal reference to an extra-insular ceramic *koiné*. The Sardinian specificities can be tentatively linked to issues involving privileged access to the island's primary obsidian resource: the locus of the developments was indeed among sites located in Gulf of Oristano near Monte Arci, and the evidence comes primarily from the cemetery of Cuccuru S'Arriu-Cabras. Here, adjacent to the eponymous settlement, burials in unprecedented shaft-access hypogeal so-called oven-tombs were accompanied by one or more skilfully carved stone statuettes, as well as fine ceramics, stone tools and bone implements. The distribution of these distinctive so-called volumetric sculptures elsewhere in the island suggests something like an overland route – one by which obsidian was channelled to select destinations in Corsica and the northern Tyrrhenian mainland, presumably to the benefit of those interred at Cuccuru S'Arriu, and carrying also some of their accoutrements.

The San Ciriaco phase

During the following San Ciriaco phase of the later fifth millennium, the island continued to support diverse and contrasting cultural expressions while sustaining engagements within a Tyrrhenian *koiné*. The ceramic industry produced an array of high-quality austere and generally unembellished forms, paralleling those in Corsica (Présien types) and in part those on the mainland (Diana-Bellavista, Chassey-Lagozzo, VBQ). The lithic industry added to its traditional blade-based repertory the rare bifacially-flaked tanged projectile point. Sardinian obsidian continued to find its way into Corsica and the northern Tyrrhenian mainland, as did Sardinian flint, in lesser amounts. In terms of subsistence regimes, mixed-livestock herding (caprines, swine, cattle) remained the norm, while agriculture, previously apparently restricted to the Bonu Ighinu valley, was established also in the Gulf of Oristano and, with less certainty, among the numerous newly founded open-air settlements in the lower Campidano valley and the Gulf of Cagliari. In terms of imagery, ovine motifs seem to have disappeared, and the volumetric idols, which had been reserved for high-status hypogeal burials, were replaced by slimmer so-called steatopygeous forms conforming to southern Italian types, and deposited in both domestic and burial contexts.

More far-reaching for its implications was the re-drawing of part of the island's social landscape during the Late Neolithic, as indicated by funerary data. While some natural shelters continued to receive burials, the hypogeal sepulchre introduced during the Bonu Ighinu phase as a repository of high-status interments was now more widely adopted as an alternative burial mode (although not, it seems, in Corsica). At the same time, the customs and architecture of a European-wide megalithic burial cult took hold in northeast Sardinia and Corsica featuring interment in necropoli of slab-cist graves with cairns and monolithic symbols. Their relative wealth in architectural and burial accompaniments leaves little doubt that these were the funerary and probably territorial expressions of a Sardinian-Corsican elite. Beyond this, interpretations remain tentative, but the placement astride the inter-insular transit point near the Straits of Bonifacio and, it would seem, along a primary obsidian trade route, has

encouraged reading the data as outlining a new network of social and commercial relations with controlling interest in the management of Sardinia's obsidian resources.

Final impressions

An overarching impression from this account of the Sardinian Neolithic corpus is that of diversity. Such an impression raises a cautionary note: it is all too easy, when fixing the archaeological gaze on a lacunous corpus of evidence such as the one just reviewed, to interpolate toward a fuller configuration. Reconstructing Neolithic subsistence regimes is perhaps particularly vulnerable, since the term and concept of 'The Neolithic' generally conjures up a picture of cultivated fields, grazing stock and stable villages. The possibility of such regimes certainly arrived in the central Mediterranean with the first Neolithic migrants of eastern heritages who possessed the resources for its realisation. But for Sardinia at least, and probably Corsica, plant cultivation was probably never a predominant subsistence mode during the Neolithic periods. Instead, these large islands supported a patchwork of more diverse regimes including herding, hunting, collecting – and also, at times, cultivation.

By all accounts, Sardinia's borders to its closest neighbour remained porous throughout the period under study. Through the Maddalena archipelago and across the Bonifacio straits, Neolithic pioneers, colonists, traders and others probably moved more or less freely and frequently, on missions of exploration, exploitation, settlement, trade, exchange, intermarriage, and probably in circumstances of social friction and mediation too. Such movement was in part facilitated by and in part reflected in parallel shifts of the inter-insular *koiné* of styles. Neolithic adaptations on Corsica varied widely, with some resembling and some contrasting those in Sardinia. At times, significant divergences are found in burial practices, artistic expressions and lithics; at other times (most notably the Late Neolithic), the parallels are sufficiently close to consider the adjacent regions as a single cultural unit. The bases of the shifting relationships are still to be explored, but Corsica's paucity of quality knapping stone relative to its larger neighbour will have been a primary conditioning factor.

Finally, it has become clear that for the period in question we cannot assume a culturally 'unified' Sardinia, nor that the adaptive undertakings revealed here were specific to Sardinia. Considering the evidence, uneven though it is, it seems more constructive to view Sardinia's Neolithic landscape rather as a collage-like patchwork of numerous sub-insular if not local modes, each addressing its own issues of adaptation, each unfolding its own history. One might liken the phenomenon to Levi-Strauss' hypothetical bricoleur: each locale drawing from its inherited (if not pre-adapted) package of tools, resources, skills and know-how – deploying those of time-honoured efficacy, adjusting some, and inventing others toward the crafting of functional adaptations aimed toward basic goals of subsistence, security, procreation, meaning and probably social recognition. Attainments will have varied by locality and circumstance, and affiliations and integrations with other locales will have shifted, expanded and been attenuated on the basis of need, desire and chance.

Epilogue

Ozieri and the End of the Sardinian Neolithic

Toward the close of the 5th millennium BC, the cultural profile referred to as San Ciriaco was replaced across the island by one that contrasted it in nearly every aspect. Pottery was often richly and expressively decorated, sometimes featuring stylised images of the human form. Figurines underwent further modification toward so-called planar styles with striking similarities to later Cycladic statuettes. Rock cut tombs (*domus de janas*) were further expanded and often intricately carved to suggest in detail the interiors of multi-roomed houses appointed with carved iconography featuring the ram and especially the bull. This new modality, known locally as Ozieri or San Michele, is understood as documenting the transition in the island from the Neolithic to the Eneolithic. This transition engendered new cultural adaptations inextricably tied to broader regional trends toward an increasingly greater exploitation of metal resources (copper and silver) and to unprecedented engagements with the distant Near East.

Ozieri sites have been identified across the island although concentrated mainly in the agricultural lowlands of Sassari and Alghero in the northwest, the Campidano plain from Cabras in the central-west to Cagliari in the south, and in the valleys of the Sulcitano-Iglesiente in the southwest. The chronology has been fairly well established based on a series radiocarbon assays which together allow us to place the facies chronologically from ca. 4050 to 3550 cal. BC (see Melis 2013, Tab. II).

Although consideration of the social implications of the Ozieri material assemblages has been limited, a certain degree of social differentiation seems to have obtained in the form perhaps of ranked families or clans, in some instances with hereditary status. Such asymmetry was probably tied to variable engagements with extra-insular trade networks. There is evidence that the more ancient obsidian and flint industries were restructured during this period toward more specialised export markets in what is now southern France, and it can be argued that successful control of these resources (Monte Arci obsidian and Perfugas flint) – their exploitation, processing, movement or specific manufacturing skills – and perhaps the control also of textile resources or industries, would likely have translated to some level of relative wealth, as for example expressed in access to the largest and most expensively decorated tombs, residence in stone-founded rectangular houses, embellished pottery, and perhaps to the still rare items of copper and silver, as well as conferring increased status and influence (Webster and Webster 2017, 9).

The Ozieri record is also punctuated by an extraordinary archaeological finding – the implications of which, for local cultural developments, have as yet been little investigated. This is the surprising and unmistakeable evidence of direct engagements with Mesopotamian spheres of influence, most notably (but not only) in the appearance of a remarkable red-plastered-stone platform temple – the so-called Red Temple at Monte D'Accoddi-Sassari. Its architectural remains were found overlying those of the late Neolithic San Ciriaco settlement there. While our data are still uneven, a consideration of architectural details, within the wider context of the ceramic, metal and textile record of the period, has led to the tentative conclusion that the Red Temple edifice does not represent an indigenous cultural expression but rather the manifestation of a migration event initiated from the Near East sometime in the early 4th millennium BC (see Webster 2019 for a detailed analysis of this extraordinary monument).

The nature of the new relations with this exotic other implied by these findings is still little understood. But it would seem significant that neither conflict nor segregated habitation or burial enclaves have so far been documented. At the same time, the close juxtaposition of the Red Temple to a presumably indigenous and operational menhir shrine suggests a degree of cult entanglement if not syncretism. Although further clues to the nature of indigenous-foreign relations in the island have been scarce so far, several observations are suggestive: while imports are rare, exotic vase forms or styles were introduced, as seen in several apparently hybrid Uruk-Ozieri-styled lugged vases. Some metal tools were probably introduced too (perhaps as a temple foundation offering), weaving looms appeared, as evinced by weights and in rare depictions, and woolly sheep may have been introduced, as well as taurine iconography, and rectangular, stone-footed buildings.

Despite uncertainties, the Ozieri facies lays bare a fundamental issue in Sardinian prehistory and indeed island prehistories in general: the relationship between insularity, its punctuation, cultural discontinuity, and the creation of insular identities. Regarding this last, for Ozieri-phase Sardinia at least, encounters with the exotic other were doubtless contributory. We have suggested that the Ozieri evidence in this regard might be served by a so-called glocal model of identity formation constituted by elements resulting from both indigenous tradition and foreign connectedness (Gordon and Kouremenos 2017). For a detailed treatment of this facies, see Webster and Webster (2017, 1-31).

Bibliography

Acquafredda, P. and I.M. Muntoni, 'Obsidian from Pulo di Molfetta (Bari, southern Italy): provenance from Lipari and first recognition of a neolithic sample from Monte Arci (Sardinia)', *Journal of Archaeological Science* 35 (2008): 947-55.

Agosti, F. et al., 'La Grotta Rifugio di Oliena (Nuoro): caverna-ossario neolitica', *Rivista di Scienze preistoriche* XXXV:1/2 (1980): 75-124.

Alba, L., 'Nuovo contributo per lo studio del villaggio neolitico di San Ciriaco di Terralba (OR)', *Studi Sardi* XXXII (1999): 7-60.

Alba, L., 'La grotta 'de su Mrajani' e la grotta di Suddomu a Monte Casula di Iglesias', in *Atti della XLIV Riunione Scientifica dell'Istituto Italiano di Preistoria e Protostoria: La preistoria e la protostoria della Sardegna (Cagliari, Barumini, Sassari 23-28 novembre 2009)*, edited by C. Lugliè and R. Cicilloni, 1247-52. Florence: IIPP, 2012.

Alba, L., 'Pitzu 'e Pudda di Iglesias (CI), un sito all'aperto del neolitico antico', *Centro Iglesiente Studi Speleo-archeologici* 10 (Iglesias notiziario 1 Settembre 2015), 1-18.

Alba, L. and G. Canino, 'L'insediamento del neolitico antico 'cardiale' di Acqua sa Canna (Gonnesa-CA). Nota preliminare', in *L'ossidiana del Monte Arci nel Mediterraneo. La ricerca archeologica e la salvaguardia del paesaggio per lo sviluppo delle zone interne della Sardegna. Atti del 2° Convegno internazionale, Pau 28-30 novembre 2003,* 211-19. Cagliari: Edizioni AV, 2004.

Alba, L. and G. Canino, 'L'insediamento del neolitico antico 'cardiale' di Perdaias Manna (Gonnesa-CA), nota preliminare', in *L'ossidiana del Monte Arci nel Mediterraneo. Le vie dell'Ossidiana nel Mediterraneo ed in Europa. Atti del 3° Convegno internazionale, Pau 25-26 settembre 2004,* 73-78. Mogoro: PTM Editrice, 2005.

Alba, L. and G. Canino, 'Gli strumenti litici dell'insediamento neolitico di S'Arrocca Abruxiada di Arbus (Breve nota)', in *L'ossidiana del Monte Arci nel Mediterraneo. Nuovi apporti sulla diffusione, sui sistemi di produzione e sulla loro cronologia, Atti del 5° Convegno internazionale, Pau 27-29 Giugno 2008,* 135-46. Ales: NUR, 2010.

Alley, R.B. and A.M. Agustsdottir, 'The 8k event: cause and consequence of a major Holocene abrupt climate change', *Quaternary Science Reviews* 24 (2005): 1123-49.

Ammerman, A. and C. Polglase, 'New evidence on the exchange of obsidian in Italy', in *Trade and Exchange in European Prehistory* (Oxbow Monograph 33), edited by F. Healy and C. Scarre, 101-107. Oxford: Oxbow Books, 1993.

Ammerman, A. and C. Polglase, 'Analyses and description of the obsidian from Arene Candide', in *Arene Candide: A Functional and Environmental Assessment of the Holocene Sequence (Excavations Bernabò Brea-Cardini 1940-50),* (Memorie dell'Istituto di Paleontologia 5), edited by R. Maggi, 573-92. Rome: Il Calamo, 1997.

Anthony, D., 'Migration in Archeology: The Baby and the Bathwater', *American Anthropologist New Series* 92:4 (1990): 895-914.

Anthony, D., 'Prehistoric migration as social process', in *Migrations and invasions in archaeological explanation,* edited by J. Chapman and H. Hamerow, 21-32. Oxford: BAR Publishing International Series 664, 1997.

Antona, A., 'Il megalitismo funerario in Gallura. Alcune osservazioni sulla necropoli di Li Muri', *Rivista di Scienze Preistoriche* LIII (2003), 358-73.

Antona Ruju, A., 'Appunti per una seriazione evolutiva delle statuette femminili della Sardegna prenuragica', in *Atti della XXII Riunione Scientifica dell'Istituto Italiano di Preistoria e Protostoria: La Sardegna centro-settentrionale (Sassari 21-27 ott. 1978),* edited by E. Contu et al., 115-47. Florence: IIPP, 1980.

Antona Ruju, A. and M.L. Ferrarese Ceruti, *Il nuraghe Albucciu e i monumenti di Arzachena* (Guida Archeologica 19). Sassari: Carlo Delfino Editore, 1992.

Antonioli, F., L. Ferranti and F. Lo Schiavo, 'The submerged Neolithic burials of the Grotta Verde at Capo Caccia (Sardinia, Italy): implication for the Holocene sea-level rise/I reperti neolitici sommersi rinvenuti presso la Grotta Verde (Capo Caccia, Sardegna), Implicazioni sulla risalita del mare olocenica', *Memorie descrittive del Servizio Geologico Nazionale* 52 (1994): 329-36.

Antonioli, F., et al., 'Sea-level change during the Holocene in Sardinia and in the northeastern Adriatic (central Mediterranean sea) from archaeological and geomorphological data', *Quaternary Science Reviews* 26 (2007): 2463-86.

Ashby, E., *Arrow Lethality Study Update–2005 Part I:* https://www.grizzlystik.com/PR/Ashby_2005_Update_1.pdf

Atzeni, E., 'Su Carroppu di Sirri (Carbonia)', *Rivista di Scienze Preistoriche* XXVII (1972): 478-79.

Atzeni, E., 'Riparo sotto roccia di Su Carroppu (Sirri-Carbonia)', *Rivista di Scienze Preistoriche* XXXII:1/2 (1978): 357-58.

Aureli, D., 'Lo studio tecnologico dell'insieme litico di Sa Pedrosa-Pantallinu (SS): nuove prospettive sul primo popolamento della Sardegna', in *Atti della XLIV Riunione Scientifica dell'Istituto Italiano di Preistoria e Protostoria: La preistoria e la protostoria della Sardegna (Cagliari, Barumini, Sassari 23-28 novembre 2009)*, edited by C. Lugliè and R. Cicilloni, 375-82. Florence: IIPP, 2012.

Bagolini, B. and P. Biagi, 'Il neolitico del Vhò di Piadena', *Preistoria Alpina* 11 (1975): 77-121.

Bakels, C., 'Plant remains from Sardinia, Italy, with notes on barley and grape', *Vegetation History and Archaeobotany* 11 (2002): 3-8.

Balossi, F. and M. Frangipane, 'La ceramica impressa del Vicino Oriente', in *Le ceramiche impresse nel Neolitico antico. Italia e Mediterraneo* (Collana del Bullettino di paletnologia italiana/Studi di Paletnologia I), edited by M.A. Fugazzola Delpino, A. Pessina and V. Tiné, 3-15. Rome: Istituto poligrafico e Zecca dello Stato, 2002.

Banchieri, D. et al., 'Il Neolitico dell'Italia settentrionale', in *Criteri di nomenclatura e di terminologia inerente alla definizione delle forme vascolari del neolitico/ eneolitico e del bronzo/ ferro. Atti del Congresso di Lido di Camaiore 26-29 marzo 1998*, edited by D. Cocchi Genick, 43-62. Florence: Octavo, 1999.

Battentier, J. et al., 'The environment of the last hunters-gatherers and first agropastoralists in the western Mediterranean region, between the Rhone and the Northern Apennines (7th - 6th millennium cal. BCE): Attractiveness of the landscape units and settlement patterns', *Quaternary Science Reviews* 184 (2017): 1-16 (https://doi.org/10.1016/j.quascirev.2017.08.013).

Benvenuti, A. and L. Metallinou, 'La ceramica impressa della Grecia', in *Le ceramiche impresse nel Neolitico antico. Italia e Mediterraneo* (Collana del Bullettino di paletnologia italiana/Studi di Paletnologia I), edited by M.A. Fugazzola Delpino, A. Pessina and V. Tiné, 17-28. Rome: Istituto poligrafico e Zecca dello Stato, 2002.

Berger, J-F. and J. Guilaine, 'The 8200 cal BP abrupt environmental change and the Neolithic transition: a Mediterranean perspective', *Quaternary International* 200 (2009), 31-49.

Bergin, S., *Mechanisms and Models of Agropastoral Spread During the Neolithic in the West Mediterranean: The Cardial Spread Model*. Arizona State University: doctoral thesis, 2016.

Bernabou Auban, J., M. Balaguer and P. García Borja, 'Le Néolithique ancien valencien. Évolution et

caractérisation des productions céramiques', in *Premières sociétés paysannes de Méditerranée occidentale. Structures des productions céramiques (Séance de la Société préhistorique française, Toulouse 11-12 mai 2007)*, (Mémoire SPF 51), edited by C. Manen et al., 215-26. Paris: CNRS, 2010.

Bertorino, G. et al., 'Insediamento all'aperto della Sardegna centro-occidentale nel Neolitico Antico: ambiente e produzione ceramica', *Bollettino dell'Accademia Gioenia di Scienze Naturali* 33:357 (2000): 121-34.

Bertorino, G. et al., 'Petrographic characterisation of polished stone axes from Neolithic Sardinia: archaeological implications', *Archaeometry and Classical Heritage/Periodico di Mineralogia* 71 (2002): 87-100.

Biagi, P. and M. Cremaschi, 'La Grotta Rifugio di Oliena', in *Sardegna centro-orientale dal Neolitico alla fine del mondo antico. Nuoro - Museo Civico Speleo-Archeologico: Mostra in occasione della XXII Riunione Scientifica dell'Istituto Italiano di Preistoria e Protostoria*, 11-15. Sassari: Soprintendenza ai Beni Archeologici per le Provincie di Sassari e Nuoro, 1980.

Biagi, P. and E. Starnini, 'La cultura della ceramica impressa nella Liguria di ponente (Italia settentrionale): Distribuzione, cronologia e aspetti culturali', in *Del neolític a l'edat del bronze en el Mediterrani occidental. Estudis en homenatge a Bernat Martí Oliver* (Serie Trabajos Varios del SIP 119), edited by H. Bonet Rosado, 35-50. Valencia: Museo de Prehistoria de Valencia, 2016.

Bigazzi, G., M. Oddone and G. Radi, 'The Italian obsidian sources', *Archeometriai Mühely* 1 (2005): 1-13.

Bignon, O. et al., 'Les restes culinaires de Cuccuru is Arrius (Oristano, Sardaigne): nouveaux apports à la connaissance des économies néolithiques en domaine littoral', *Bulletin de la Société préhistorique française* 105:4 (2008): 773-85.

Binder, D., *Le néolithique ancien Provencal: typologie et technologie des outillages lithiques* (24e Supplement à Gallia Préhistoire). Paris: CNRS, 1987.

Binder, D., 'Mesolithic and Neolithic interaction in southern France and northern Italy: new data and current hypotheses', in *Europe's First Farmers*, edited by T.D. Price, 117-43. Cambridge: Cambridge University Press, 2000.

Binder, D. and R. Maggi, 'Le Neolithique ancien de l'arc liguro-provençal', *Bulletin de la Societé préhistorique française* 98 (2001): 411-22.

Binder, D. and I. Sénépart, 'La séquence de l'Impresso-Cardial de l'abri Pendimoun et l'évolution des assemblages céramiques en Provence', in *Premières sociétés paysannes de Méditerranée occidentale. Structures des productions céramiques (Séance de la Société préhistorique française, Toulouse 11-12 mai*

2007), (Mémoire SPF 51), edited by C. Manen et al., 149-67. Paris: CNRS, 2010.

Binder, D., G. Bernard and J. Vaquer, 'La circulation de l'obsidienne dans le sud de la France au Néolithique', in *Actes del Congres Internacional Xarxes al Neolitic. Circulacio i intercanvi de matèries, productes i idees a la Mediterrània occidental, VII-III millennia a.C. Gavà/Bellaterra, 2-4/2/2011 (Rubricatum. Revista del Museo de Gavà* 5), edited by M. Borrell et al., 189-99. Gavà: Museo de Gavà, 2012.

Binder, D. et al., 'L'abri Pendimoun a Castellar (Alpes-Maritimes). Nouvelles données sur le complexe culturel de la ceramique imprimée mediterranéenne dans son contexte stratigraphique', *Gallia Préhistoire* 35 (1993): 177-251.

Binder, D. et al., 'Pressure-Knapping Blade Production in the North-Western Mediterranean Region During the Seventh Millennium cal B.C.', in *The Emergence of Pressure Blade Making: From Origin to Modern Experimentation*, edited by P.M. Desrosiers, 199-217. New York: Springer, 2003 (https://doi.org/10.1007/978-1-4614-2003-3-7).

Binder, D. et al., 'Modelling the earliest north-western dispersal of Mediterranean Impressed Wares. New dates and Bayesian chronological model', *Documenta Praehistorica* XLIV (2017): 54-77.

Bonifay, E., 'Circonscription de la Corse', *Gallia Préhistoire* 26:2 (1983): 511-25.

Bonifay, E. et al., 'La grotte de La Coscia (Roggiano, Macinaggio): étude préliminaire d'un nuoveau site du Pléistocène supérieure de Corse', *Paléo* 10 (1998): 17-41.

Boschian, G. et al., 'Prime ricerche nell'abitato neolitico di Contraguda (Perfugas, Sassari)', *Rivista di Scienze Preistoriche* LI (2001): 235-87.

Bourgeois-Pichat, J., 'Social and biological determinants of human fertility in nonindustrial societies', *Proceedings of the American Philosophical Society* 111 (1967): 160.

Brandaglia, M., 'Il neolitico a ceramica impressa dell'Isola del Giglio. L'industria litica', *Studi per l'Ecologia del Quaternario* 7 (1985): 53-76.

Brandaglia, M., 'Isola Del Giglio. Toscana', in *Le ceramiche impresse nel Neolitico antico. Italia e Mediterraneo* (Collana del Bullettino di paletnologia italiana/Studi di Paletnologia I), edited by M.A. Fugazzola Delpino, A. Pessina and V. Tiné, 407-23. Rome: Istituto poligrafico e Zecca dello Stato, 2002.

Bressy-Leandri, C., 'Caractérisation et provenance des silex de sites néolithiques corses' in *Ressources lithiques, productions et transferts entre Alpes et Méditerranée. Actes de la journée de la Société préhistorique française de Nice, 28-29 mars 2013* (Séances de la Société préhistorique française 5), edited by A. Tomasso et al., 277-88. Paris: SPF, 2016.

Briois, F., 'Portiragnes – Peiro-Signado', *CNRS: ADLFI Informations* 1996/2004 (https://journals.openedition.org/adlfi/11740).

Briois, F. and C. Manen, 'L'habitat Néolithique ancien de Peiro Signado à Portiragnes (Hérault)', in *De la maison au village dans le Néolithique du sud de la France et du nord-ouest méditerranéen (Journées de la SPF 2003)*, (Mémoire SPF 48), edited by A. Beeching and I. Sénépart, 31-37. Marseille: SPF, 2009.

Briois, F., C. Manen and B. Gratuze, 'Nouveaux résultats sur l'origine des obsidiennes de Peiro Signado à Portiragnes (Hérault)', *Bulletin de la Société préhistorique française* 106:4 (2009): 809-11.

Brizzi, V., 'The Elusive Transverse Arrowhead: a lithic projectile point...on the reversible side' (www.academia.edu/11591024).

Broodbank, C., *The Making of the Middle Sea*, Thames and Hudson 2015 (2nd ed.).

Calo, C.M. et al., 'Sardinian population (Italy): a genetic review', *International Journal of Modern Anthropology* 1 (2008): 39-65.

Calvi Rezia, G. and L. Sarti, 'Pienza', in *Le ceramiche impresse nel Neolitico antico. Italia e Mediterraneo* (Collana del Bullettino di paletnologia italiana/Studi di Paletnologia I), edited by M.A. Fugazzola Delpino, A. Pessina and V. Tiné, 333-39. Rome: Istituto poligrafico e Zecca dello Stato, 2002.

Canino, G. et al., 'Catalogo dei materiali', in *La Sardegna preistorica. Storia, materiali, monumenti* (Corpora delle antichità della Sardegna), edited by A. Moravetti et al., 255-376. Sassari: Regione Autonoma della Sardegna/Carlo Delfino Editore, 2017.

Caponi, G. and G. Radi, 'La ceramica di Cala Giovanna Piana', in in *Préhistoire et protohistoire de l'aire tyrrhénienne*, edited by C. Tozzi and M.C. Weiss, 89-100. Ghezzano-Pisa: Felici Editore, 2007.

Carlson, A.E., 'The younger Dryas climate event', in *The Encyclopedia of Quaternary Science*, Volume 3, edited by S.J. Elias and C.J. Mock, 126-34. Amsterdam: Elsevier 2013.

Carneiro, R.L. and D.F. Hilse, 'On determining the probable rate of population growth during the Neolithic', *American Anthropologist* 68:1 (1966): 177-81 (https://doi.org/10.1525/aa.1966.68.1.02a00230).

Castaldi, J., *Arzachena. Monumenti archeologici. Breve itinerario*, Sassari: Carlo Delfino, 1984.

Cavulli, F., 'Le strutture del Neolitico antico in Italia settentrionale: considerazioni e proposte interpretative', *Rivista di Scienze Preistoriche* LVIII (2008): 75-98.

Ceruleo, P., 'Le vie dell'ossidiana dalle isole al continente: approvvigionamento, diffusione e commercio. Il caso della Sabina e della valle dell'Aniene', *Annali della*

Associazione Nomentana di Storia e Archeologia 4 (2003): 22-57.

Cesari, J. et al., 'Note préliminaire sur le Néolithique cardial de l'abri no 1 du gisement de Campu Stefanu (Sollacaro, Corse-du-Sud)', in *EPI OINOPA PONTON. Studi sul Mediterraneo antico in ricordo di Giovanni Tore*, edited by C. Del Vais, 79-95. Oristano: S'Alvure, 2012a.

Cesari, J. et al., 'Note préliminaire sur l'habitat pré- et protohistorique de Campu Stefanu (Sollacaro, Corse-du-Sud)', in *Atti della XLIV Riunione Scientifica dell'Istituto Italiano di Preistoria e Protostoria: La preistoria e la protostoria della Sardegna (Cagliari, Barumini, Sassari 23-28 novembre 2009)*, edited by C. Lugliè and R. Cicilloni, 435-54. Florence: IIPP, 2012b.

Cesari. J. et al., 'Le site de Campu Stefanu (Sollacaro, Corse-du-Sud): une occupation du Mesolithique et du Neolithique ancien', in *Transitions in the Mediterranean. When hunters became farmers. Transitions en Mediterranee. Ou comment des chasseurs devinrent collecteurs*, edited by C. Manen, T. Perrin and J. Guilaine, 283-306. Toulouse: Archives d'écologie préhistorique, 2014.

Cherry, J., 'The first colonization of the Mediterranean islands: a review of recent research', *Journal of Mediterranean Archaeology* 3/2 (1990): 145-221.

Cherry, J., 'Paleolithic Sardinians? Some questions of evidence and methods', in *Sardinia in the Mediterranean: A Footprint in the Sea. Studies in Sardinian Archaeology presented to Miriam S. Balmuth*, edited by R.H. Tykot and T.K. Andrews, 29-39. Sheffield: Sheffield Academic Press, 1992.

Cherry, J. and P.T. Leppard, 'Patterning and its causation in the pre-neolithic colonization of the Mediterranean islands (late Pleistocene to early Holocene)', *The Journal of island and coastal archaeology* 2017, 1-15.

Chiang, C.W.K. et al., 'Genomic history of the Sardinian population', *Nature Genetics* 50 (2018): 1426-34 (https://doi.org/10.1038/s41588-018-0215-8).

Chikhi, L. et al., 'Y genetic data support the Neolithic demic diffusion model', *Proceedings of the National Academy of Science of the U.S.A.* 99:17 (2002): 11008-11013 (https://doi.org/10.1073/pnas.162158799).

Ciancio, A. and F. Radina, 'Madonna delle Grazie (Rutigliano-Bari): campagna di scavo 1979', *Taras. Rivista di archeologia* 1-2 (1979): 7-61.

Cicilloni, R., M. Serra and G. Tanda, 'Indagini archeologiche presso la grotta di Su Mrajani di Monte Casula-Iglesias (Sardegna meridionale). Relazione preliminare (campagne 2011-2012-2013)', *The Journal of Fasti Online* 2014 (www.fastionline.org/docs/FOLDER-it-2014-311.pdf).

Clark, J.D., J.L. Phillips and P.S. Staley, 'Interpretations of prehistoric technology from ancient Egyptian and other sources. Part 1: Ancient Egyptian Bows and Arrows and their Relevance for African Prehistory', *Paleorient* 2:2 (1974): 323-88.

Clutton-Brock. J., *Domesticated animals from early times*. London: Heinemann, 1981.

Cocchi Genick, D., *Manuale di preistoria II: Neolitico*. Florence: Octavo, 1994.

Contu, D. et al. 'Y-Chromosome based evidence for pre-neolithic origin of the genetically homogeneous but diverse Sardinian population: inference for association scans', *PlosOne* 2008:3 (https://doi.org/10.1371/journal.pone.0001430).

Contu, E. 'L'ipogeismo della Sardegna pre- e protostorica', in *L'Ipogeismo nel Mediterraneo: Origini, Sviluppo, Quadri Culturali. Atti del Congresso Internazionale, 23-28 Maggio 1994, Sassari-Oristano, Italia*, edited by G. Tanda, M.G. Melis and P. Melis, 313-66. Sassari: Università degli Studi di Sassari/Muros: Stampacolor, 2000.

Costa L.J., *Espaces et productions lithiques taillées en Corse (ixe-iie millénaires avant J.-C. cal. BC)*. Université de Paris X (Nanterre): doctoral thesis, 2001.

Costa, L.J., *Corse préhistorique. Peuplement d'une île et modes de vie des societés insulaires (IX-II millénaires av. J.C.)*, Paris: Errance, 2004.

Costa, L.J. et al., 'Analyses de provenance des matériaux exploités à Strette (Barbaghju, Haute-Corse): approche du fonctionnement du site au Néolithique ancien', *Bulletin de la Société préhistorique française* 99/4 (2002): 765-74.

Dag, Z.Ö. and B. Dilbaz, 'Impact of obesity on infertility in women', *Journal of the Turkish-German Gynecological Association* 16 (2005): 111-7.

de Lanfranchi, F., 'La grotte sépulcrale de Curacchiaghiu (Levie, Corse)', *Bulletin de la Société préhistorique française* 64:2 (1967): 587-612.

de Lanfranchi, F., 'Préneolithique ou Mésolithique insulaire?', *Bulletin de la Société préhistorique française* 95:4 (1998): 537-46.

de Lanfranchi, F., 'Un vase néolithique en roche dure, à anse zoomorphe, trouvé en Corse méridionale dans les années trente', *Bulletin de la Société préhistorique française* 97:3 (2000): 481-83.

de Lanfranchi, F. and J. Alessandri, 'Le mésolithique de la Corse et de la Sardaigne a-t-il fait l'objet d'un peuplement continu ou à contraire n'est-il q'une terre d'escale de pêcheurs-navigateurs continentaux?', in *Atti della XLIV Riunione Scientifica dell'Istituto Italiano di Preistoria e Protostoria: La preistoria e la protostoria della Sardegna (Cagliari, Barumini, Sassari 23-28 novembre 2009)*, edited by C. Lugliè and R. Cicilloni, 407-15. Florence: IIPP, 2012.

de Lanfranchi, F. and M.C. Weiss, *La civilisation des Corses. Les origins*, Ajaccio: Editions Cyrnos et Méditerranée, 1973.

Depalmas, A., 'L'Industria litica del Neolitico antico in Sardegna', *Interreg préhistoire Corse-Sardaigne* 2 (1995): 3-10.

Di Cristofaro, J. et al., 'Prehistoric migrations through the Mediterranean basin shaped Corsicn Y-chromosome diversity', *PlosOne* 13:8 (2018), (https://doi.org/10.1371/journal.pone.0200641).

Dini, M., *'L'industria in ossidiana dei siti neolitici di Santa Caterina di Pittinuri e Torre Foghe sulla costa occidentale della Sardegna'*, in *Préhistoire et protohistoire de l'aire tyrrhénienne*, edited by C. Tozzi and M.C. Weiss, 195-202. Ghezzano-Pisa: Felici Editore, 2007.

Doan, K. et al., 'Phylogeography of the Tyrrhenian red deer (*Cervus elaphus corsicanus*) resolved using ancient DNA of radiocarbon-dated subfossils', Scientific Reports 7:1 (2017): 2331 (https://doi.org/10.1038/s41598-017-12272-z).

Driscoll, C. et al., 'The Near Eastern Origin of Cat Domestication', *Science* (July 2007): 1-3 (https://doi.org/10.1126/science.1139518).

Ducci, S. and P. Perazzi, 'Il Neolitico antico dell'Arcipelago Toscano', in *Il primo popolamento olocenico dell'area corso-toscana* (Interreg. II, Corsica 1997-99), edited by C. Tozzi and M.C. Weiss, 53-56. Pisa: Edizioni ETS, 2000.

Falchi, P. et al., 'L'insediamento neolitico di Contraguda (Perfugas, Sassari): aggiornamento delle ricerche', in *Atti della XLIV Riunione Scientifica dell'Istituto Italiano di Preistoria e Protostoria: La preistoria e la protostoria della Sardegna (Cagliari, Barumini, Sassari 23-28 novembre 2009)*, edited by C. Lugliè and R. Cicilloni, 503-08. Florence: IIPP, 2012.

Fanti, L., *La fonction des récipients céramiques dans les sociétés du Néolitique moyen B (4500-4000 cal BC) en Sardaigne centre-occidentale (Italie): Indices fonctionnels, économiques, interculturels à partir de l'analyse des caractéristiques morphométriques, des résidus organiques et des traces d'usure des poteries.* Université Cote d'Azur: doctoral thesis 2015.

Fanti, L., C. Lugliè and A. Usai, 'Piccole fosse e 'depositi strutturati' del Neolitico Medio B in Sardegna (4500-4000 cal BC)', in *Pozzetti, buche, piccole fosse, silos... Le strutture in negativo neolitiche di piccole dimensioni: metodi di indagine e problemi interpretativi. Abstract Book, Terzo Incontro Annuale di Preistoria e Protostoria, Firenze, Museo Archeologico Nazionale, 8-9 maggio 2017*, edited by C. Lugliè, A. Beeching and I.M. Muntoni, 29-32. Florence: IIPP, 2017 (http://www.iipp.it/wp-content/uploads/2017/05/IAPP3_Abstract-Book_4.pdf).

Fanti, L. et al., 'The role of pottery in Middle Neolithic societies of western Mediterranean (Sardinia, Italy, 4500-4000 cal BC) revealed through an integrated morphometric, use-wear, biomolecular and isotopic approach', *Journal of Archaeological Science* 93 (2018): 110-28.

Fenu, P., F. Martini and G. Pitzalis, 'Gli scavi nella grotta Su Coloru (Sassari): primi risultati e prospettive di ricerca', *Rivista di Scienze Preistoriche* L (1999-2000): 165-87.

Fenu, P. et al., 'Le datazioni radiometriche della grotta Su Coloru (Sassari) nella transizione Mesolitico-Neolitico', *Rivista di Scienze Preistoriche* LII (2002): 327-35.

Fenu, P. et al., 'Le industrie litiche di aspetto paleolitico inferiore rinvenute nel territorio di Ottana, Nuoro', in *Atti della XLIV Riunione Scientifica dell'Istituto Italiano di Preistoria e Protostoria: La preistoria e la protostoria della Sardegna (Cagliari, Barumini, Sassari 23-28 novembre 2009)*, edited by C. Lugliè and R. Cicilloni, 369-74. Florence: IIPP, 2012.

Ferrarese Ceruti, M.L., 'Un vasetto con decorazione a spirali da Orgosolo (Nuoro)', *Bullettino di Paletnologia Italiana* XVI:74 (1965): 53-57.

Ferrarese Ceruti, M.L. and G. Pitzalis, 'Il tafone di Cala Corsara nell'isola di Spargi (La Maddalena-Sassari)', in *Atti della XXVI Riunione Scientifica: Il Neolitico in Italia (Firenze, 7-10 novembre 1985)*, 871-86. Florence: IIPP, 1987.

Ferrarese Ceruti, M.L. and O. Fonzo, 'Nuovi elementi dalla grotta funeraria di Tanì (Carbonia)', in *Carbonia e il Sulcis. Archeologia e territorio*, edited by V. Santoni, 95-115. Oristano: S'Alvure, 1995.

Fiedel, S. and D. Anthony, 'Deerslayers, pathfinders and icemen: origins of the European Neolithic as seen from the frontier', in *Colonization of unfamiliar landscapes – The archaeology of adaptation*, edited by M. Rockman and J. Steele, 144-68. London: Routledge, 2003.

Fiori, F., 'L'insediamento neolitico di Tresnuraghes', *Sardegna Antica* 15 (1999): 26-27.

Fiori, F., 'L'insediamento neolitico di Tresnuraghes: l'industria litica', *Sardegna Antica* 17 (2000): 13-15.

Floris, R. et al., 'La presenza umana nella Sardegna centro occidentale durante l'Olocene antico: il sito di S'Omu e S'Orcu (Arbus, VS)', in *Atti della XLIV Riunione Scientifica dell'Istituto Italiano di Preistoria e Protostoria: La preistoria e la protostoria della Sardegna (Cagliari, Barumini, Sassari 23-28 novembre 2009)*, edited by C. Lugliè and R. Cicilloni, 999-1004. Florence: IIPP, 2012.

Forestier, H., 'Le Clactonien: mise en application d'une nouvelle methode de débitage s'inscrivant dans la variabilité des systèmes de production lithique au Paléolithique ancien', *Paléo* 5 (1993): 53-82.

Formicola, V., 'Neolithic transition and dental changes: the case of an Italian site', *Journal of Human Evolution* 16:2 (1987): 231-39.

Foschi Nieddu, A., 'La Grotta Sa Korona di Monte Majore (Thiesi, Sassari): primi risultati dello scavo 1980', in *Atti della XXVI Riunione Scientifica dell'Istituto Italiano di Preistoria e Protostoria: Il Neolitico in Italia. Firenze, 7–10 Novembre 1985*, edited by R. Grifoni Cremonesi et al., 859-70. Florence: IIPP, 1987.

Foschi Nieddu, A., 'Utensili di società neolitiche dalla Grotta di Monte Majore (Thiesi, Sassari)', *Atti del XIII Congresso U.I.S.P.P., Forlì 8-14 settembre 1996*, edited by C. Peretto and C. Giunchi, 295-300. Forlì: ABACO Edizioni, 1998.

Fowler, C., J. Harding and D. Hofmann (eds.), *The Oxford Handbook of Neolithic Europe,* Oxford: Oxford University Press, 2015.

Francalacci, P. et al., 'Peopling of three Mediterranean islands (Corsica, Sardinia and Sicily) inferred by Y-chromosome biallelic variability', *American Journal of Physical Anthropology* 121:3 (2003): 270-79.

Freund, K., *The politics of obsidian consumption in the West Mediterranean.* McMaster University (Hamilton, Ontario): doctoral thesis, 2014.

Freund, K. and Z. Batist, 'Sardinian obsidian circulation and early maritime navigation in the Neolithic as shown through social network analysis', *Journal of Island & Coastal Archaeology* 9 (2014): 364-80.

Fugazzola Delpino, M.A., 'Le facies a ceramica impressa dell'area medio-tirrenica', in *Le ceramiche impresse nel Neolitico antico. Italia e Mediterraneo* (Collana del Bullettino di paletnologia italiana/Studi di Paletnologia I), edited by M.A. Fugazzola Delpino, A. Pessina and V. Tiné, 97-116. Rome: Istituto poligrafico e Zecca dello Stato, 2002.

Garstang, J., *Prehistoric Mersin. Yumuk Tepe in southern Turkey.* Oxford: Clarendon Press, 1953.

Gassin, B. and C. Luglià, 'Delle frecce, per far cosa?', in *Atti della XLIV Riunione Scientifica dell'Istituto Italiano di Preistoria e Protostoria: La preistoria e la protostoria della Sardegna (Cagliari, Barumini, Sassari 23-28 novembre 2009)*, edited by C. Luglià and R. Cicilloni, 485-93. Florence: IIPP, 2012.

Germanà, F., 'Forme umane medioneolitiche dalla grotta Rifugio di Oliena (Nuoro). Antropologia e paleopalologia', *Quaderni di Scienze Antropologiche* 6 (1981): 5-68.

Germanà, F., 'Paleosardi e Protosardi dal Paleolitico all'età del Bronzo Recente (tentativo di analisi dell'avvincendarsi di forme umane nell'isola di Sardegna)', *in Sardinia in the Mediterranean: a footprint in the sea. Studies in Sardinian archaeology presented to Miriam S. Balmuth*, edited by R.H. Tykot and T.K. Andrews, 137-56. Sheffield: Sheffield Academic Press, 1992.

Germanà, F. and V. Santoni, 'La necropoli di Cuccuru S'Arriu (Cabras) e i paleosardi medio-neolitici', *Quaderni della Soprintendenza Archeologica per le Provincie di Cagliari e Oristano* 9 (1992): 5-30.

Gibaja, J. and A. Palomo, 'Geométricos usados como proyectiles. Implicaciones economicas, sociales e ideológicas en el noreste de la península Ibérica', *Trabajos de prehistoria* 61:1 (2004): 81-97.

Gilabert, C. et al. 'Le site du Monte Revincu: nouvelles données sur un village néolithique moyen du nord de la Corse', in *Huitièmes Rencontres de Préhistoire Récente, Marseille Nov. 2008*, edited by I. Sénépart et al., 283-97. Toulouse: Archives d'écologie préhistorique, 2011.

Gilabert, X.R., J. Martínez-Moreno and R. Mora Torcal, 'Ground stone tools and spatial organization at the Mesolithic site of font del Ros (southeastern Pre-Pyrenees, Spain)', *Journal of Archaeological Science - Reports* 5 (2016): 209-24 (https://doi.org/10.1016/j.jasrep.2015.11.023).

Gimbutas, M., *The Language of the Goddess: Unearthing the hidden symbols of Western Civilization*, San Francisco: Harper & Row, 1989.

Ginesu, S. et al., 'Morphological evolution of the Nurighe cave (Logudoro, northern Sardinia, Italy) and the presence of man: first results', *Supplementi di Geografia fisica e dinamica quaternaria* 26:1 (2003): 41-48.

Gordon, J.M. and A. Kouremenos., 'Insulae Coniunctae: Mediterranean Archaeologies of Insularity in the Age of Globalization', paper presented at the 118th Annual Meeting of the Archaeological Institute of America, Toronto, Ontario, Jan. 5-8, 2017. *Archaeological Institute of America 118th Annual Meeting Abstracts* 40 (2017): 2A (https://www.academia.edu/25582946).

Gravina, A., 'Caratteri del Neolitico medio-finale nella Daunia centro-settentrionale', in *Atti del 6 convegno nazionale sulla preistoria-protostoria-storia della Daunia (San Severo 14-15-16 dicembre 1984)*, edited by B. Mundi and A. Gravina, 21-42. San Severo: Archeoclub d'Italia, 1988.

Gravina, A., 'Coppa Pocci. La frequentazione nel neolitico antico e medio', in *Atti del 12 convegno nazionale sulla preistoria-protostoria-storia della Daunia (San Severo 14-15-16 dicembre 1990)*, edited by G. Clemente, 49-62. San Severo: Archeoclub d'Italia, 1991.

Gravina, A., 'Alcune manifestazioni 'artistiche' preistoriche nella Daunia centro-occidentale', in *Atti del 28 convegno nazionale sulla preistoria-protostoria-storia della Daunia (San Severo 25-26 novembre 2007)*, edited by A. Gravina, 11-28. San Severo: Archeoclub d'Italia, 2008.

Grifoni Cremonesi, R., 'Le Néolithique ancien de Toscane et de l'Archipel toscane', *Bulletin de la Société préhistorique française* 98:3 (2001): 423-29.

Guilaine, J., *De la vague à la tombe. La conquête néolithique de la Méditerranée (8000-2000 avant J.-C.)*. Paris: Le Seuil, 2003.

Guilaine, J., 'The Neolithic transition: From the Eastern to the Western Mediterranean', in *Times of Neolithic Transition along the Western Mediterranean* (Fundamental Issues in Archaeology), edited by O. Garcia-Puchol and D.C. Salazar-Garcia, 15-32. Boston: Springer, 2017.

Guilaine, J. and R. Grifoni Cremonesi, *Torre Sabea. Un établissement du Néolithique ancien en Salento* (Collection de l'École française de Rome 315). Rome: École française de Rome, 2003.

Guilaine, J. and C. Manen, 'La ceramica impressa della Francia meridionale', in *Le ceramiche impresse nel Neolitico antico. Italia e Mediterraneo* (Collana del Bullettino di paletnologia italiana/Studi di Paletnologia I), edited by M.A. Fugazzola Delpino, A. Pessina and V. Tiné, 373-95. Rome: Istituto poligrafico e Zecca dello Stato, 2002.

Guilaine, J. and C. Manen, 'From the Mesolithic to Early Neolithic in the Western Mediterranean', in *Going over: the Mesolithic-Neolithic transition in north-west Europe* (Proceedings of the British Academy 144), edited by A. Whittle and V. Cummings, 21-51. London: OUP, 2007.

Guilbeau, D., *Les grandes lames et les lames par pression au levier du Néolithique et de l'Énéolithique en Italie*. Université Paris Ouest: doctoral thesis, 2010.

Halstead, P. and V. Isaakidou, 'Revolutionary secondary products: the development and significance of milking, animal-traction and wool-gathering in later prehistoric Europe and the Near East', in *Interweaving Worlds: Systemic Interactions in Eurasia, 7th to 1st Millennia BC*, edited by T. Wilkinson, S. Sherratt and J. Bennet, 61-76. Oxford: Oxbow Books, 2011.

Hammann, S. and L. Cramp, 'Towards the detection of dietary cereal processing through absorbed lipid biomarkers in archaeological pottery', *Journal of Archaeological Science* 93 (2018): 74-81.

Hassan, F.A. and R.A. Sengel, 'On mechanisms of population growth during the Neolithic', *Current Anthropology* 14/5 (1973): 535-42.

Hmwe, S. et al., 'Conservation genetics of the endangered red deer from Sardinia and Mesola with further remarks on the phylogeography of *Cervus elaphus corsicanus*', *Biological Journal of the Linnean Society* 88 (2006): 691-701.

Holmes, K. and R. Whitehouse, 'Anthropomorphic figurines and the construction of gender in Neolithic Italy', *Accordia Research Papers* 7 (1998): 95-126.

Horejs, B, et al., 'The Aegean in the Early 7th Millennium BC: Maritime Networks and Colonization', *Journal of World Prehistory* 28 (2015): 289-330.

Hurcombe, L., 'The restricted function of Neolithic Obsidian Tools at Grotta Filiestru, Sardinia', in *Traces et Fonction: Les Gestes Retrouvés. Colloque International de Liège* (Études et Recherches Archéologique de L'Université de Liège 50), edited by P. Anderson et al., 87-96. Liège: CNRS, 1992.

Ibba, M.A. et al., 'Indagini archeologiche sul Capo Sant'Elia a Cagliari', *QUADERNI. Rivista di Archeologia* 28 (2017): 353-86.

Inizan, M.-L. et al., *Technology and Terminology of Knapped Stone* (Préhistoire de la Pierre Taillée Tome 5), Nanterre: CREP, 1999.

Insoll, T., 'Miniature possibilities? An introduction to the varied dimensions of figurine research', in *The Oxford Handbook of Prehistoric Figurines*, edited by T. Insoll, 3-15. Oxford: Oxford University Press, 2017.

Ivanova, M., 'Tells, invasion theories and warfare in fifth millennium B.C. north-eastern Bulgaria', in *War and Sacrifice. Studies in the Archaeology of Conflict*, edited by T. Pollard and I. Banks, 33-48. Leiden: Brill, 2007.

Jarmen, M., 'European deer economies and the advent of the Neolithic', in *Papers in European Prehistory*, edited by E. Higgs, 125-47. Cambridge: Cambridge University Press, 1972.

Klein Hofmeijer, G. et al., 'Indications of pleistocene man on Sardinia', *Nuclear instruments and methods in physics research B29* (1987): 166-68.

Klein Hofmeijer, G. et al., 'La fine del Pleistocene nella Grotta Corbeddu in Sardegna. Fossili umani, aspetti paleontologici e cultura materiale', *Rivista di Scienze Preistoriche* XLI (1990): 29-64.

Lai, L. et al., 'Frammenti di ecologia neolitica: i dati isotopici delle Grotta Rifugio (Oliena, Sardegna orientale)', paper delivered at the conference Preistoria del Cibo. 50ma Riunione Scientifica dell'Istituto Italiano di Preistoria e Protostoria: L'uomo è ció che mangia?, Session 1: Oct. 6, 2015 (http://docplayer. it/10519700-2-frammenti-di-ecologia-neolitica-i-dati-isotopici-della-grotta-rifugio-oliena-sardegna-orientale.html).

Lambeck, K. et al., 'Sea level change along the Italian coast for the past 10,000 yrs.', *Quaternary Science Reviews* 23 (2004): 1567-98.

Lanfranco, L.P. and S. Eggers, 'Caries through time: an anthropological overview', in *Contemporary Approach to Dental Caries*, edited by Ming-Yu Li, 3-34. London: IntechOpen, 2012 (https://doi.org/10.5772/38059).

Latini, V. et al., 'Beta-globin gene cluster haplotypes in the Corsican and Sardinian populations', *Human Biology* 75 (2003): 855-71.

Laviano, R. and I.M. Muntoni, 'Produzione e circolazione della ceramica 'Serra d'Alto' nel V millennio a.C. in Italia sud-orientale', in *Le classi ceramiche: situazione degli studi. Atti della 10a Giornata di Archeometria della Ceramica (Roma, 5-7 aprile 2006)*, edited by S. Gualtieri, B. Fabbri and G. Bandini, 57-72. Bari: Edipuglia, 2009.

Le Bourdonnec, F.-X. et al., 'The circulation of obsidian in western Mediterranean during the Neolithic. The Early Neolithic site of Sa Punta (Sardinia) and the Middle to Upper Neolithic site of A Fuata (Corsica)', poster for the Groupe des Méthodes Pluridisciplinaires Contribuant à l'Archéologie, Montpellier 2009 (https://www.academia.edu/2171158).

Le Bras-Goude, G. et al., 'Stratégies de subsistance et analyse culturelle de populations Néolithiques de Ligurie: Approche par l'étude isotopique (δ13C and δ15N) des restes osseux', *Bulletins et Mémoires de la Société d'Anthropologie de Paris* 18:1-2 (2006): 43-53.

Leandri, F. et al., 'Le site du Monte-Revincu (Santo-Pietro-di-Tenda, Haute-Corse): contribution à la connaissance du Néolithique moyen de la Corse', in *Corse et Sardaigne préhistoriques. Relations et échanges dans le contexte méditerranéen, Actes du 128e Congrès national des sociétés historiques et scientifiques, Bastia 14-21 avril 2003* (Documents préhistoriques 22), edited by A. D'Anna et al., 165-83. Paris: CTHS, 2007.

Leppard, T.P., 'Modeling the impacts of Mediterranean island colonization by archaic hominins: the likelihood of an insular lower Palaeolithic', *Journal of Mediterranean Archaeology* 27:2 (2014): 231-53.

Levine, M.A., 'La fauna di Filiestru (Trincea D)', in *La Grotta Filiestru a Bonu Ighinu, Mara (SS). (Quaderni della Soprintendenza Archeologica per le Province di Sassari e Nuoro 13)*, edited by D.H. Trump, 109-31. Sassari: Dessì, 1983.

Levi-Strauss, C., *The Savage Mind* (transl. G. Weidenfield and Nicholson Ltd.). Chicago: University of Chicago Press, 1962.

Lewthwaite, J., 'Nuragic foundations: an alternative model of development in Sardinian prehistory, ca. 2500-1500 BC.', *Studies in Sardinian Archaeology* 3, edited by M.S. Balmuth, 57-74. Oxford: BAR Publishing International Series 387, 1986.

Liebermeister, H., 'Prognose der Adipositas, was hat sich geändert?', *Versicherungsmedizin* 47 (1995): 17-23.

Lilliu, G., *La Civiltà dei Sardi dal neolitico all'età dei nuraghi.* Torino: RAI, 1963.

Lilliu, G., *La Civiltà dei Sardi dal paleolitico all'età dei nuraghi.* Torino: Nuova Eri, 1988.

Lilliu, G., *Arte e religione della Sardegna prenuragica.* Sassari: Carlo Delfino Editore, 1999.

Lo Schiavo, F., 'La preistoria', in *Il Museo Sanna in Sassari*, Sassari: Banco di Sardegna, 1986.

Lo Schiavo, F., 'Grotta Verde 1979: Un contributo sul Neolitico antico della Sardegna', in *Atti della XXVI Riunione Scientifica dell'Istituto Italiano di Preistoria e Protostoria: Il Neolitico in Italia (Firenze 7-10 novembre 1985)*, 839-58. Florence: IIPP, 1987.

Lo Vetro, D. and F. Martini, 'Mesolithic in Central-Southern Italy: Overview of lithic productions', *Quaternary International* 423 (2016), 279-302.

Locci, M.C., 'L'industria su pietra scheggiata, scheggioide e lavigata (vetrine C-D)', in *Le collezioni litiche preistoriche dell'Università di Cagliari*, edited by E. Atzeni, 29-36. Cagliari: Edizioni AV, 2000.

Lorenzi, F., 'Bilan des opérations archéologiques effectuées de 2004 a 2006 sur le site néolithique de A Guaita (Morsiglia, Haute-Corse)', in *Préhistoire et protohistoire de l'aire tyrrhenienne*, edited by C. Tozzi and M.C. Weiss, 23-33. Ghezzano-Pisa: Felici Editore, 2007.

Loria, R. and D.H. Trump, *Le scoperte a 'Sa 'Ucca de su Tintirriolu' e il Neolitico sardo* (Monumenti Antichi dell'Accademia dei Lincei, Serie miscellanea, vol. II-2/49). Rome: Accademia Nazionale dei Lincei, 1978.

Losi, S., 'Le forme del corpo nella Sardegna neolitica', in *Atti della XLIV Riunione Scientifica dell'Istituto Italiano di Preistoria e Protostoria: La preistoria e la protostoria della Sardegna (Cagliari, Barumini, Sassari 23-28 novembre 2009)*, edited by C. Lugliè and R. Cicilloni, 525-34. Florence: IIPP, 2012.

Lugliè, C., 'L'industria su pietra scheggiata (vetrine A-B)', in *Le collezioni litiche preistoriche dell'Università di Cagliari*, edited by E. Atzeni, 17-27. Cagliari: Edizioni AV, 2000.

Lugliè, C., 'La ceramica di facies S. Ciriaco nel Neolitico Superiore della Sardegna: evoluzione interna e apporti extrainsulari', in *Atti della XXXV Riunione Scientifica dell'Istituto Italiano di Preistoria e Protostoria: Le comunità della preistoria italiana. Studi e ricerche sul Neolitico e le età dei metalli, in memoria di Luigi Bernabò Brea (Lipari, 2-7 giugno 2000)*, edited by P. Bianchi, 723-33. Florence: IIPP, 2003.

Lugliè, C., 'La produzione lamellare in ossidiana nel Neolitico medio della Sardegna: un caso di studio da Bau Angius (Terralba, OR)', *Aristeo. Quaderni del Dipartimento di Scienze Archeologiche e Storico-Artistiche dell'Università di Cagliari* 1 (2004): 33-46.

Lugliè, C., *Risorse litiche e tecnologia della pietra scheggiata nel Neolitico antico della Sardegna.* Università di Roma La Sapienza: doctoral thesis, 2006.

Lugliè, C., 'L'inconsueto maschile: una raffigurazione fallica del neolitico medio da Bau Angius (Sardegna centro-occidentale)', in *Il Segno e l'Idea. Arte preistorica in Sardegna*, edited by G. Tanda and C. Lugliè, 53-64. Cagliari: CUEC, 2008.

Lugliè, C., 'Il mesolitico', in *Atti della XLIV Riunione Scientifica dell'Istituto Italiano di Preistoria e Protostoria: La preistoria e la protostoria della Sardegna (Cagliari, Barumini, Sassari 23-28 novembre 2009)*, edited by C. Lugliè and R. Cicilloni, 31-36. Florence: IIPP, 2009a.

Lugliè, C., ' L'obsidienne néolithique en Méditerranée Occidentale', in *L'homme et le précieux: matières minérales précieuses*, edited by M-H. Moncel and F. Fröhlich, 213-24. Oxford: BAR Publishing International Series 1934, 2009b.

Lugliè, C., 'The site of Su Forru de is Sinzurreddus', project presentation 2010: http://www.fastionline.org/excavation/micro_view.php?fst_cd=AIAC_329&curcol=sea_cd-AIAC_3711

Lugliè, C., 'From the Perspective of the Source. Neolithic Production and Exchange of Monte Arci Obsidians (Central-Western Sardinia)', in *Actes del Congres Internacional Xarxes al Neolitic. Circulacio i intercanvi de matèries, productes i idees a la Mediterrània occidental, VII-III millennia a.C. Gavà/Bellaterra, 2-4/2/2011 (Rubricatum. Revista del Museo de Gavà 5)*, edited by M. Borrell et al. 173-80. Gavà: Museo de Gavà, 2012.

Lugliè, C., 'The Su Carroppu rock shelter within the process of neolithisation of Sardinia', in *Transitions in the Mediterranean. When hunters became farmers. Transitions en Méditerranée. Ou comment des chasseurs devinrent collecteurs*, edited by C. Manen, T. Perrin and J. Guilaine, 307-26. Toulouse: Archives d'écologie préhistorique, 2014.

Lugliè, C., 'La comparsa dell'economia produttiva e il processo di neolitizzazione in Sardegna', in *La Sardegna preistorica. Storia, materiali, monumenti (Corpora delle antichità della Sardegna)*, edited by A. Moravetti et al., 37-49. Sassari: Regione Autonoma della Sardegna/Carlo Delfino Editore, 2017.

Lugliè, C., 'Your path led trough [sic] the sea... The emergence of Neolithic in Sardinia and Corsica', *Quaternary International* 470 (2018): 285-300.

Lugliè, C. and F. Lo Schiavo, 'Risorse e tecnologia: le rocce e i metalli', in *Atti della XLIV Riunione Scientifica dell'Istituto Italiano di Preistoria e Protostoria: La preistoria e la protostoria della Sardegna (Cagliari, Barumini, Sassari 23-28 novembre 2009)*, Vol. 1, edited by C. Lugliè and R. Cicilloni, 247-67. Florence: IIPP, 2009.

Lugliè, C. and V. Pinna, 'Alla soglia del gesto: sequenze operative in incisioni su ciottolo del Neolitico Antico della Sardegna', in *Atti della XLIV Riunione Scientifica dell'Istituto Italiano di Preistoria e Protostoria: La preistoria e la protostoria della Sardegna (Cagliari, Barumini, Sassari 23-28 novembre 2009)*, edited by C. Lugliè and R. Cicilloni, 477-83. Florence: IIPP, 2012.

Lugliè C. and V. Santoni, forthcoming, 'La necropoli ipogeica di Cuccuru is Arrius (Cabras - Oristano). Nuovi elementi di cronologia assoluta' in *Vasi a Bocca Quadrata. Evoluzione delle conoscenze, nuovi approcci interpretativi, Atti del Convegno di Studi (Riva del Garda, 13-15 maggio 2009)*, edited by E. Mottes.

Lugliè, C., F.-X. Le Bourdonnec and G. Poupeauet, 'Neolithic Obsidian Economy Around the Monte Arci Source (Sardinia, Italy): The Importance of Integrated Provenance/Technology Analyses', in *Proceedings of the 37th International Symposium on Archaeometry, 13th - 16th May 2008, Siena, Italy*, edited by I. Turbanti-Memmi, 255-60. Berlin/Heidelberg: Springer, 2011.

Lugliè, C. et al., 'Early Neolithic obsidians in Sardinia (Western Mediterranean): the Su Carroppu case', *Journal of Archaeological Science* 34 (2007): 428-39.

Lugliè, C. et al., 'Obsidians in the Rio Saboccu (Sardinia, Italy) campsite: Provenance, reduction and relations with the wider Early Neolithic Tyrrhenian area', *Comptes Rendus Palevol* 7 (2008): 249-58.

Lugliè, C. et al., 'Il Neolitico antico terminale di Sa Punta - Marceddì (Terralba, OR)', in *Atti della XLIV Riunione Scientifica dell'Istituto Italiano di Preistoria e Protostoria: La preistoria e la protostoria della Sardegna (Cagliari, Barumini, Sassari 23-28 novembre 2009)*, edited by C. Lugliè and R. Cicilloni, 463-70. Florence: IIPP, 2012.

Maggi, R., 'Le facies a ceramica impressa dell'area ligure', in *Le ceramiche impresse nel Neolitico antico. Italia e Mediterraneo (Collana del Bullettino di paletnologia italiana/Studi di Paletnologia I)*, edited by M.A. Fugazzola Delpino, A. Pessina and V. Tiné, 91-96. Rome: Istituto poligrafico e Zecca dello Stato, 2002.

Mallegni, F. et al., 'La falange nella grotta di Nurighe presso Cheremule: revisione e nuove informazioni', *Sardinia, Corsica et Baleares antiquae* IX, 2011, 9-12.

Malone, C., 'The Italian Neolithic: A synthesis of research', *Journal of World Prehistory* 17:3 (2003): 235-312.

Manca, L., 'Considerazioni sui manufatti in osso nella Preistoria sarda', in *Atti della XXXIX riunione scientifica dell'Istituto Italiano di Preistoria e Protostoria: Materie prime e scambi nella preistoria italiana (Firenze 25-27 novembre 2004)*, edited by A.M. Bietti Sestieri, 933-43. Florence: IIPP, 2006.

Manen, C., 'Implantations de faciès d'origine italienne au Néolithique ancien: l'exemple des sites 'liguriens' du Languedoc', in *Sociétés et espaces. Actualité de la recherche. Actes des troisièmes rencontres méridionales de préhistoire récente, Toulouse, 6-7 novembre 1998*, edited by M. Leduc, N. Valdeyron and J. Vaquer, 35-42. Toulouse: Archives d'écologie préhistorique, 2000.

Manen, C., 'Émergence, développement et évolution des styles céramiques du Languedoc-Roussillon au 6ème millénaire avant notre ère', in *Actes des IVe Rencontres Méridionales de Préhistoire Récente, Nîmes, France,*

2000 (Monographies d'Archéologie Méditerranéenne 15), edited by J. Gasco, X. Gutherz and P.-A. De Labriffe, 43-55. Lattes: Édition de l'Association pour le Développement de l'Archéologie en Languedoc-Roussillon, 2003.

Manen, C., 'La production céramique de Pont de Roque-Haute: Synthèse et comparations', in *Pont de Roque-Haute. Nouveaux regards sur la néolithisation de la France Méditerranéenne*, edited by J. Guilaine, C. Manen and J.D. Vigne, 151-66. Toulouse: Archives d'écologie préhistorique, 2007.

Manen, C. and F. Covertini, 'Neolithization of the western mediterranean: pottery productions, circulation and recombination', in *Actes del Congres Internacional Xarxes al Neolitic. Circulacio i intercanvi de matèries, productes i idees a la Mediterrània occidental, VII-III millennia a.C. Gavà/Bellaterra, 2-4/2/2011* (*Rubricatum. Revista del Museo de Gavà* 5), edited by M. Borrell et al., 363-68. Gavà: Museo de Gavà, 2012.

Manen, C. and P. Sabatier, 'Chronique radiocarbone de la néolithisation en Méditerranée occidentale', *Bulletin de la Société préhistorique française* 100:3 (2003): 479-504.

Manfredini, A., 'Rituali funerari e organizzazione sociale: una rilettura di alcuni dati della facies Diana in Italia meridionale', in *Studi di Preistoria e Protostoria in onore di Luigi Bernabò Brea*, edited by M.C. Martinelli and U. Spigo, 71-87. Messina: Edas, 2001.

Marchand, G. and C. Manen, 'Mésolithique final et Néolithique ancien autour du détroit: une perspective septentrionale (Atlantique/Méditerranée)', in *The last hunter-gatherers and the first farming communities in the South of the Iberian peninsula and North Morocco, Workshop, Faro, Nov. 2009* (Promontoria Monográfica 15), edited by J.F. Gibaja and A. Faustino Carvalho, 173-79. Faro: Universidade do Algarve, 2010.

Martini, F., 'Il paleolitico in Sardegna. Evidenze, problem e ipotesi a trent'anni dalla scoperta', in *Atti della XLIV Riunione Scientifica dell'Istituto Italiano di Preistoria e Protostoria: La preistoria e la protostoria della Sardegna (Cagliari, Barumini, Sassari 23-28 novembre 2009)*, Vol. I, edited by C. Lugliè and R. Cicilloni, 17-27. Florence: IIPP, 2009.

Martini, F., 'Il paleolitico e il mesolitico in Sardegna', in *Sardegna preistorica. Storia, materiali, monumenti* (Corpora delle antichità della Sardegna), edited by A. Moravetti et al., 11-36. Sassari: Regione Autonoma della Sardegna/Carlo Delfinol Editore, 2017.

Martini, F. and A. Palma di Cesnola, 'L'industria litica di Riu Altana (Sassari): il complesso clactoniano arcaico', *Rivista di Scienze Preistoriche* XLV:1 (1993): 3-22.

Martini, F. and F. Saliola, 'I siti paleolitici: i complessi industriali. Sa Coa de sa Multa', in *Sardegna Paleolitica: Studi sul più antico popolamento dell'isola*, edited by F.

Martini, 45-79. Florence: Museo fiorentino di preistoria P. Graziosi, 1999.

Martini, F. and C. Tozzi, 'Il Mesolitico in Sardegna', in *Atti della XLIV Riunione Scientifica dell'Istituto Italiano di Preistoria e Protostoria: La preistoria e la protostoria della Sardegna (Cagliari, Barumini, Sassari 23-28 novembre 2009)*, edited by C. Lugliè and R. Cicilloni, 399-406. Florence: IIPP, 2012.

Martini, F. et al., 'Il Mesolitico di Su Coloru (Laerru, Sassari): nuovi dati', in *Atti della XLIV Riunione Scientifica dell'Istituto Italiano di Preistoria e Protostoria: La preistoria e la protostoria della Sardegna (Cagliari, Barumini, Sassari 23-28 novembre 2009)*, edited by C. Lugliè and R. Cicilloni, 417-22. Florence: IIPP, 2012.

Masala, S., 'La fauna della grotta di Su Coloru: scavi 1996-98', *Aidu Entos* 5-6 (2008): 4-17.

Masala, S., *I cambiamenti delle faune oloceniche legati all'attività antropica: nuove introduzioni, evoluzioni interne, cambiamenti climatici: il caso della Sardegna e di Creta*. Università degli Studi di Sassari: doctoral thesis, 2013.

Masseti, M., 'Domestic fauna and anthropochorous fauna', *Journal of Human Evolution* 21:2 (2006): 85-93 (https://doi.org/10.1007/s11598-006-9009-6).

Masseti, M., 'Holocene endemic and anthropochorous wild mammals of the Mediterranean islands', *Anthropozoologica* 28 (1998): 3-20.

Mazzieri, P. et al., 'Contatti e scambi tra la cultura Serra d'Alto e i vasi a bocca quadrata: il caso delle ollette tipo San Martino', in *Actes del Congres Internacional Xarxes al Neolitic. Circulacio i intercanvi de matèries, productes i idees a la Mediterrània occidental, VII-III millennia a.C. Gavà/Bellaterra, 2-4/2/2011* (*Rubricatum. Revista del Museo de Gavà* 5), edited by M. Borrell et al., 351-61. Gavà: Museo de Gavà, 2012.

Melis, M.G., 'Monte d'Accoddi and the end of the Neolithic in Sardinia (Italy)', *Documenta Praehistorica* XXXVIII (2011): 207-19.

Melis, M.G., 'Sardinian prehistoric burials in a Mediterranean perspective, symbolic and socio-economic aspects', in *Neolithic Monuments: Functions, Mentalité and the Social Construction of the Landscape*, edited by B. Schulz Paulsson and B. Gaydarska, 7-23. Oxford: BAR Publishing International Series 2625, 2014.

Melis, P., 'Lo scavo della Tomba X nella necropoli ipogeica di Santu Pedru (Alghero-Sassari): una *domus de janas* delle prime fasi del Neolitico Recente', *Rivista di Scienze Preistoriche* LIX (2009): 93-114.

Melis, R.T. and M. Mussi, 'Mesolithic burials at S'Omu e S'Orku (SOMK) on the southwestern coast of Sardinia', in *Mesolithic burials. Rites, symbols and social organization of early postglacial communities.*

International conference at Halle (Saale), Germany, 18th to 21st of September 2013, edited by J.M. Grünberg et al., *Tagungen des Landesmuseum für Vorgeschichte Halle* 13/II, 2016, 733-40.

Melis, R.T. et al., 'Popolamento e ambiente nella Sardegna centro occidentale durante l'Olocene antico: primi risultati', in *Atti della XLIV Riunione Scientifica dell'Istituto Italiano di Preistoria e Protostoria: La preistoria e la protostoria della Sardegna (Cagliari, Barumini, Sassari 23-28 novembre 2009)*, edited by C. Luglię and R. Cicilloni, 427-34. Florence: IIPP, 2012.

Mellaart, J., *Catal Huyuk: a Neolithic town in Anatolia*. London: Thames and Hudson, 1967.

Micheli, R., 'Ornamenti in conchiglia del Neolitico dell'Italia settentrionale', in *Conchiglie e Archeologia: contributi scientifici in occasione della mostra Dentro la Conchiglia: sezione archeologica, Museo Tridentino di Scienze Naturali, Trento, 13 settembre 2003-25 gennaio 2004*, (Preistoria Alpina 40:1, 2004), edited by M.A. Borrello, 53-70. Trento: Alcione, 2004.

Modi, A. et al., 'Complete mitochondrial sequences from Mesolithic Sardinia', *Scientific Reports* 7:42869 (2017), (https://www.ncbi.nlm.nih.gov/pmc/articles/PMC5335606/).

Moravetti, A., *Sardegna archeologica dal cielo, dai circoli megalitici alle torri nuragiche*, Sassari: Carlo Delfino Editore, 2012 (2nd. ed.).

Moravetti, A., 'Ceramiche decorate della cultura di Ozieri', in *La Sardegna preistorica. Storia, materiali, monumenti* (Corpora delle antichità della Sardegna), edited by A. Moravetti et al., 65-82. Sassari: Regione Autonoma della Sardegna/Carlo Delfino Editore, 2017.

Mussi, M., 'La Venere di Macomer nel quadro del Pleistocene superiore finale europeo', in *Atti della XLIV Riunione Scientifica dell'Istituto Italiano di Preistoria e Protostoria: La preistoria e la protostoria della Sardegna (Cagliari, Barumini, Sassari 23-28 novembre 2009)*, edited by C. Luglię and R. Cicilloni, 383-90. Florence: IIPP, 2012.

Mussi, M. and R.T. Melis, 'Santa Maria Is Acquas e le problematiche del paleolitico superiore in Sardegna', *Origini* 24 (2002): 67-94.

Nakamura, C. and L. Meskell, 'Articulate Bodies: Forms and Figures at Çatalhöyük', *Journal of Archaeological Method and Theory* 16:3 (*The Materiality of Representation*), (2009): 205-30.

Narroll, R., 'Floor area and settlement population', *American Antiquity* 27:4 (1962): 587-89.

Natali, E., 'Gli insediamenti neolitici di Valle Messina e Serra dei Canonici (San Nicola di Melfi - Potenza)', in *Atti del 23 convegno nazionale sulla preistoria-protostoria-storia della Daunia (San Severo 23-24 novembre 2002)*, edited by A. Gravina, 81-96. San Severo: Archeoclub d'Italia, 2003.

Natali, E., 'Typologie des décors de la céramique imprimée archaïque du Sud-Est de l'Italie', in *Premières sociétés paysannes de Méditerranée occidentale. Structures des productions céramiques (Séance de la Société préhistorique française, Toulouse 11-12 mai 2007)*, (Mémoire SPF 51), edited by C. Manen et al., 43-56. Paris: CNRS, 2010.

Nussey, D.H. et al., 'Genetic consequences of human management in an introduced island population of red deer (Cervus elaphus)', *Heredity* 97 (2006): 56-65.

Olivieri, A. et al., 'Mitogenome diversity in Sardinia: a genetic window onto an island's past', *Molecular biology and evolution* 34:5 (2017): 1230-39.

Omrak, A. et al., 'Genomic evidence establishes Anatolia as the source of the European Neolithic gene pool', *Current Biology* 26 (2016): 270-75.

Orsoni, F., 'Ricerche paletnologiche nei dintorni di Cagliari', *Bullettino di Paletnologia Italiana* V (1879): 44-46.

Paglietti, G., 'La piccola statuaria femminile della Sardegna neolitica. Proposta di una seriazione evolutiva attraverso l'applicazione di metodi stilistici e dimensionali', in *Il Segno e l'Idea. Arte preistorica in Sardegna*, edited by G. Tanda and C. Luglię, 11-52. Cagliari: CUEC, 2008.

Paglietti, G., 'All'origine del megalitismo nell'occidente mediterraneo: le tombe a circolo', in *Atti del III Convegno Nazionale dei Giovani Archeologi: Uomo e Territorio. Dinamiche di frequentazione e di sfruttamento delle risorse naturali nell'antichità, Sassari 27-30 settembre 2006*, edited by M.G. Melis, 97-103. Muros: Nuova Stampa Color, 2009.

Paglietti, G., 'La madre mediterranea della Sardegna neolitica', in *La Sardegna preistorica. Storia, materiali, monumenti* (Corpora delle antichità della Sardegna), edited by A. Moravetti et al., 97-110. Sassari: Regione Autonoma della Sardegna/Carlo Delfino Editore, 2017.

Pala, M. et al., 'Mitochondrial haplogroup U5b3: a distant echo of the epipaleolithic and the legacy of the early Sardinians', *The American Journal of Human Genetics* 84 (2009): 814-21.

Palmiotti, L., *Il popolamento antico nella Puglia centrale. Frequentazione antropica, cultura materiale, concettualità tra il VII e il II millennio a.C.* Trani: Regione Puglia/C.R.S.E.C./Antonio Cortese Editore, 2004.

Palombo, M.R. et al., 'The late Pleistocene to Holocene palaeogeographic evolution of the Porto Conte area: Clues for a better understanding of human colonization of Sardinia and faunal dynamics during the last 30 ka', *Quaternary International* 439A (2017): 117-40.

Paolini-Saez, H., 'Les productions céramiques du Néolithique ancien tyrrhénien', *in Premières sociétés paysannes de Méditerranée occidentale. Structures des productions céramiques (Séance de la Société préhistorique française, Toulouse 11-12 mai 2007)*, (Mémoire SPF 51), edited by C. Manen et al., 89-104. Paris: CNRS, 2010.

Pardo, L.M. et al., 'Dissecting the genetic make-up of North-East Sardinia using a large set of haploid and autosomal markers', *European Journal of Human Genetics* 20 (2012): 956-64.

Pasquet, A. and F. Demouche, 'Le Mésolithique à Punta di Caniscione (Monacia d'Aullène, Corse-du-Sud)', in *Historie de la Corse Vol 1: Des origines à la veille des révolutions: occupations et adaptations*, edited by A-M. Graziani, 45-48. Ajaccio: Éditions Alain Piazzola, 2013.

Patroni, G., 'S. Bartolomeo in Italia. Grotta preistorica rinettata nell'aprile 1901', *Notizie degli Scavi* 1901: 381-389.

Pearson, J. and L. Meskell, 'Biographical bodies. Flesh and food at Catalhöyük', *Proceedings of the British Academy* 198 (2014): 233-50.

Pesce, G., 'La 'Venere' di Macomer', *Rivista di Scienze Preistoriche* IV (1949): 123-37.

Pittau, P. et al., 'Palynological interpretation of the Early Neolithic coastal open-air site at Sa Punta (central-western Sardinia, Italy)', *Journal of Archaeological Science* 39 (2012): 1260-70.

Puglisi, S.M., 'Villaggi sotto roccia e sepolcri megalitici della Gallura', *Bullettino di Paletnologia Italiana Nuova serie* V (1941): 123-41.

Puglisi, S.M. and E. Castaldi, 'Aspetti dell'accantonamento culturale nella Gallura preistorica e protostorica', *Studi Sardi* XIX (1964): 59-148.

Radina, F., 'Strutture d'abitato del Neolitico lungo il basso corso ofantino. Il silos di S. Giovanni-Setteponti', in *Atti del 23 convegno nazionale sulla preistoria-protostoria-storia della Daunia (San Severo 23-24 novembre 2002)*, edited by A. Gravina, 59-70. San Severo: Archeoclub d'Italia, 2003.

Radina, F. and L. Sarti, 'Le strutture d'abitato', in *Le ceramiche impresse nel Neolitico antico. Italia e Mediterraneo* (Collana del Bullettino di paletnologia italiana/Studi di Paletnologia I), edited by M.A. Fugazzola Delpino, A. Pessina and V. Tiné, 196-207. Rome: Istituto poligrafico e Zecca dello Stato, 2002.

Renfrew, C., 'Megaliths, territories and populations', in *Acculturation and continuity in Atlantic Europe*, edited by S.J. de Laet, 198–220. Brugge: De Tempel, 1976.

Richards, M., 'The Neolithic Invasion of Europe', *Annual Review of Anthropology* 32 (2003): 135-62.

Robb, J.E., *The early Mediterranean village. Agency, material culture and social change in Neolithic Italy*. Cambridge: Cambridge University Press, 2007.

Romagnoli, F. and F. Martini, 'Sistemi tecnici del Paleolitico sassarese: Sa Coa de Sa Multa', in *Atti della XLIV Riunione Scientifica dell'Istituto Italiano di Preistoria e Protostoria: La preistoria e la protostoria della Sardegna (Cagliari, Barumini, Sassari 23-28 novembre 2009)*, edited by C. Lugliè and R. Cicilloni, 361-68. Florence: IIPP, 2012.

Rootsi, S. et al., 'Phylogeography of Y-chromosome haplogroup I reveals distinct domains of prehistoric gene flow in Europe', *The American Journal of Human Genetics* 75 (2004): 128-37.

Runnels, C. et al., 'Warfare in Neolithic Thessaly: A Case Study', *Hesperia* 78:2 (2009): 165-94.

Salque, M. et al., 'Earliest evidence for cheese making in the sixth millennium BC in northern Europe', *Nature* 493 (2013): 522-25 (https://doi.org/10.1038/nature11698).

Sanges, M., 'Gli strati del Neolitico antico e medio nella Grotta Corbeddu di Oliena (Nuoro). Nota preliminare', in *Atti della XXVI Riunione Scientifica dell'Istituto Italiano di Preistoria e Protostoria: Il Neolitico in Italia (Firenze 7-10 novembre 1985)*, 825-30. Florence: IIPP, 1987.

Santoni, V., 'Nota preliminare sulla tipologia delle grotticelle artificiali funerarie della Sardegna', *Archivio Storico Sardo* XXX (1976): 3-49.

Santoni, V., 'Notiziario. Sardegna', *Rivista di Scienze Preistoriche* XXXII:2 (1977): 353-54.

Santoni, V., 'Il mondo del sacro in età neolitica', *Le Scienze* 170 (1982): 70-80.

Santoni, V., *Le tombe neolitiche di Cuccuru S'Arriu di Cabras* (Quaderni didattici della Soprintendenza Archeologica per le provincie di Cagliari e Oristano 1), 1988.

Santoni, V., 'Cuccuru S'Arriu-Cabras. Il sito di cultura San Michele. Dati preliminari', in *La cultura di Ozieri. Problematiche e nuove acquisizioni, Atti del I Convegno di Studi (Ozieri, gennaio 1986-aprile 1987)*, edited by L. Dettori Campus, 169-200. Ozieri: Il Torchietto, 1989.

Santoni V., 'Il neolitico medio di Cuccuru s'Arriu di Cabras (Or) - Nota preliminare', in *La ceramica racconta la storia. Atti del Convegno La ceramica artistica, d'uso e da costruzione nell'Oristanese dal neolitico ai giorni nostri (Oristano 1994)*, 7-18. Oristano: S'Alvure, 1995.

Santoni, V., 'Il Neolitico superiore di Cuccuru S'Arriu di Cabras (Oristano)', in *La ceramica nel Sinis dal Neolitico ai giorni nostri. Atti del II Convegno La ceramica racconta la storia (Oristano 25 Ottobre-Cabras 26 Ottobre 1996)*, edited by C. Cossu and R. Melis, 97-105. Oristano: Condaghes, 1998.

Santoni, V., 'Le Néolithique moyen supérieur de Cuccuru S'Arriu (Cabras-Oristano, Sardaigne)', in *Le Néolithique du Nord-ouest méditerranéen, Actes du*

XXIV Congrès Préhistorique de France, Carcassonne 26-30 septembre 1994, edited by J. Vacquer, 77-87. Paris: SPF, 1999.

Santoni, V., 'Alle origini dell'ipogeismo in Sardegna: Cabras-Cuccuru-S'Arriu, la necropoli del Neolitico medio', in *L'Ipogeismo nel Mediterraneo: Origini, Sviluppo, Quadri Culturali. Atti del Congresso Internazionale, 23-28 Maggio 1994, Sassari-Oristano, Italia*, edited by G. Tanda, M.G. Melis and P. Melis, 369-91. Sassari: Università degli Studi di Sassari/ Muros: Stampacolor, 2000.

Santoni, V. and A. Doria, 'Cabras (Oristano). Necropoli neolitica sull'isolotto di Cuccuru S'Arriu', in *Memorabilia: Il futuro della memoria. 3: Laboratori per il progetto*, edited by F. Perego, 451-56. Bari: Laterza, 1987.

Santoni V., G. Bacco and D. Sabatini, 'L'orizzonte Neolitico Superiore di Cuccuru S'Arriu di Cabras. Le sacche C.S.A. nn. 337, 380/1979 e n. 2/1989', in *La cultura di Ozieri: la Sardegna e il Mediterraneo nel IV e III millennio a.C. Atti del II convegno di studi, Ozieri 15-17 ottobre 1990*, edited by L. Campus, 227-95. Ozieri: Il Torchietto, 1997.

Santoni, V. et al., 'Cabras: Cuccuru S'Arriu. Nota preliminare di scavo 1978-79-80', *Rivista di Studi Fenici* 10:1 (1982): 103-27.

Sarti, L. et al., 'Il neolitico di Grotta Su Coloru (Laerru, Sassari): nuovi dati', in *Atti della XLIV Riunione Scientifica dell'Istituto Italiano di Preistoria e Protostoria: La preistoria e la protostoria della Sardegna (Cagliari, Barumini, Sassari 23-28 novembre 2009)*, edited by C. Lugliè and R. Cicilloni, 455-62. Florence: IIPP, 2012.

Saxe, A.A., *Social dimensions of mortuary practices*. University of Michigan at Ann Arbor: doctoral thesis, 1970.

Schulting, R. and L. Fibiger (eds.), *Sticks, Stones, and Broken Bones. Neolithic Violence in a European Perspective*. Oxford: Oxford University Press, 2012.

Sebis S., C. Lugliè and V. Santoni, 'Il Neolitico medio di Cuccuru is Arrius (Cabras, OR) nella struttura abitativa 422', in *Atti della XLIV Riunione Scientifica dell'Istituto Italiano di Preistoria e Protostoria: La preistoria e la protostoria della Sardegna (Cagliari, Barumini, Sassari 23-28 novembre 2009)*, edited by C. Lugliè and R. Cicilloni, 495-502. Florence: IIPP, 2012.

Shah, D., *God and Goddess in Neolithic period*. Izmir: University Institute of Social Sciences Archaeology Department of Anatolia: master's thesis, 2007.

Simmons, A.H., *Stone Age sailors. Paleolithic seafaring in the Mediterranean*, Routledge 2016 (2nd ed.).

Skeates, R., 'Caves in need of context: prehistoric Sardinia', in *Caves in context: the cultural significance of caves and rockshelters in Europe*, edited by K. Bergsvik and R. Skeates, 166-87. Oxford: Oxbow Books, 2012.

Skeates, R., 'Italian enclosures', in *The Oxford handbook of Neolithic Europe*, edited by C. Fowler, J. Harding and D. Hofmann, 779-93. Oxford: Oxford University Press, 2015.

Skeates, R., 'Prehistoric figurines in Italy', in *The Oxford Handbook of Prehistoric Figurines*, edited by T. Insoll, 776-78. Oxford: Oxford University Press, 2017.

Smith, B.H., 'Patterns of molar wear in hunter-gatherers and agriculturalists', *American Journal of Physical Anthropology* 63 (1984): 39-56.

Sondaar, P.Y., 'Palaeolithic Sardinians: palaeontological evidence and methods', in *Sardinian and Aegean Chronology: Toward the Resolution of Relative and Absolute Dating in the Mediterranean. Proceedings of the International Colloquium 'Sardinian Stratigraphy and Mediterranean Chronology', Tufts University, Medford, MA, March 17-19, 1995* (Studies in Sardinian Archaeology 5), edited by M.S. Balmuth and R.H. Tykot, 45-51. Oxford: Oxbow Books, 1998.

Sondaar, P.Y. and S.A.E. van der Geer, 'Mesolithic environment and animal exploitations on Cyprus and Sardinia/Corsica', in *Archaeozoology of the Near East IV A: Proceedings of the IVth International Symposium on the Archaeozoology of Southwestern Asia and Adjacent Areas* (ARC Publicatie 32), edited by M. Buitenhuis et al., 67-72. Groningen: CARC, 2000.

Sondaar, P.Y. et al., 'The human colonization of Sardinia: a late-pleistocene human fossil from Corbeddu cave', *Comptes rendus de l'Academie de Sciences de Paris* 320:IIa (1995): 145-50.

Soro, L. and A. Usai, 'Between necessity and economy: the archaeological field excavation at Gribaia (Sardinia, Italy). A photogrammetrical solution to document a small archaeological heritage', contribution to *Workshop 13 (Archäologie und Computer) of the international congress 'Cultural heritage and new technologies', Vienna 2-5 November 2008*. Vienna: Phoibos Verlag, 2009 (https://www.academia.edu/371063).

Soro, P., 'Aspetti storici e archeologici', in *Le grotte di Monte Maiore*, edited by M. Mucedda et al., 38-46. Thiesi: Comune di Thiesi, 2013.

Spoor, F., 'The human fossils from Corbeddu Cave, Sardinia: a reappraisal', in *Elephants have a snorkel! Papers in honour of Paul Y. Sondaar*, Vol. 7, edited by J.W.F. Reumer and J. De Vos, 297-302. Rotterdam: Deinsea 1999.

Spoor, F. and P.Y. Sondaar, 'Human fossils from the endemic island fauna of Sardinia', *Journal of human evolution* 15/5 (1986): 399-408.

Stanton, D., J. Mulville and M. Bruford, 'Colonization of the Scottish islands via long-distance Neolithic transport of red deer (Cervus elaphus), *Proceedings* of the Royal Society B (Biological Sciences) 283/1828 (2016): https://doi.org/10.1098/rspb.2016.0095.

Starnini, E., 'L'industria litica scheggiata', in *Il Neolitico nella Caverna delle Arene Candide: Scavi 1972-77* (Monografie Preistoriche ed Archeologiche 10), edited by S. Tiné, 219-36 and 450-71. Bordighera: Istituto internazionale di studi liguri, 1999.

Starnini, E., P. Biagi and N. Mazzucco, 'The beginning of the Neolithic in the Po Plain (northern Italy): Problems and perspectives', *Quaternary International* 470 (2018): 301-17.

Tagliacozzo, A., 'Animal exploitation in the Early Neolithic in Central-Southern Italy', in *Homenaje a Jesús Altuna. Trabajos sobre Paleontología, Arqueozoología, Antropología, Arte, Arqueología y Patrimonio arqueológico* (MUNIBE Antropologia-Arkeologia 57), 429-39. San Sebastian: Aranzadi 2005-2006.

Tanda, G., 'Gli anelloni litici italiani', *Preistoria Alpina* 13 (1977): 111-55.

Tanda. G., 'Il Neolitico Antico e Medio della Grotta Verde, Alghero', in *Atti della XXII Riunione Scientifica dell'Istituto Italiano di Preistoria e Protostoria: La Sardegna centro-settentrionale, Sassari 21-27 ott. 1978*, edited by E. Contu et al., 46-94. Florence: IIPP, 1980.

Tanda, G., 'Il Neolitico Antico della Sardegna', in *Le Néolithique ancien Méditerranéen. Actes du Colloque International de Préhistoire, Montpellier 1981* (Archéologie en Languedoc n. special 1982), edited by J. Bousquet, 333-37. Lattes: Fédération archéologique de l'Hérault, 1982.

Tanda, G., 'Nouveaux éléments pour une définition culturelle des matériaux de la Grotta Verde (Alghero, Sassari, Sardaigne)', in *Premières communautés paysannes en Méditerranée Occidentale. Actes du Colloque International du C.N.R.S. Montpellier, 26–29 Avril 1983*, edited by J. Guilaine et al., 425-31. Paris: CNRS, 1987.

Tanda, G., 'I Siti del Neolitico antico e l'ambiente: strategie di sussistenza', *Interreg préhistoire Corse-Sardaigne 2* (1995): 17-29.

Tanda, G., 'Articolazione e cronologia del Neolitico Antico', in *Sardinian and Aegean Chronology: Toward the Resolution of Relative and Absolute Dating in the Mediterranean. Proceedings of the International Colloquium 'Sardinian Stratigraphy and Mediterranean Chronology', Tufts University, Medford, MA, March 17-19, 1995* (Studies in Sardinian Archaeology 5), edited by M.S. Balmuth and R.H. Tykot, 77-92. Oxford: Oxbow Books, 1998.

Tanda, G., 'Grotta Verde, Sardegna', in *Le ceramiche impresse nel Neolitico antico. Italia e Mediterraneo* (Collana del Bullettino di paletnologia italiana/Studi di Paletnologia I), edited by M.A. Fugazzola Delpino, A.

Pessina and V. Tiné, 441-44. Rome: Istituto poligrafico e Zecca dello Stato, 2002.

Tanda, G., 'Il bucranio nella Sardegna preistorica: origine, sviluppo, cronologia, significato', *The Valcamonica Symposium* (2007): 479-483 (https://www.ccsp.it/web/INFOCCSP/VCS%20storico/vcs2007pdf/tanda.pdf

Tanda, G., 'L'ipogeismo funerario in Sardegna', in *La Sardegna preistorica. Storia, materiali, monumenti* (Corpora delle antichità della Sardegna), edited by A. Moravetti et al., 111-35. Sassari: Regione Autonoma della Sardegna/Carlo Delfino Editore, 2017.

Taramelli, A., 'Esplorazione archeologiche e scavi nel promontorio di S. Elia', *Notizie degli Scavi* 1904: 19-37.

Taramelli, A., 'Alghero: nuovi scavi nella necropoli preistorica di Anghelu Ruju', *Monumenti Antichi della Reale Accademia dei Lincei* 19 (1909): 397-540.

Tchernov, A., 'Sex differences in energy balance, body composition, and body fat distribution', in *Diabetes in women. Pathophysiology and therapy*, edited by A. Tsatsoulis, J. Wyckoff and F. Brown, 1-24. London: Humana Press, 2009.

Terradas, X. et al., 'Neolithic diffusion of obsidian in the western Mediterranean: new data from Iberia', *Journal of Archaeological Science* 41 (2014): 69-78 (https://doi.org/10.1016/j.jas.2013.07.023).

Tiberi, I. and S. Dell'Anna, 'Usi funerari nel Salento del V millennio a.C.: le tombe di Carpignano Salentino (Lecce)', in *Atti del Convegno: Il pieno sviluppo del Neolitico in Italia, Finale Ligure Borgo, 8-10 giugno 2009* (Rivista di Studi Liguri 77/79), edited by M. Bernabò Brea, R. Maggi and A. Manfredini, 353-57. Bordighera: Istituto internazionale di studi liguri, 2014.

Tiné, S. and A. Traverso, *Monte D'Accoddi: 10 Anni di Nuovi Scavi,* Genova: Del Cielo, 1992.

Tozzi, C. and M. Dini, 'L'industria mesolitica del Riparo di Porto Leccio (Trinità d'Agultu, SS). Analisi tecnologica', in *Atti della XLIV Riunione Scientifica dell'Istituto Italiano di Preistoria e Protostoria: La preistoria e la protostoria della Sardegna (Cagliari, Barumini, Sassari 23-28 novembre 2009)*, edited by C. Lugliè and R. Cicilloni, 423-26. Florence: IIPP, 2012.

Tozzi, C. and M.C. Weiss, 'Nouvelle données sur le Néolithique ancien de l'aire corso-toscane', *Bulletin de la Société préhistorique française* 98:3 (2001): 445-58.

Tramoni P. and A. D'Anna, 'Le Néolithique moyen de la Corse revisité: nouvelles données, nouvelles perceptions', in *Le Chasséen, des Chasséens... Retour sur une culture nationale et ses parallèles, Sepulcres de fossa, Cortaillod, Lagozza, Actes de colloque (18-20 novembre 2014, Paris)*, edited by T. Perrin et al., 59-72. Toulouse: Archives d'écologie préhistorique, 2016.

Tramoni, P. et al., 'Le site de Tivulaghju (Porto-Vecchio, Corse-du-Sud) et les coffres mégalithiques du sud de la Corse, nouvelles données', *Bulletin de la Société préhistorique française* 104:2 (2007): 245-74.

Traverso, A., 'Arene Candide (Liguria)', in *Le ceramiche impresse nel Neolitico antico. Italia e Mediterraneo* (Collana del Bullettino di paletnologia italiana/Studi di Paletnologia I), edited by M.A. Fugazzola Delpino, A. Pessina and V. Tiné, 91-96. Rome: Istituto poligrafico e Zecca dello Stato, 2002.

Traverso, A., 'Il santuario prenuragico di Monte d'Accoddi (Sassari): tipologia e cronologia dei materiali ceramici dai saggi di scavo sul monumento (1984-2001)', *Bullettino di Paletnologia Italiana* XCVI (2005-2007): 63-108.

Tresset, A. and J-D. Vigne, 'Substitution of species, techniques and symbols at the Mesolithic-Neolithic transition in Western Europe', in *Going over: the Mesolithic-Neolithic transition in north-west Europe* (Proceedings of the British Academy 144), edited by A. Whittle and V. Cummings, 189-210. London: OUP, 2007.

Trump, D.H., '*The Grotta Filiestru, Bonu Ighinu*, Mara (Sassari)', in *Le Néolithique ancien Méditerranéen. Actes du Colloque International de Préhistoire, Montpellier 1981* (Archéologie en Languedoc n. special 1982), edited by J. Bousquet, 327-31. Lattes: Fédération archéologique de l'Hérault, 1982.

Trump, D.H., *La Grotta di Filiestru a Mara-SS* (Quaderni della Soprintendenza ai Beni Archeologici per le Provincie di Sassari e Nuoro 13), 1983.

Trump, D.H., *Nuraghe Noeddos and the Bonu Ighinu Valley: excavation and survey in Sardinia*. Oxford: Oxbow Books, 1990.

Turchi, D., 'Venerette e pippias', *Sardegna Antica* 1 (1992): 2-4.

Tykot, R., *Prehistoric Trade in the Western Mediterranean: The Sources and Distribution of Sardinian Obsidian*. Harvard University (Boston): doctoral thesis, 1995.

Tykot, R., 'Obsidian procurement and distribution in the Central and Western Mediterranean', *Journal of Mediterranean Archaeology* 9:1 (1996): 39-82.

Tykot, R., 'Islands in the Stream. Stone Age Cultural Dynamics in Sardinia and Corsica', in *Social Dynamics of the Prehistoric Central Mediterranean*, edited by R. Tykot, J. Morter and J. Robb, 67-82. London: Accordia Research Institute, 1999.

Tykot, R., 'Determining the source of lithic artifacts and reconstructing trade in the ancient world', in *Written in stone: The multiple dimensions of lithic analysis*, edited by P.N. Kardulias and R.W. Yerkes, 59-85. Lanham, MD: Lexington Books, 2003.

Ucchesu, M., M.R. Manunza and L. Peña-Chocarro, 'New archaeobotanical evidence for the Chalcolithic period in Sardinia (Italy)', poster for the 6th Conference of the International Workgroup for Palaeoethnobotany, Thessaloniki, 17-22 June 2013 (https://www.academia.edu/4345060).

Ucchesu, M., S. Sau and C. Lugliè, 'Crop and wild plant exploitation in Italy during the Neolithic period: New data from Su Mulinu Mannu, Middle Neolithic site of Sardinia', *Journal of Archaeological Science - Reports* 14 (2017): 1-11.

Ucelli Gnesutta, P., 'Grotta di Settecannelle, Lazio', in *Le ceramiche impresse nel Neolitico antico. Italia e Mediterraneo* (Collana del Bullettino di paletnologia italiana/Studi di Paletnologia I), edited by M.A. Fugazzola Delpino, A. Pessina and V. Tiné, 342-49. Rome: Istituto poligrafico e Zecca dello Stato, 2002.

Ugas, G., *La tomba dei guerrieri di Decimoputzu*, Cagliari: Edizioni della Torre, 1990.

Ugas, G., 'Strutture insediative seminterrate e ipogeismo sepolcrale nella Sardegna preistorica', in *L'Ipogeismo nel Mediterraneo: Origini, Sviluppo, Quadri Culturali. Atti del Congresso Internazionale, 23-28 Maggio 1994, Sassari-Oristano, Italia,* edited by G. Tanda, M.G. Melis and P. Melis, 887-910. Sassari: Università degli Studi di Sassari/Muros: Stampacolor, 2000.

Usai, L., 'Su Stangioni, Sardegna', in *Le ceramiche impresse nel Neolitico antico. Italia e Mediterraneo* (Collana del Bullettino di paletnologia italiana/Studi di Paletnologia I), edited by M.A. Fugazzola Delpino, A. Pessina and V. Tiné, 445-52. Rome: Istituto poligrafico e Zecca dello Stato, 2002.

Usai, L., 'Il Neolitico medio', in *Atti della XLIV Riunione Scientifica dell'Istituto Italiano di Preistoria e Protostoria: La preistoria e la protostoria della Sardegna. Cagliari, Barumini, Sassari 23-28 novembre 2009,* Vol. I, edited by C. Lugliè and R. Cicilloni, 49-58. Florence: IIPP, 2009.

Usai, L., M. Migaleddu and C. Lugliè, 'La stazione del Neolitico Antico di Su Stangioni (Portoscuso)', *Studi Sardi* XXXIV (2009): 11-71.

Vaquer, J., 'Le role de la zone nord-tyrrhenienne dans la diffusion de l'obsidienne en Mediterranée nord-occidentale au Neolithique', in *Corse et Sardaigne prehistoriques. Relations et échanges dans le contexte mediterraneen. Actes du 128e Congrès national des sociétés historiques et scientifiques, Bastia 14-21 avril 2003,* edited by A. D'Anna et al., 99-119. Paris: CTHS, 2007.

Vella Gregory, I., 'Embodied materiality: The human form in pre-Nuragic Sardinia', *Archaeological Review from Cambridge* 21:2 (2006): 9-31.

Vella Gregory, I., 'Thinking through the body: the use of images as a medium of social expression', *Journal of Mediterranean Studies* 17:1 (2007): 23-46.

Vella Gregory, I., 'Mediterranean – Sardinia', in *The Oxford Handbook of Prehistoric Figurines*, edited by

T. Insoll, 799-822. Oxford: Oxford University Press, 2017.

Vigne, J.-D., 'Biogeographie insulaire et anthropzoologie des societes Neolithiques Mediterraneenes: Herisson, Renard et Micromammiferes', *Anthropozoologica* 8 (1988): 31-52.

Vigne, J.-D., 'Le peuplement paléolithique des îles: le débat s'ouvre en Sardaigne', *Les Nouvelles de l'archeologie* 35 (1989): 39-42.

Vigne, J.-D., 'Domestication ou appropriation pour la chasse: histoire d'un choix socio-culturel depuis le Neolithique. L'exemple des cerfs (*Cervus*)', in *Exploitation des animaux sauvages à travers le temps. Actes des XIIIe rencontres internationals d'archéologie et d'histoire d'Antibes/IV colloque de l'homme et l'animal*, edited by J. Desse and F. Audoin-Rouzeau, 201-20. Antibes: Éditions APDCA, 1993.

Vigne, J.-D., 'Préhistoire du Cap Corse: les abris de Torre d'Aquila, Pietracorbara (Haute-Corse). La Faune', *Bulletin de la Société préhistorique française* 92:3 (1995): 381-89.

Vigne, J.-D., 'Preliminary research on the exploitation of animal resources in Corsica during the pre-neolithic', in *Sardinian and Aegean Chronology: Toward the Resolution of Relative and Absolute Dating in the Mediterranean. Proceedings of the International Colloquium 'Sardinian Stratigraphy and Mediterranean Chronology', Tufts University, Medford, MA, March 17-19, 1995* (Studies in Sardinian Archaeology 5), edited by M.S. Balmuth and R.H. Tykot, 57-62. Oxford: Oxbow Books, 1998.

Vigne, J.-D., 'Accumulations de lagomorphes et de rongeurs dans les sites mésolithiques corso-sardes: origines taphonomiques, implications anthropologiques', in *Petits animaux et sociétés humaines. Du complément alimentaire aux ressources utilitaires. Actes des XXIVe rencontres internationales d'archéologie et d'histoire d'Antibes*, edited by J.-P. Brugal and J. Desse, 285-305. Antibes: Éditions APDCA, 2004.

Vigne, J.-D., 'Exploitation des animaux et Néolithisation en Méditerranée Nord-Occidentale', in *Pont de Roque-Haute. Nouveaux regards sur la néolithisation de la France Méditerranéenne*, edited by J. Guilaine, C. Manen and J.D. Vigne, 221-301. Toulouse: Archives d'écologie préhistorique, 2007.

Volante, N., 'Il Neolitico', in *Introduzione allo studio della ceramica in archeologia (Dipartimento di Archeologia e Storia delle Arti, Università degli Studi di Siena)*, 115-36. Florence: Centro Editoriale Toscano, 2007.

Walter, P., 'La genèse des hypogées en Méditerranée centrale et le commerce de l'obsidienne', in *L'Ipogeismo nel Mediterraneo: Origini, Sviluppo, Quadri Culturali. Atti del Congresso Internazionale, 23-28 Maggio 1994, Sassari-Oristano, Italia*, edited by G. Tanda, M.G.

Melis and P. Melis, 607-20. Sassari: Università degli Studi di Sassari/Muros: Stampacolor, 2000.

Webster, G., *A prehistory of Sardinia 2300-500 BC* (Monographs in Mediterranean Archaeology 5), Sheffield: Sheffield Academic Press, 1996.

Webster, G., 'Identifying Monte D'Accoddi: Sardinia's 4th-millennium ziggurat, *Sardinia, Corsica et Baleares Antiquae* XVII (2019): 39-59.

Webster, G. and M. Webster, *Punctuated insularity. The archaeology of 4th and 3rd millennium Sardinia*. Oxford: BAR Publishing International Series 2871, 2017.

Weiss, M.C., 'Armatures tranchantes et microlithes: étude des pièces géométriques de petites dimensions et a bords abattus du Néolithique ancien de A Petra', in *Il primo popolamento olocenico dell'area corso-toscana* (Interreg. II, Corsica 1997-99), edited by C. Tozzi and M.C. Weiss, 201-23. Pisa: Edizioni ETS, 2000.

Weiss, M.C., 'Habitation et modèle d'occupation du sol de l'horizon IIb2 du site du Néolithique ancien de A Petra (L'Ile-Rousse, Haute-Corse)', in *Préhistoire et protohistoire de l'aire tyrrhénienne*, edited by C. Tozzi and M.C. Weiss, 9-18. Ghezzano-Pisa: Felici Editore, 2007.

Wilkens, B., 'Small carnivores and their prey in holocenic Sardinia', poster for the 2010 conference of the International Council for Archaeozoology/Bone Commons, The Alexandria Archive Institute (Item #1649; http://alexandriaarchive.org/bonecommons/items/show/1649).

Wilkens, B., *Archeozoologia. Manuale per lo studio dei resti faunistici dell'area mediterranea*. Sassari: EDES, 2003.

Zohary, D., E. Tchernov and L. Kolska Horwitz, 'The role of unconscious selection in the domestication of sheep and goat', *Journal of Zoology* 245:2 (1998): 129-35 (https://doi.org/10.1111/j.1469-7998.1998.tb00082.x).